Ethics, Justice and International Relations

This topical and timely book critically explores contemporary liberal international relations theory. In the fifty years since the declaration of human rights, the language of international relations has come to incorporate the language of justice and injustice. The book argues that if justice is to become the governing principle of international politics, then liberals must recognise that their political preferences cannot be the preconditions of global ethics. The hierarchy of international political ethics must be constructed afresh so that the first principles of justice are accessible to all agents as political and ethical equals.

Ethics, Justice and International Relations systematically examines the current empirical and theoretical debates surrounding globalisation, interdependence and the philosophical justification of international relations theory, and argues that constructivist reasoning provides the only secure grounding for a political theory of international relations. This book offers the only full treatment available of the most recent contributions of some of the major thinkers in the contemporary canon including Mervyn Frost, Onora O'Neill, Michael Walzer and John Rawls. In seeking to establish a genuinely constructivist liberal theory, this book reveals that the universalist aspirations of the communitarian tradition offers the only way forward for a just liberal solution to the problems of contemporary international politics. This book will be essential reading for students and scholars in politics, international relations, political theory and ethics.

Peter Sutch is Lecturer in the School of European Studies at the University of Wales, Cardiff.

Routledge Advances in International Relations and Global Politics

1 **Foreign Policy and Discourse Analysis**
France, Britain and Europe
Henrik Larsen

2 **Agency, Structure and International Politics**
From ontology to empirical enquiry
Gil Friedman and Harvey Starr

3 **The Political Economy of Regional Co-operation in the Middle East**
Ali Carkoglu, Mine Eder, Kemal Kirisci

4 **Peace Maintenance**
The evolution of international political authority
Jarat Chopra

5 **International Relations and Historical Sociology**
Breaking down boundaries
Stephen Hobden

6 **Equivalence in Comparative Politics**
Edited by Jan W. van Deth

7 **The Politics of Central Banks**
Robert Elgie and Helen Thompson

8 **Politics and Globalisation**
Knowledge, ethics and agency
Martin Shaw

9 **History and International Relations**
Thomas W. Smith

10 **Idealism and Realism in International Relations**
Robert M. A. Crawford

11 **National and International Conflicts, 1945–1995**
New empirical and theoretical approaches
Frank Pfetsch and Christoph Rohloff

12 **Party Systems and Voter Alignments Revisited**
Edited by Lauri Karvonen and Stein Kuhnle

13 **Ethics, Justice and International Relations**
Constructing an international community
Peter Sutch

14 **Democracy and National Pluralism**
Edited by Ferran Requejo

15 **Capturing Globalization**
Edited by James H. Mittelman and Norani Othman

Ethics, Justice and International Relations

Constructing an international community

Peter Sutch

Routledge
Taylor & Francis Group

London and New York

First published 2001
by Routledge
11 New Fetter Lane, London EC4P 4EE

Simultaneously published in the USA and Canada
by Routledge
29 West 35th Street, New York, NY 10001

Routledge is an imprint of the Taylor & Francis Group

Typeset in Baskerville by Taylor & Francis Books Ltd
Printed and bound in Great Britain by Biddles Ltd,
Guildford and King's Lynn

British Library Cataloguing in Publication Data
A catalogue record for this book is available from the British Library

Library of Congress Cataloging in Publication Data
Sutch, Peter
Ethics, justice, and international relations: constructing an international community / Peter Sutch.
p. cm. – (Routledge advances in international relations and politics; 13)
Includes bibliographical references and index.
1. International relations–Moral and ethical aspects. 2. Internationalism. 3. Justice. 4. Communitarianism. 5. Liberalism. I. Title. II. Series.
JZ1306.S88 2001
172'.4–dc21

00-051820

ISBN 0–415–23274–0

To Nicola, Victoria and Matthew

Contents

Acknowledgements

This book is the product of several years work. During that time I have received support and encouragement from many people. I would like to thank all those in the department of Political Theory and Government at the University of Wales, Swansea where this project was conceived and developed and to those in the European School, Cardiff, University of Wales where it was completed. I owe particular debts to David Boucher who guided me through every stage of this project, and to Bruce Haddock and Rex Martin for their unfailing enthusiasm and shining example. I have been fortunate enough to have been able to test aspects of this argument in many forums. My thanks go to the editors and reviewers at the *Review of International Studies* where I first published my thoughts on the work of Mervyn Frost, to Howard Williams and the UK Kant Society who helped me refine my views on the nature of contemporary cosmopolitanism and the work of Onora O'Neill, and to Mark Evans, editor of *The Edinburgh Companion to Contemporary Liberalism* where I first explored the idea of a constructivist and communitarian liberal international relations theory. I also owe much to the less formal, but valuable, encouragement of friends and colleagues, in particular to Peri Roberts for countless hours of discussions. Any shortcomings that remain are entirely my own.

Abbreviations

O'Neill, *TJV*	O. O'Neill, *Towards Justice and Virtue: A Constructive Account of Practical Reason*, Cambridge, Cambridge University Press, 1996.
O'Neill, *CR*	O. O'Neill, *Constructions of Reason: Explorations of Kant's Practical Philosophy*, Cambridge, Cambridge University Press, 1989.
O'Neill, *FH*	O. O'Neill, *Faces of Hunger: An Essay on Poverty, Justice and Development*, London, Allen and Unwin, 1986.
Rawls, 'LOP'	J. Rawls, 'The Law of Peoples', in S. Shute and S. Hurley (eds) *On Human Rights. The Oxford Amnesty Lectures*, New York, Basic Books, 1993.
Rawls, *PL*	J. Rawls, *Political Liberalism*, New York, Columbia University Press, 1993.
Rawls, *TJ*	J. Rawls, *Theory of Justice*, Oxford, Clarendon Press, 1972.
Walzer, *JUW*	M. Walzer, *Just and Unjust Wars: A Moral Argument with Historical Illustrations*, New York, Basic Books, 1977.
Walzer, *SJ*	M. Walzer, *Spheres of Justice: A Defence of Pluralism and Equality*, Oxford, Blackwell, 1983.
Walzer, 'MSS'	M. Walzer, 'The Moral Standing of States: A Response to Four Critics', in *Philosophy and Public Affairs*, Vol. 9, No. 18, 1980, 209–229.

Introduction

The vast majority of the key phrases in recent international politics have included the expression 'the international community'. This phrase is used both to describe something and to justify major (and very often controversial) international ventures. Recent events such as the Gulf war or the bombing of Belgrade as well as major parts of recent international history (such as the restrictions on trade with South Africa during the final years of the apartheid regime) all rest on the authority of the international community. Hopes for a future free from imperialism and free from the anarchy of a purely state-oriented international system appear to be realistic if we are witnessing the genesis of a real 'international community'. Clearly there is a vital issue to explore here. The questions I pursue in this book include inquiries such as '*how* could an "international community" be the source of legitimate action in global politics?'; or 'is the development of the prevailing human rights culture an unconditional good?'; or 'what principles must we commit to in order to ensure that the term "international community" lives up to its name?'. These are some of the most important questions thrown up by contemporary international politics.

It will be immediately apparent that these questions are not those associated with the empirical study of international relations or political science. Understanding the key actors in this 'international community', the laws and instruments of their power or how this entity differs from previous power centres in world politics is undoubtedly an important undertaking. Equally important, however, are the normative questions thrown up by the escalation in appeals to the authority of this 'international community'. In international relations theory these normative questions are of recent origin. For almost 300 years the highest authority in international politics was thought to be the sovereign state. Any ethical issues were thought to arise only within the confines of the state and the issues of international politics were thought to be merely functional. But the half-century since the end of the last world war has seen a dramatic change in the way we expect international politics to be conducted. Normative international relations theory is now hard to avoid for anyone who wishes to ask questions of the world around us. To contribute to discussions on the NATO response to ethnic cleansing in the Kosovo region of Serbia requires that we take a moral stand on a complex issue. In political theory questions concerning the ethics of what we now call international relations have been asked almost continuously since the time of the Peloponnesian Wars.[1] Political theory is thus extraordinarily well equipped to explore issues relating to the moral standing of states, the priority of shared human rights in relation to social or cultural rights, or the first principles of an international community. In this book contemporary political theory meets international politics.

Is this the right way to pursue such a series of inquiries? It is sometimes claimed that political theory is too esoteric a tool to be of relevance to the grim realities of international relations. The claim is that political theory privileges the principle over the practical. There are two fundamental ways in which this might be the case. The first is that a political theory might offer a rather utopian view. It might offer an image of a perfect way of life attainable only by agents who possess virtues or attributes that all (or many) real agents do not. Similarly it might offer an ideal that can be satisfied only by material conditions that cannot be realised. The second way in which political theory might privilege the principle over the practical is that a political theory might offer a position that sets, or articulates, ethical standards and uses them to test the legitimacy of practical politics. The first of these approaches is clearly irrelevant to the study of politics, international or otherwise. Principles of political ethics must be, to use the phrase of one influential author examined in this book, accessible to and followable by all relevant agents and agencies.[2] The second approach, however, attacks the fundamental issues at stake in the development of international relations. When politicians, journalists, generals or those claiming that their human rights have been violated appeal to the authority of the international community they are not merely appealing to a practically effective power. Rather they are appealing to a normative authority. Not only can the international community solve some key problems in world politics (i.e. it has the resources to do so) but, so it is claimed, it has the *right* and often the *duty* to do so. The ethical standards of the international community claim legitimate moral superiority. The purpose of exploring this claim is to discover the basis upon which a very influential alliance of military powers asserts its right to act against the interests of governments that do not meet the ethical and political standards of the international community.

The background to the questions this book explores is permeated by deep-running political and theoretical divisions. Politically there is a deep division between those who argue that human rights should be the prime concern in contemporary world politics and others who argue that the system of sovereign states is the only guarantor of cultural and political freedom. Theoretically there are divisions over the kinds of chains of reasoning that can generate authoritative ethical principles. What criteria must ethical principles reach? What gives such principles their authority? The answers to these theoretical questions often underwrite answers to the concrete political questions. Some theorists, often (but not always) termed cosmopolitan, argue that ethical principles must attach to all human beings equally. This position, rather unsurprisingly, is often cited in favour of the political argument that supports a universal human rights culture.

Other theorists (sometimes labelled communitarian) argue that the cosmopolitan position cannot make sense of the variety of the human condition.[3] They argue that the category 'human' is meaningless and that concrete categories such as 'liberal', 'Muslim', 'American' or 'Slavic' have far more content and should thus be accorded ethical superiority. Such positions are often wary of broad-ranging claims to ethical universality and rely instead on political categories such as sovereign autonomy and the principle of non-intervention. Exploring these issues is vital to developing a full understanding of current developments in international relations.

In the following chapters I have two goals. Firstly I explore this debate by examining the arguments of several of the most influential thinkers in contemporary political theory. This offers some vital insights into the sorts of arguments one can put forward in defence of a political theory of international relations. It also gives us an informed understanding of the ethical and political claims that the 'international community' relies upon if its claim to moral and political authority is to be successful. In offering a detailed, critical examination of modern thinking on issues of international political theory I hope to highlight the key issues that underpin our hopes for a qualitative progression towards a just and functional international community. Secondly I attempt to formulate a defensible argument that takes an explicit position on the development of the international community. I argue that if the international community is to be the source of legitimate authority in world politics then the basic principles that guide it have to be altered. I suggest that, for political and philosophical reasons, the dominant liberal-cosmopolitan conception of international justice has to be replaced or, at the very least, modified. Furthermore I argue that it must be replaced by an account of ethics that, while mirroring the genuine need and desire for a transnational response to world crises, can accommodate the greater diversity of ethical and political positions evident in the world today. Real political issues motivate this exploration of theoretical themes. Ethnic cleansing, NATO-led military interventions that bomb political targets, UN trade embargoes that threaten the political stability of entire nations, famine, natural disasters, ecological destruction, chemical weapons capabilities; these are all part of contemporary international relations. How do we respond? From one perspective it seems clear that the international community is opposed to gross violations of human rights. Yet all too often this community cannot agree upon what constitute human rights. The liberal west claims personal, political, cultural and economic rights for each individual that, if adopted by the international community, require that many cultures and societies give up certain practices. How do we decide which claims are just? This is a political and a philosophical question. Hence the need for a contemporary political theory of international relations.

There are two key developments in contemporary international relations theory that inform much of what follows. The first is a political development, the second a philosophical development. The political change centres on what is often described as globalisation or interdependence. The increasing interconnectedness of our everyday lives requires that we take account of a wider political and social arena when we build new political and social institutions or act through existing ones. The philosophical change centres on a concept often termed 'constructivism'. This concept attempts to confront the moral scepticism of the antifoundationalist traditions (postmodernism, critical theory, poststructuralism) and recognises that justifiable principles must be built from predicates that are themselves accessible to all the relevant parties. In many respects constructivism is simply an attempt to come to terms with the plurality of moral convictions in an interconnected world. Metaphysical disputes about the nature of ultimate reality or the ontological disputes about the nature of God are, in many cases, irresolvable. To some extent constructivist arguments sidestep these issues by relying only upon arguments that are justifiable before the relevant parties. The pattern that this evasion takes is particularly important both to contemporary political theory and to our understanding of how our cultures might interact with others. These theories seek to tell a realistic story about what it is to live by universal principles in today's world. I believe that this revised story is particularly important to the success or failure of contemporary political theories of international relations. In particular I think that the new way that Walzer and Rawls look upon universalism in ethics and politics is what gives their international theory such persuasive force. It is no longer possible to view the universal as an absolute moral principle understood in the abstract and then applied. We, the multifarious peoples of the world, have to build a universal standpoint from which we can regulate our political interactions. Understanding that constructive process is, perhaps, the chief goal of political theory at the beginning of the twenty-first century. The genesis of this theoretical process is the conviction that we should not ask individuals or societies to act on principles that they cannot or will not accept. The subtitle of this book reflects my conviction that we need to construct the principles and the institutions of the international community if we are to advance world politics.

Structure and content

Generating and defending a moral and political theory is a complex process. It requires a critical examination of the problem at hand and of the most relevant responses to that problem. It also requires a critical examination of our own ethical intuitions. Finally, and perhaps the most difficult of all, it requires that we take a stand.

To this end chapter 1 will begin by examining the context within which this book will work. It will look at the growing difficulties in using the guiding concepts of global politics (sovereignty, national interest, non-intervention, human rights and international justice) and will then go on to argue that a philosophical/normative approach to international relations theory, identified as the cosmopolitan/communitarian distinction in the work of Brown (among others),[4] has the potential to answer the questions thrown up by contemporary international relations. Examining the most innovative approaches to this problem found in international relations theory and political theory really offers us a way in to this debate. I argue in the opening chapters of the book that the approaches offered by international relations theory (from the globalisation/interdependence debates to realism, idealism, postmodernism and critical theory) leave unanswered some of the most vital questions that we must ask of international justice. Furthermore I show that political theory confronts these vital issues head on and that therefore we must marry the political concerns of international relations theory with the philosophical concerns of political theory: that we need a normative political theory of international relations. This much is simply groundwork. Developing this line of thought I argue that the philosophical and practical problems associated with normative political theory require that we develop the idea, increasingly popular in contemporary political thought, that we need a constructivist normative political theory. Here constructivism argues that we may not rely on the highly contested metaphysical, political or theological assumptions that the intellectual ancestors of liberal thought (and thus of contemporary human rights theory) relied upon to ground political ethics. This fact is easily demonstrated in world politics where principles of justice must be accessible to a wide variety of political, religious and moral cultures. The deep-seated concern of many that the move to universalise a liberal human rights culture is value imperialism via the back door is rigorously developed here to show that human rights theory needs to be updated if it is to successfully claim to be a drive to justice rather than a drive to liberalism.

Building on the final arguments of chapter 1 I then relate the cosmopolitan and communitarian traditions to international relations and show how constructivist cosmopolitanism and constructivist communitarianism attack the most urgent theoretical problems of international politics. The first tradition I examine is the dominant Kantian liberal-cosmopolitan tradition. This tradition is the historically accepted theoretical underpinning of human rights theory. In chapter 2 I explore its philosophical provenance, its deployment in the current debates (principally through the work of T.W. Pogge and C. Beitz) and its most recent expression in O'Neill's critical and constructivist cosmopolitanism. O'Neill's work also has a separate chapter dedicated to a full exploration of the constructivist cosmopolitan position. Here my claim is that cosmopolitanism does not stay within the limits of constructivism (i.e. it assumes an ethical and philosophical standpoint that is unacceptable to many actual or potential members of the nascent international community). Therefore, I argue, there is no justification for treating the accepted (UN) version of human rights as the correct tool for fashioning a just world order.

The second tradition is often portrayed as communitarianism.[5] This tradition is commonly thought to be opposed to a universal conception of justice that could govern international politics and to mount a staunch defence of sovereign independence to the exclusion of human rights. Yet what this widely accepted distinction obscures are non-Kantian strands of the liberal tradition that seek to construct universal principles of political ethics in a way that is significantly different from (and, I argue in chapter 3, more successful than) both liberal cosmopolitanism and traditional communitarianism. This claim informs the central argument of my book – that the developmental communitarianism exhibited by Rawls, Walzer and Frost offers the key to the evolution of international ethics. This tradition is highlighted and developed to present the Hegelian-liberal theory of Mervyn Frost (*Ethics in International Relations*, 1996), the communitarian-liberal theory of Michael Walzer (*Just and Unjust Wars*, 1977 and *Thick and Thin: Moral Arguments at Home and Abroad*, 1994) and the *political* liberalism of John Rawls (*Political Liberalism*, 1993, 'The Law of Peoples', 1993 and *Law of Peoples*, 1999) as important alternatives to the current orthodoxy of Kantian-cosmopolitanism.

Chapters 4 to 7 develop the argument still further. In offering a critical exegesis of four constructivist thinkers, one cosmopolitan and three communitarian, this book shows that developmental communitarianism can supply the answers to the political and philosophical problems engendered by the current composition of international and transnational interaction. Chapter 4 examines Onora O'Neill's constructivist cosmopolitanism and argues that she does not (and that her philosophical tradition cannot) overcome the tensions between problems associated with the dichotomy between sovereignty and universal ethics. Chapter 5 reintroduces the work of Mervyn Frost arguing that his 'secular Hegelian' reinterpretation of human rights offers more to contemporary international relations theory than has been recognised. I argue that in positing a basic connection between the development of human rights and a developing understanding of sovereignty Frost avoids the paralysing antithesis often ascribed to the role of these two concepts in international theory. Ultimately, however, I believe Frost's secular Hegelianism overreaches the potential of developmental communitarianism. Therefore in chapters 6 and 7 I examine the ethical minimalisms of Michael Walzer and John Rawls. Here I argue that their accounts of a developing ethical minimalism in the international politics of the 'here and now' advances our understanding of the role of justice and human rights in international relations in a way that offers a route beyond the stalemate of current theoretical divisions. The principal claim of this book is that a developmental communitarianism, similar to that of Rawls (and to a lesser but still significant extent of Frost and Walzer), can offer us an invaluable and theoretically sustainable link between the concepts of sovereignty, international ethics and human rights that international relations theory needs if it is to take account of the problems and possibilities that confront global politics. This book does not set out to develop a new way of understanding international relations. Still less does it claim to have discovered previously unheard voices in the philosophical tumult. The four central thinkers examined by this book are all well-known proponents of political philosophy. However I do claim that the marked relevance of the work of Walzer, Rawls and Frost, their method and approach to international relations theory, has been misunderstood or ignored to the detriment of the political theory of international relations.

Finally, all the thinkers examined in this book are, in a broadly conceived sense, liberal. This, it could be said, can only maintain the western hegemony (perhaps the most obvious structural component of international politics in the modern age) and continue to privilege, without justification, the moral standards and practices of liberalism. Yet within liberal international relations theory there is a tradition of thought that has the potential to overcome these theoretical and political problems. This potential is not, I shall argue, found in the dominant tradition of liberal theory in international ethics but in the developmental communitarian tradition constructed in chapters 3, 5, 6 and 7. In this book I suggest that a successful constructivist international relations theory, if it is to produce a political theory suited to world politics, must take proper account of the way it constructs or portrays international community. My reasons for making this argument stem from several sources. Firstly a belief that the justifications that liberals are obliged to construct for their theory are not strong enough to ignore the facts of pluralism. Secondly an uneasiness with the cosmopolitan-liberal assumption that sovereignty, one of the political key stones of international relations, is irrelevant to an understanding of international justice; and thirdly my belief that the assumption that sovereignty is hostile to concepts such as human rights which are thought to be, by definition *both* universal *and* cosmopolitan in character is obscuring a very fruitful scam in international relations theory.

The central argument: a brief overview

One of the most theoretically complete examples of constructivist cosmopolitanism is to be found in the work of Onora O'Neill.[6] Her constructivist cosmopolitanism is examined in chapter 5 as the most precise expression of contemporary Kantian liberal international relations theory. It comprises both the latest and most sustainable form of theoretical justification and the most popular liberal theory of international justice. It is constructivist because the historically accepted foundations of liberal theory have been modified to take account of the now widely recognised fact that improbable, unprovable, inaccessible or non-universalisable premises are unable to provide sufficient grounds for political theory. It is resolutely cosmopolitan because O'Neill, like many liberals, argues that despite the necessary changes in liberalism's justificatory strategy it is possible and necessary to continue to develop the idea of *Ius Cosmopoliticum* outlined in Kant's *Perpetual Peace*[7] but cultivated to champion human rights and global justice as the first principles of world politics. In this work I am concerned to show that while the constructivist theoretical project offers a sustainable and accessible approach to international ethics, cosmopolitanism cannot be thought of as the product of constructivist reasoning. Cosmopolitanism includes too many exclusively liberal assumptions to claim the kind of universality appropriate to the idea of a truly *international* community. My principal counter-claim against O'Neill (and cosmopolitanism more generally) is that the pattern of argument used to justify a liberal, individualist account of international justice is incomplete. Put more technically, the typical claim of cosmopolitanism that if it is true that principles of ethics must be universalisable then principles of ethics must be cosmopolitan is incomplete. The space between these two important concepts (universality and cosmopolitanism) is highlighted by contemporary criticisms of foundational moral judgments. We can only build in this space, we can only construct a just international community, if we go some way towards recognising the diversity of the agents and agencies of contemporary world politics. This argument, which springs from a detailed examination of contemporary cosmopolitan arguments, concludes that it is the political development of international relations that underwrites the often-heard claim that international ethical principles should be universal in scope and that to ignore the character of the international community when developing these principles is therefore sheer folly.

Having made this argument I seek to discover precisely what we can build in this new political space. In doing this I go on to argue that the constructivist and developmental communitarianism of thinkers such as Rawls,[8] Walzer[9] and Frost[10] offers this invaluable link between international politics and constructivist liberal theory. In this argument I use the phrase developmental communitarianism to describe a tradition of thought to which I believe Rawls, Walzer and Frost belong for two primary reasons. Firstly I wish to point out how far removed the justifications of their liberal ideas are from those of liberal cosmopolitanism. Cosmopolitan liberals believe that the first principles of liberalism should apply to all individuals irrespective of their historical and political situation. For the developmental communitarians however the justification of the principles of liberalism are themselves contingent upon history, upon consensus or the shared development of a background justification for the principles of international relations. This I believe to be a vital fact and one that feeds into the second reason for my having chosen developmental communitarianism as the signifier for the work of Frost, Walzer and Rawls. The 'communitarian method' of these thinkers is not an argument about the essential primacy of community over the individual. Rather it is intended to show that individualistic theories of rights or interventionist political policies are not justified unless the circumstances of justice and a general consensus of actors coincide to produce such a justification. In this they share much with the constructivist cosmopolitanism of O'Neill. Where they differ is in the fact that they do not feel justified in abstracting from the present circumstances of justice to a strong notion of interconnectedness that licenses principles of a cosmopolitan-liberal international theory. Rather, argue the developmental communitarians, we may abstract to the existent plurality of political communities and to the consensus upon principles of international justice implicit in the actions and norms they share and only go on to show how important the norms of human rights and other liberal principles are to the existence of international politics if these values can be said to be a necessary part of our developing international community. This distinction, I will contend, makes a significant difference to claims to have legitimately reached universal principles of international justice. The liberalism of Walzer and Rawls, and to a more limited extent that of Frost, is a conclusion rather than an assumption and it is this fact, one that stems from their general method, that marks them off from traditional liberal and cosmopolitan theory. Throughout this book I will argue that it is only developmental communitarianism that can successfully claim to have constructed principles of international justice that can be fairly and legitimately universalised to form the basis of a just international community.

Notes and references

1 See D. Boucher, *Political Theories of International Relations: From Thucydides to the Present*, Oxford, New York, Oxford University Press, 1998.

2 This phrase characterises the requirements of political theory articulated by O. O'Neill. See particularly, O. O'Neill, *Towards Justice and Virtue: A Constructive Account of Practical Reason*, Cambridge, Cambridge University Press, 1996 (O'Neill, *TJV*).

3 For an introduction to the content and scope of what has become known as the cosmopolitan/communitarian debate see C. Brown, *International Relations Theory: New Normative Approaches*, New York, London, Harvester-Wheatsheaf, 1992.

4 Brown, *International Relations Theory*. For further reading see chapter 2.

5 See, for example, Brown, *International Relations Theory*, also S. Mulhall and A. Swift, *Liberals and Communitarians*, Oxford, Blackwell, 1992, and S. Avineri and A. de-Shalit (eds), *Communitarianism and Individualism*, Oxford, Oxford University Press, 1992.

6 O'Neill, *TJV*.

7 Kant, 'To Perpetual Peace: A Philosophical Sketch', third definitive article, in T. Humphrey (trans.), *Perpetual Peace and other Essays*, Indianapolis, Hackett, p. 118.

8 See particularly J. Rawls, 'The Law of Peoples', *On Human Rights: the Oxford Amnesty Lectures*, S. Shute and S. Hurley (eds), Basic Books, 1993; J. Rawls, *The Law of Peoples*, Harvard University Press, 1999 and J. Rawls, *Political Liberalism*, Columbia University Press, 1993 (Rawls, 'LOP' and Rawls, *PL* respectively).

9 See particularly M. Walzer, *Just and Unjust Wars: A Moral Argument with Historical Illustrations*, Basic Books, 1977 (Walzer, *JUW*) and M. Walzer, *Thick and Thin: Moral Arguments at Home and Abroad*, University of Notre Dame Press, 1994.

10 M. Frost, *Ethics and International Relations: A Constitutive Theory*, Cambridge University Press, 1996.

1 Setting the scene

International relations as political theory

If one were to sketch a history of the development of *inter*national politics one might date its codified beginning at 1648, the beginning of its crisis in 1914 and chart its demise over the fifty years that followed 1945. There would, of course, be debate over the precise dating of the most important events but nevertheless this sketch would not be thought of as particularly controversial.[1] While any empirical claim that we now live in a post-international world is untenable, the philosophical and political claims that we should accept post-internationalism as the way forward or that we have developed (or are developing) a transnational politics are both respectable and commonplace. In fifty years there has been a radical move away from an international system that took over three hundred years to develop.[2]

The recent history of what Held terms the United Nations system has begun, and has proceeded with remarkable rapidity, to erode some of the central features of an international system that takes the territorial nation-state as the dominant unit of analysis in international politics. Globalisation is the watchword of contemporary empirical and theoretical analysis that argues forcefully that political practice is leaving the Westphalian order behind.

> Information, pollution, migrants, arms, ideas, images, news, crime, narcotics, disease, amongst other things, readily and frequently flow across national boundaries. In addition, global transport and communications infrastructures, from airlines to the internet, facilitate the emergence of global and transnational networks linking peoples and organisations in different parts of the world.[3]

Increasingly the problems facing the international system transcend or cut through national boundaries leaving political units whose sole concern is sovereign autonomy unable to deal with the most pressing problems. The myriad of accounts of the political consequences of globalisation offer a variety of opinions on the theme of change and disjuncture which are all empirically straightforward and rarely contested. One particularly prominent theme in both the empirical analysis of globalisation and the philosophical and theoretical treatment of international relations theory is interconnectedness. The exploration of this theme, an idea with a great deal of observable weight behind it but also a huge and contested literature concerning its consequences for international politics, must form an important part of any examination of the construction of an international community.

Without delving too deeply into the complexities of the arguments surrounding globalisation, arguments tangential to the aims of this book, it is important to distinguish between the relatively uncontested facts of international politics and the much contested treatment of these facts. Held and McGrew each develop five points about current trends in international politics. Held focuses on five major disjunctures in international theory that are at the centre of conceptual and political disputes. He focuses on:

1 The increasing force and scope of international law, focusing particularly on the increased acceptance of human rights as a universal boundary upon state action and upon the recent surge of transnational environmental legislation.
2 The internationalisation of political decision making, focusing on the upsurge in international governmental organisations (such as the UN, EU, IMF, the World Bank and UNESCO) and international non-governmental organisations (the Red Cross, Amnesty, Greenpeace etc.).
3 The proliferation of military power that means a) that military action is more often a global problem rather than a state's private decision and b) that the hegemony of the superpowers is necessarily eroded and dispersed into IGOs such as NATO and WTO.
4 Cultural globalisation and the fact that the state no longer has the monopoly on culture production. Media proliferation and transnational communications infrastructures combined with increased migration has dissolved the notion of the homogenous ethnic and cultural 'Nation'.
5 The globalisation of the world economy. The globalisation of production and international finance has developed a transnational market that no single nation-state can advantageously or successfully control.[4]

These empirical observations are rarely disputed and translate into McGrew's more generalised 'distinctive attributes' of the contemporary international system that can be summed up as increased and established interconnectedness.[5] None of the above is particularly controversial and even the ensuing claims concerning the decline or development of the concept and practice of state sovereignty such as Held's comment that:

> [a]ny conception of sovereignty which interprets it as an illimitable and indivisible form of public power – entrenched securely in individual nation-states – is undermined. Sovereignty itself has to be conceived today as

> already divided among a number of agencies – national, regional and international – and limited by the very nature of this plurality.[6]

are rarely disputed. It is clear that contemporary international politics has moved away from the idea that whatever a state might do in international politics is perfectly legitimate.

If this introductory sketch of prevailing conditions in international politics is uncontroversial it is unique in attaining this status. For at this point academics and practitioners begin to disagree fervently on some empirical questions concerning how the international system has changed but more often on the normative and theoretical questions about how we should account for and respond to such changes. Even the terminology becomes disputed. Is, for example, the term 'globalisation' loaded? Does it not obscure *a priori* cosmopolitan principles, principles that are themselves philosophically contestable? As Williams notes:

> To what extent does globalisation erode sovereignty? Or is the endlessly shifting concept of sovereignty reconstituted and reformulated in a manner likely to maintain its centrality in international relations? … The death of the state has often been reported in international relations. Globalisation is the latest in a long line of assassins.[7]

Rather than talk of globalisation some theorists (mainly realists and communitarians) prefer to talk of interdependence, a conception of interconnectedness that is more reticent about (and in some cases openly hostile to) the idea that the state is becoming increasingly irrelevant to the practice and norms of international relations. Again Williams, in 'Rethinking Sovereignty', draws out the central aspects of the dispute.

> One way of thinking about this difference is to define interdependence as interconnectedness which erodes the effectiveness of national policy and threatened national autonomy. … A key feature of globalisation as already outlined is interconnectedness, not unlike interdependence, which stresses mutuality, globalisation also refers to the possibility of dependence. Crucially, the conceptualisation of globalisation refers to the reordering of time and space. Interdependence theorists have focused on the internationalisation of international relations whereas writers within the paradigm of globalisation argue for a more global society.[8]

This division of concerns in international relations theory features in most of the debates and finds its most useful expression, I will suggest, within the cosmopolitan/communitarian debate in normative international theory. What is at stake here is not simply the empirical data concerning how individuals and associations are interconnected but the normative pressure such data can legitimately exert upon the authority of the arguments and practices surrounding sovereignty and human rights. Put simply the most pressing questions facing us today focus upon whether a realist or communitarian (state-oriented) international politics or a more universalist or cosmopolitan (perhaps human rights-oriented) international politics is best suited to the contemporary situation.

Despite the controversies surrounding the concept one thing is clear, interconnectedness is a theme that requires examination. All sides of the debate surrounding interconnectedness stress the dangers and possibilities of the development of this social phenomenon. The potential globalisation of a liberal order is often contrasted with the unevenness of globalisation that promises integration but threatens fragmentation. The basic ethical principles of the dominant liberal-cosmopolitan position are not universally shared, particularly outside of the more powerful, economically developed western states. Yet as McGrew notes 'political and economic elites in the world's major metropolitan areas are much more tightly integrated into and have much greater control over global networks'.[9] This well-charted political phenomenon combined (importantly in the view of this work) with the philosophical crisis in liberal foundationalism threatens the optimism of many commentators. The questions facing liberal scholars and practitioners who believe that the prevailing international political climate offers the requisite conditions for the removal of 'power theory' from the centre of international political analysis and its replacement with universally justifiable normative argument are manifold. A new-found awareness of the particularity of 'our' ethico-political position combined with the historical dominance of that position in world politics obliges us to consider carefully what is necessary to the development of a just international community. The central, if general, question of current attempts to understand the implications of the last fifty years of international history is simply 'given that the international system has developed leaving agents and agencies interconnected in ways unimagined by the Westphalian system of international politics what rights and duties have we incurred and how must we rethink international politics in order to enact them?'

Understanding interconnectedness

Given the centrality of interconnectedness it is necessary to find a way to conceptualise and analyse the impact of this concept on international relations theory. There are a number of competing accounts of the debate surrounding interconnectedness and a wide variety of positions within these accounts. However, it is clear that the debates surrounding the changing shape of world politics go far beyond the empirical.

All four of the principal thinkers examined in the following chapters accept that interconnectedness is a feature of a changing international political scene. Walzer argues that interconnectedness leads to the (transient) instantiation of universal rights to life and liberty;[10] Frost believes that interconnectedness is leading to the transposition of the norms of sovereignty and the norms of human rights and thus to a global civil society;[11] Rawls argues that interconnectedness leads to international consensus upon a new understanding of human rights and political autonomy;[12] and O'Neill argues that interconnectedness requires that we recognise our cosmopolitan obligations to humanity.[13] Each of these positions are generated to answer the key questions of modern international relations. All these thinkers, like others in their field, are seeking to redefine ethical and political boundaries in light of new empirical and theoretical developments. The political map of international interaction has changed so that any, even vaguely realistic, portrayal of interconnectedness (the interaction of agents and agencies) forces the recognition that political and thus ethical boundaries are more comprehensive and tractable than previously allowed. This much is not at issue between the theorists examined in this study but it does represent a fundamentally different approach to the study of international relations than that taken by the majority of those engaged in the study of world politics. The fundamental debate is not whether the world system has changed but what such changes, empirical and theoretical, license. At the heart of the debates concerning interconnectedness and international politics are normative and ethical issues.

While the scope of analysis has necessarily widened there is still an underlying reluctance to examine the ethical issues. As Brown notes:

> [t]he prevailing philosophy in the social sciences – taken from economics but influential everywhere – drew a sharp distinction between positive and normative analysis, in effect eliminating the latter. Normative concerns were translated into 'value-judgments'; it was deemed to be possible to study the effect of value-judgments on behaviour and action but impossible to subject their contents to rational analysis.[14]

Yet it is precisely these value judgments that people rely upon when they seek to understand and theorise the political prominence and development of concepts such as sovereignty and human rights. Such judgments must be subjected to critical analysis. Justifications of state and non-state action in international politics require and receive normative buttresses and assessing these justifications is something that has traditionally taken place in the often separate but cognate discipline of political theory. Yet assessing the normative claims made on behalf of states, cultures, individuals and citizens must form the groundwork of international politics today. Focusing on interconnectedness offers the debate the opportunity to bring the dynamic normative issues to the forefront of international relations theory, to acknowledge that the claims agents (both governmental and other) make in order to justify their international actions have normative dimensions far beyond the sovereign 'I shall' which could theoretically brook no argument.

As international politics developed historically the theories that fed into, and off, this development also underwent dramatic changes. The development of international relations theory is usually characterised as three 'Great Debates' where 'realism' does battle with 'idealism', 'neorealism' with 'neoliberalism' and 'rationalism' with 'reflectivism'. However, in the context of the present argument, the evolution of international relations theory is better described as the process that (quite literally) shook the foundations of the discipline and led to the philosophical primacy of the critical theoretical, postmodernist and constructivist accounts of international politics. This sketch of the development of a discipline can be seen to lead on from the so-called 'third debate'. The claims, voiced by critical theorists or reflectivists,[15] that the epistemological and methodological assumptions of realists, neo-realists and neo-liberals unwittingly sustained the *status quo* have been taken on board by a wide variety of thinkers. It is among this number that constructivists, writing in the cosmopolitan/communitarian genre (if this area of discourse is developed enough to be so described) are to be situated. These two perspectives and the subsequent debate about international justice, whether it is couched in terms of state legitimacy or human rights, form a fascinating dialogue. As Brown argues, fittingly setting out the terms of the debate for us, the terms cosmopolitan and communitarian:

> have many points of contact with moral and social philosophy taken in general, unlike such distinctively international relations categories as 'realism' or 'pluralism'. The cosmopolitan/communitarian divide relates directly to the most central question of any normative international relations theory, namely the moral value to be credited to particularistic political collectivities as against humanity as a whole. Communitarianism either denies that there is an opposition here, or is prepared to assign central value to the community; cosmopolitan thought refuses this central status to the community, placing the ultimate source of moral value elsewhere.[16]

It is an aspect of this potentially more fruitful avenue of enquiry that forms the context of this book.

Steps towards a reconstruction of international politics

By unfortunate coincidence just as the need for a normative approach to international relations became clear the legitimacy of normative political theory was itself being questioned. Hand in hand with the criticisms of traditional theorising in international politics have gone more general critiques of the structure of political and philosophical justification. Thus the move from considering international politics as the consequence of certain unalterable facts to conceiving of international action as the consequence of moral and political decisions does not immediately suggest a move from traditional international theory to normative political theory. Questions raised concerning the epistemology and ontology of traditionally accepted forms of theorising in international studies are clearly applicable to some forms of normative theory. This is, in part, the reason why the academic discipline of international relations theory developed without incorporating normative political theory into its intellectual armoury. More famous among the challengers to the dominant orthodoxy of realism are the positions of postmodernism and critical theory. It is the 'deconstruction' of traditional international relations theory that these two varieties of analysis effected that really opened up the normative debate in contemporary thought and forms the background to the work of constructivist theory in the cosmopolitan/communitarian debate. The two traditions are both critical in approach. Indeed they share so much common ground that Linklater distinguishes them as 'Marxian-inspired critical theory' and 'postmodernism-inspired critical theory'.[17] In order to complete this introductory circle and to introduce the idea that a critical and constructivist normative theory viewed through the cosmopolitan/communitarian distinction is the most viable way forward in international relations theory, I intend to examine briefly the development of these two 'critical' enterprises and their impact on the analysis of international politics. In conclusion and in subsequent chapters I will argue that a third critical enterprise, one that combines the aspirations of critical theory with a more powerful theoretical pedigree, also contains the philosophical wherewithal to be of service in understanding international politics.

The predominance of the sovereign state in international relations theory is challenged by theorists of interdependence, by critical theorists, postmodernists and normative theorists. The empirical claims of writers such as Herz, or more recently McGrew and Held are supported by new critical understandings of the role of concepts such as sovereignty. The critical claims of both postmodernists and critical theorists aim to problematise the foundations of the realist international order. The work of Hoffman, Linklater and Cox on the emancipatory potential of the process of reflecting on theorising as a practice (rather than concentrating on problem solving within a given theoretical practice) forms the mainstream of critical theory in international relations.[18] Ashley's rendering of the 'anarchy problematique', Rorty's 'unjustifiable hope' for a future human rights culture and the idea of casting international theory as 'intertext' informs much of postmodern thinking in international relations as a field of study (although postmodernists consciously defy categorisation).[19] The central idea is that we must understand how dominant norms and concepts are created and reiterated in order to prevent exclusionary and oppressive ideas gaining an undeserved ontological, methodological and often political primacy.[20] Empirical change has led to theoretical change. Theories that developed during the enlightenment have come under close scrutiny as a direct consequence of this change and this includes normative theory as well as realist theory. As V. Spike Peterson notes, '[c]ontemporary empirical and epistemological developments reveal significant problems with [positivist and enlightenment] ways of knowing'.[21] Yet while the damning critique of traditional approaches to international politics offered by postmodernists and critical theorists represents a valuable step forward for international relations theory, this benefit is in danger of dissipating unless it is still possible to construct an accessible and practical political theory from the ruins of the traditional approaches to international relations. The danger that critical theorists and postmodernists see with traditional international relations theory is that it artificially and unjustly privileges certain fallacies about the international sphere. For example, realism is seen as not just explaining the international world order but as actively constituting its character in its reiteration of concepts such as sovereignty and anarchy. If this can be shown to be the case some of the 'truths' of international relations can be shown to be mere contingencies. Presenting sovereignty as the guiding 'fact' of international politics can be shown to be empirically inaccurate. Presenting sovereignty and anarchy as essential to any account of the present and future of international politics can be shown to be ontologically dubious and as perpetuating some of the structural aspects of international politics that, when taken as a given, prevent us (as politicians, citizens, interest groups and members of the human race sharing the political space of the international arena) from solving certain problems and removing certain barriers to whatever we might see as progress. This concern is eminently valid. Deconstructing international relations is a precondition of accurately constructing an account of interconnectedness. However the attempt to construct a viable account of interconnectedness (of international community and therefore of the basis of international politics) is frustrated by the postmodern rejection of all normative theory and the critical theorists' *a priori* adoption of cosmopolitan ideals. Deconstructing the old order is a vital task and one that the current literature in international studies has lent its full force. However the reconstruction of international relations theory is something that can be better achieved within the confines of constructivist normative theory. My central claim here is that while the antifoundational critique has made an important point the subsequent claim that we should now give up the search for justifiable ethical and political principles is not a necessary one. The familiar claims that we should abandon mainstream political thought and conduct life experiments 'in the margins' of human experience is not suited to the issues of international politics.

Postmodern readings of international relations and the projects of critical theory vary widely. They are linked in their concern to problematise and transcend traditional understandings of international relations but to attempt to capture the programme of either broadly defined method is too huge a project to begin here. However this chapter, and this book more generally, intends to introduce the argument that constructivist normative theory, rather than critical theory or postmodernism, is the best way forward 'here and now'. It does so by acknowledging the force of the postmodern critique of 'bad-foundationalism' and the critical theoretical enterprise of reflecting upon theorising itself but rejecting the non-cognitivist conclusions of some postmodernists and the immediate relevance of the 'yet-to-be-created' theoretical projects of others. I go on to suggest that the theoretical project of critical theory is more relevant but that it can, or should, be incorporated into the general framework that is the cosmopolitan/communitarian distinction if its relevance is to be fully realised.[22] In order to meet this burden it is important to examine certain aspects of critical and postmodern theory to see how this work transcends traditional ways of looking at international relations theory, to see what must be taken on board and to show why developmental communitarianism has the potential to offer more to international politics.

Postmodern readings in an international context

The two aspects of postmodernity I wish briefly to examine here are intended to show firstly the critical force of postmodern writing on international relations theory and secondly a vision of what a postmodern intra, inter, trans or sub-national political existence might look like. The first section of this argument focuses on deconstruction, the problematisation of traditional discourse, using Ashley's double reading of the 'anarchy problematique'. While there is an emerging mass of literature on the subject and a number of alternative sources, Ashley's article has the dual advantages of being concise and well known. There is some debate as to whether this article is indeed postmodern. As Brown notes, Ashley's work on,

> geopolitics and the 'anarchy problematique' were clearly moving in a post-modern direction but, equally clearly, still related to a pre-Morgenthauian, practice-oriented realism. ... The first fully postmodern Ashleyan work is his deconstruction of Waltz in Der Derian and Shapiro.[23]

However, Ashley's article does develop, with appealing brevity, several important postmodern themes among them the idea of 'making strange' traditional debates, treating them as 'intertextual' and then 'deconstructing' them. Also there seems to be an important sense in which Ashley's dialogic reading of the 'anarchy problematique' underwrites the later work.

The general thrust of Ashley's 'anarchy problematique', indeed of the majority of postmodern international relations theory, is the attempt to 'make strange' what Ashley calls a 'heroic practice'.[24] A heroic practice is Ashley's version of a common target for postmodern critiques of modernity. In this case the heroic practice models the modernist attitude towards what Frost calls the 'settled norms' of international relations (below). The traditional or heroic way of explaining international relations sets up a dichotomy between sovereignty and anarchy where sovereignty is the ideal of order, rationality and homogeneity and anarchy threatens this idea being characterised as contingent, disordered, lacking any coherent sense of truth; as something to be assimilated into the ordered world. Far from being an empirical observation of the international arena the modernist, rational, understanding of world politics is elevated to the status of ontological truth by the modernist heroic practice. It is treated as a foundational truth that allows them to discriminate between normal and abnormal, necessary from arbitrary.[25]

> And so, calling upon the heroic practice they do what must be done if modernist discourse is here to proceed: they 'find' a sovereign presence that

> must itself be immunised from reasoned criticism because it must be taken to be the principle of reasoning discourse in itself.[26]

The heroic practice, in this case the attachment of the status of foundational to the concept of Sovereignty in international relations theory, puts what is essentially a constructed concept beyond deconstruction or analysis. Progress must be in terms supportive to sovereignty, a fact which sustains the *status quo* (nation-states system, power, national interest, war rather than law) on the grounds that sovereignty is foundational or absolutely necessary to the politics that is played out in the space designated *inter*national by modernist discourse. '"Making strange" this sovereignty versus anarchy discourse is a postmodernist tactic, the attempt to "denaturalise" the debates within international relations theory.... The first step in showing how a process, a perspective, a concept, or a fact is socially constructed is to distance it, to make it seem strange.'[27] In order to do this Ashley offers two readings of the traditional view of international relations theory or the 'anarchy problematique'. The first reading Ashley offers is monological. That is, it mimics the heroic practice, follows the traditional discourse in order to accentuate 'its supposed boundaries, coherence and purity of purpose at the expense of its historicity, its vitality and dependence upon the arbitrary play of knowledgeable practices in its relations to the other texts of a pluralistic culture'.[28] In reaffirming traditional international relations theory in this way Ashley highlights the way in which that discourse provides a circular argument that unconsciously treats sovereignty as a generative principle, a foundation, yet still 'finds' the importance of sovereignty to international relations. The second reading is dialogical. Rather than mimic the heroic practice the interpretative model of the dialogue is used to show that there is no eternal referent or foundation for an idea. Instead the discourse is treated as an intertext.

> It follows ... that the supposed fixity and 'deep structuring' of a sovereign presence, and the resultant 'hard core' homogeneity and continuity of meaning ascribed to a text, is always to be grasped as a problematical historical effect.[29]

The dialogical reading deconstructs the sovereignty/anarchy dichotomy using a standard postmodern strategy. It shows that you cannot know something by what it is not without elevating its antithesis (illegitimately) to a foundational position. Recognising this leaves the reader free from the 'blackmail of the heroic practice' and free to explore new approaches and new questions.

> The reader can also explore ways in which, under various circumstances, these practices might be resisted or disabled; boundaries might be put in doubt and transgressed; representations might be subverted, deprived of the presumption of self-evidence, and politicised and historicised; new

> connections among diverse cultural elements might become possible; and new ways of thinking and doing global politics might be opened up.[30]

Ashley's project, and the projects of likeminded thinkers,[31] are important to the development of thinking about global and international politics. The conclusions they reach are by no means exclusive to postmodernism (indeed I believe that constructivist political theory builds upon the conclusions of the critical traditions) but they do highlight an important methodological flaw in realist readings of international relations theory. However there is, as Detevak notes, more to postmodernism than simply challenging the ontological assumptions of realism: 'It also has an abiding ethical concern which hinges on state sovereignty. State Sovereignty, as the dominant mode of subjectivity in international relations, holds significant ethico-political implications.'[32]

However the difficulties inherent in the construction of a postmodern ethics are many. Ashley's critique of the heroic practices of international relations leads on to a critique of the geopolitical limitations of ethics.[33] Nevertheless his claim that 'where ethics is rigorously practised, no totalitarian order could ever be'[34] still holds more promise for the deconstruction of a flawed order than for a redefined political programme. A recognition of the idea of 'different but equal' that Brown sees as potentially the most positive outcome of a postmodern interpretation of politics[35] cannot (or cannot yet) fill the political void left by the problematisation of the status of the sovereignty/anarchy dichotomy. The direction suggested by postmodernists such as Ashley and reflected in the ideal of the ironist in Rorty's work is an acceptance of flux and a recognition of a lack of universal meaning combined with an ordered political existence, a political existence that does not become the source of power. The postmodern agent (the liberal ironist of Rorty or the itinerate *condottiere* of Ashley)[36] struggles against orthodoxy of any kind. For Ashley, 'the IC conducts himself "virtu-ally", that is according to a general ethos or art of life in which one endlessly struggles amidst contingency and chance to somehow make it possible to live an inherently virtuous ideal *in effect*'.[37] If the critique of traditional understandings of international relations hits home what is the next step? For Ashley there is no definite answer but a series of ethical hopes the substance and problems of which are reflected more fully in Rorty's postmodern attempt to construct a human rights culture.

Rorty's account of a postmodern human rights culture rests on a different but comparable critique of the way we have traditionally theorised and acted in international relations. The idea that the philosophical search for truth is and always has been part of the problem rather than part of the solution reappears in order to replace it with post-philosophical hermeneutic textualism and thereafter with postmodern pragmatism. Here Rorty expresses the postmodernist hope, similar to that of Ashley, 'that the cultural space left by the demise of epistemology will not be filled – that our culture should be one in which the demand for constraint and confrontation is no longer felt'.[38] To be brutally concise, as any introduction must, Rorty develops his critique of 'bad foundationalism' to endorse a non-foundational pragmatism (qua Dewey) and to develop various accounts of the consequences of pragmatism. In later writings Rorty begins to do something quite unusual. While Rorty's work is usually labelled postmodern it often has the designation postmodern modified by riders such as 'communitarian'[39] or 'liberal'.[40] This is largely because, as Cochran vividly puts it, 'he does not share the belief of Michel Foucault and others that the baby, liberal democratic institutions, must go out with the Enlightenment rationalist bathwater'.[41] Rorty's anti-foundationalism does not lead him to a nihilist or a purely critical position. Indeed his adoption of the pragmatism of Dewey and his rejection of the postmodernism of Foucault is premised on an explicitly politically constructive agenda: 'Although Foucault and Dewey are trying to do the same thing, Dewey seems to have done it better, simply because his vocabulary allows room for unjustifiable hope and an ungroundable but vital sense of human solidarity.'[42]

Rorty bases the importance of this unjustifiable hope on the claim, taken from J. Shklar's definition of a liberal, that 'cruelty is the worst thing we can do'.[43] The central idea at work here is that once we have exploded the epistemological myths of modernist international relations theory we will no longer be able to discriminate between cruelty inflicted on 'people like us' and that inflicted upon 'others' not like us. Such a change, Rorty believes (or hopes) will elicit a fuller emotive response and the postmodern ironist will become a liberal ironist. The development of the 'liberal ironist', Rorty's postmodern hero, is fascinating and not a little unnerving. The liberal ironist is civilised in Rorty's terms where 'what distinguishes a civilised man from a barbarian is the ability to recognise the relative validity of one's convictions and yet stand for them unflinchingly'.[44] Recognising that our final vocabularies (conceptual frameworks) have no privileged status is vital. It is vital because the privileged standing we have historically given our ethical and political theories has led to the indefensible discrimination between black and white, Chosen and Infidel and ultimately in these cases between 'true humans and pseudohumans'.[45] This recognition leads us to become ironists, agents aware of our contingency yet empowered with the knowledge that we are self-creators. Yet even though our intellectual irony refuses the possibility of the development of moral knowledge, Rorty fuses his account of the ironist with a post-foundational liberalism. Rorty's position here stems from two principal ideas. Firstly he argues that the emergence of a human rights culture owes more to 'sad and sentimental stories' than to increased moral knowledge.[46] We are no longer as 'safe' and isolated from the horrors of the world as we once were and globalisation and interdependence have 'expanded the reference of the terms "our kind of people" and "people like us"'.[47] By manipulating and educating the sentiments of our fellow humans we further this expansion, indeed for Rorty this observable phenomenon is the 'best, and probably the only, argument for putting foundationalism behind us'.[48] Human rights, the principal aspiration of foundational liberalism, is the only appropriate mechanism for dealing with a world in which the artificial distinctions generated by rationalism have been exploded. It is this unjustifiable hope that human solidarity will be supported by irony that underpins Rorty's second argument for a post-foundational liberalism. As Cochran notes,

> [b]eliefs in freedom, toleration, and procedural justice constituted within liberal institutions are well suited to dealing with cultural diversity. As Rorty writes, there are 'practical advantages of liberal institutions in allowing individuals and cultures to get along without intruding on each others privacy, without meddling with each others conception of the good'.[49]

Postmodern irony requires continual encounters with other 'final vocabularies', a recognition that self-creation does not have any 'true' form. Rorty's unjustifiable hope in liberal institutions protects this ideal of self-creation as

> [t]he social glue holding together the ideal liberal society ... consists in little more than a consensus that the point of social organisation is to let everybody have a chance at self creation to the best of his or her abilities, and that goal requires, besides peace and wealth, the standard bourgeois freedoms.[50]

This sparse and introductory exposition cannot do full justice to Rorty's position but there are already tensions within Rorty's political programme. Perhaps the most obvious difficulty is the remaining tension between the modernist political project and Rorty's postmodern reading of the possibility and desirability of sustaining that project. The liberal ironist exhibits the kind of intellectual schizophrenia characteristic of postmodern attempts to engage with contemporary politics. Recalling Ashley's deconstruction of international relations theory is useful here. The modernist obsession with dualisms such as anarchy/sovereignty leads to a circularity of argument where anarchy is defined in relation to sovereignty (which is then treated as foundational) and vice versa. In Rorty's rendering of the liberal-ironist ideal something similar happens. The private ironist is defined in terms of pluralism, toleration, of our capacity for self-creation; in short irony *requires* the liberal institutional virtues. These virtues, Rorty claims, are already present in the ever expanding 'we group' in Rabossi's insistence that a human rights culture is characteristic of the here and now[51] and in the historical predominance of 'we' the 'Rawlsian seekers of consensus'.[52] Similarly the liberal is defined in terms of irony. Her mindset is premised on the belief that in deconstructing the discriminating practices of modernity, in ridding ourselves of the distinction between human and pseudo-human, we find that 'cruelty is the worst thing we can do' and thereby increase our desire to construct the political grounds of human solidarity. There are a number of problems here. As Bernstein notes,

> his official position is to denigrate the concept of universality ... but his vocabulary depends on all sorts of controversial and universal claims – for example we all have the capacity for self creation, we should all try to avoid

> cruelty and humiliating others, we should all strive to strengthen liberal institutions and increase human solidarity.[53]

Rorty the postmodernist rests his deconstruction of modernity on the non-cognitive function of our moral intuitions. Therefore Rorty the liberal must face up both to the fact that, 'the demand to diminish cruelty is an empty abstraction unless we give a concrete example of what we take to be examples of cruelty'[54] and to the point that an ironist may engage in a 'strong misreading' of cruelty, or humanity, or liberalism. This point is elaborated by Guignon and Hiley.

> So long as he was merely criticising foundationalist philosophy he could be content to have no answer to the question 'where do you stand when you say all these terrible things about other people?' But when he is presenting his own views, he must take responsibility for where he stands. ... His detached stance means it becomes increasingly difficult to make sense of why we have the commitments we have or why we should take one path into the future rather than another.[55]

Rorty argues that he is separating two questions. Firstly the public question 'is the absence of metaphysics politically dangerous?' Secondly, the private question, 'is ironism compatible with a sense of human solidarity?'[56] Yet this public/private distinction is required if Rorty is to have his postmodern cake and, in eating it, develop the outline of a political programme.[57] As Wain points out,

> the mechanism by which he now reconciles the growing political/cultural tensions in his work between the edifying language of aestheticist subversion and the normal pragmatic conversation of democratic politics, between the marginalisation of the intellectual and the demand for solidarity within the community from the same individual ... is the dichotomous division of life and action into public-private spheres with the strong poet being an ironist in private and engaged in commonsensical pragmatist debate in public.[58]

Yet Rorty can offer no non-circular reason why this should be so.

The difficulties in developing a political programme having first deconstructed the foundations of the political arena are many. Given that the claims of Rabbossi and Rorty, that we live in a human rights culture and think of cruelty as an evil, appear somewhat exaggerated and that only a few intellectuals think in non-foundationalist terms, it seems unlikely that Rorty's political project can speak to the here and now. Rorty's anti-realism, his critique of 'bad-foundationalism' makes a very important point (as does Ashley's critique of the heroic practice). But attempts to marry a deconstruction of politics to a relevant political agenda have proved exceptionally difficult. Rorty's unjustifiable hope appears to represent the outcome of much deconstructionist writing that resists nihilist conclusions. A well-worked rejection of the sovereignty/anarchy distinction or the human/pseudohuman distinction does not easily underwrite cosmopolitanism or human solidarity. This is not to suggest that postmodern 'dialogic' readings of international politics or global politics must confine themselves to deconstruction at the expense of theory. Ashley's negativism and Rorty's failure to sustain an appropriate vision of a human rights culture are not signifiers of the end of the usefulness of the tactic of 'making strange' the heroic practices of modernity. As Brown notes there is more to postmodern writing than arguments concerning the closure of modernity, far more at stake in international theory, as Smith notes, than epistemology.[59] The idea of a yet-to-be-created politics while promising is unhelpful here and now.

The most positive aspect of postmodern theory is the idea of irony, an idea divorced from Rorty's unjustifiable liberalism in the work of Connolly. Connolly's postmodernism aims toward a constructive general theory. He intends to compete with established theories, to produce a postmodernist theory that competes, 'not only through its ability to show how they subvert themselves ... but it must also compete with them at the level of affirmative constructions. In this case constructions that establish new possibilities in the play of identity and difference.'[60]

Connolly's irony struggles to resist the urge to ontologise identity. It challenges (as Rorty's ironist should) Rorty's claim that liberalism provides the best means of politicising identity, while appearing to recognise that irony's development has the weight of history and traditional ways of managing the political against it.

> A postmodern identity assumes an ironic stance toward what it is even while affirming itself in its identity. And this changes both the experience of identity and its *possible* range of relationships with other identities. It would not rule out of course, particular historical circumstances that spawn or intensify conflicts between opposing identities, but it would support new *possibilities* that establish new terms of comparison and debate and that place new pressures upon the established field of actualities and possibilities.[61]

There are political gaps between tradition, irony and possibility and Connolly illuminates these gaps and the potential problems more fully than Rorty. Between deconstruction and construction lies a world that has not accepted irony and while Connolly believes that 'time itself moves faster than it used to'[62] the political animal is still a ponderous beast. Nevertheless to accept the challenge of building a political world on top of pluralism (a more adequate representation of the contemporary international arena than irony) is to accept the challenge of bridging the gap between an international arena consisting of successive hegemonies now thought unjustifiable and an inter-sub-transnational politics that is justifiable in the face of pluralism. It is this challenge that postmodernism has yet to meet but that constructivism in political theory confronts head on.

A note on critical theory

Remaining, for the time being, within established convention in international studies there is one other body of literature that must be seen to leave space for constructivist normative theory before any exploration of the cosmopolitan/communitarian distinction is warranted. As Smith remarks, the majority of the discipline of international studies proceeds without noticing the cosmopolitan/communitarian distinction in normative theory.[63] The same cannot be said for critical theory. Like the postmodern theories introduced above critical theorists in international relations theory take neo-realism as their primary target and such a stance demands and has elicited a variety of responses from within the discipline. With this target in their sights critical theory has not, as Brown notes, 'been primarily concerned to engage with normative theorists'.[64] However in this introductory note I will suggest[65] that the political agenda voiced by some critical theorists does connect with the wider and more general project of normative political theory. In doing this I hope to invite the inference that the type of normative theory that this book argues is vital to international relations theory can play an important role in the formulation of critical theoretical approaches to international relations. I do not intend to put forward a comprehensive view of the critical theoretical project or to attempt to do justice to any single example of the category but to infer that critical theory starts from a basic commitment to the emancipation of humanity as a whole that rests on assumptions that are contested in the cosmopolitan/communitarian debate.

Following Linklater it is possible to distinguish that body of work referred to as 'critical theory' from postmodernism not so much by its critical approach to international theory but by its normative starting point: 'Since critical theory begins with a prima facie commitment to human equality, the first question to ask concerning the normative question of the state concerns the justification for excluding any human being from any social arrangement.'[66]

It is this aspect of the critical theoretical project I wish to glance at here as it is my contention that while the critical projects of postmodernism and critical theory bear similarities, critical theory like postmodernism leaves significant problems for a construction of an international theory that responds adequately to contemporary problems. If postmodernism fails to bridge the gap between positivist international relations and the needs of contemporary international relations then so does critical theory in assuming *a priori* the validity of cosmopolitanism. As an introductory sketch of both postmodernism and critical theory this chapter must be rather brutal with what is a large body of work. However it is not too controversial to suggest that the critical project of attacking traditional ways of theorising international relations (indeed of theorising in general) in both traditions are very similar. The task of problematising traditional ways of knowing (sketched out above) is central to the project of critical theorists who like the postmodernists seek to highlight the unjustifiable nature of the traditional political and epistemological structures that mark out the boundaries of social inclusion and exclusion. This much is clear on any basic reading of critical theory. Also clear is that the conclusions and hopes of critical theory and postmodernism are very different. The hopes of Ashley and Rorty that somehow a 'yet-to-be-created politics' that never elevates any form of knowledge or understanding to the position of truth will lead to a peaceful human rights culture cannot be equated with the project of critical theory. The basic normative standpoint that critical theory generates/assumes is simply a version of cosmopolitanism. This brief note does not purport to show whether critical theory is right or wrong but to suggest that it be subsumed under (rather than negated by) the critical standards of the cosmopolitan/communitarian debate.

Like postmodernism critical theory argues that knowledge is not a description of objective reality but reflects pre-existing social interests and therefore opposes the claim that existing social structures are necessarily justified and immutable.[67] Unlike postmodernism, critical theory attempts to recover and rejuvenate the enlightenment project in political theory.[68] For critical theorists the crisis in foundationalism does not mean that there can be no rigorous conception of (for example) international justice but just that the traditional models are flawed and need rethinking. Yet while their position is important to post-realist/post-positivist international theory, what is particularly striking is the fact that beyond the critique of epistemology

> it becomes difficult to distinguish critical theory from other varieties of progressive social thought. Thus Hoffman's cosmopolitan ethics are difficult to distinguish from those generated by Beitz, Shue or Onuf, the first two of whom are critical theorists only in the sense that they are critical of the existing order. ... It is not surprising that critical theory merges with a wider 'progressive literature' – the aim is to recast rather than abandon the enlightenment project.[69]

The goal of critical theory is simply to expose those systems of governance and distribution that rely upon foundations that are shown to be unjustifiable in the light of new understandings of interconnectedness and the epistemological critique and then to posit reformed systems of governance that do not share such problems. Critical theory, as Detevak puts it, 'opts for a revised version of cosmopolitanism'.[70] It is revised only in the sense that the foundations of its cosmopolitanism are supposed to be subject to the same critical scrutiny as the grounding assumptions of any political system. Yet cosmopolitanism is itself a diverse theory of international relations capable of many different interpretations and has many origins, all of which must be examined. What does such a claim entail? What evidence do cosmopolitans bring to the discussion? Is cosmopolitanism an underlying assumption, rather than a conclusion, of critical theory? It is precisely these questions that must be examined within contemporary liberal international relations theory. Indeed without a foray into the cosmopolitan/communitarian debate critical theory seems incomplete. The central issue is 'whether and how statecraft can be otherwise'.[71] Whether an argument is pitched from within the critical theory camp, the poststructuralist camp, the liberal or the socialist camps, its fundamental premises and conclusions are tied in with the normative arguments associated with the cosmopolitan/communitarian debate.

Opening out the normative theories

It must be noted that the cosmopolitan/communitarian debate has itself come under critical fire. The chief reasons for this criticism are twofold. First, it is suggested that this framework, like most in the academic history of international studies, creates rigid opposition between types of theory that tell us more about academia than they do about international politics. While there is some truth to this, we must recall that most intellectual traditions are subject to this charge and provided that we remember that this distinction is a starting point for analysis no real harm is done. The core distinction is quite real and while any suitably ambitious theory will transcend this stylised starting point (indeed the tradition termed developmental communitarianism is recommended precisely because it overcomes the limitations of both cosmopolitanism and communitarianism) all analytical adventures require a solid base camp from which to begin. Second (and perhaps more importantly) the cosmopolitan/communitarian debate is criticised because it is said to rely upon enlightenment reasoning and values that the critical traditions believe they have exposed as flawed. To be sure the basic tenets of the cosmopolitan/communitarian debate are drawn from the history of political thought. If normative theorists were to do no more than recommend the teachings of Kant or Hegel then their efforts may indeed have been wasted and this tradition subject to this criticism. However, contemporary, constructivist theorists (who can usefully be viewed as contributing to the cosmopolitan/communitarian debate as a way of orienting our thinking) are building upon the methodological criticisms of enlightenment ethics. The theoretical space created by the critical work of postmodernism and critical theory is outlined with appealing clarity by M. Frost. In *Ethics and International Relations*, Frost charts the development of concepts such as sovereignty, human rights and democratisation. Interesting here is the way in which Frost models the developing political and conceptual contestability surrounding the role of sovereignty in international politics. One vital consequence of the increase in epistemological uncertainty is the tendency to treat the characteristics and rules of international relations as norms rather than facts and thus as requiring justification rather than acknowledgment. Such norms exist because there is good reason for them to exist and not because they are an immutable part of the world and uncovering these good reasons and debunking a few bad ones is the principal task of normative theory. For Frost the starting point for an analysis of international relations is the modern state domain of discourse, an image of contemporary practices that recognises the tensions between the remnants of the Westphalian order and a post-Westphalian system.[72] Frost explains these tensions by referring to the settled norms that are shared within this practice. Frost lists those norms that he considers settled within the modern state domain of discourse under the sub-headings '*the sovereignty (S) norms, international law (L) norms, modernisation (M) norms and domestic (D) norms*' and summarises them thus:

> it is settled that the following are goods:
>
> S1. The preservation of the society of states.
> S2. State sovereignty.
> S3. Anti-imperialism.
> S4. The balance of power.
> S5. Patriotism.
> S6. Protecting the interests of a state's citizens.
> S7. Non intervention.
> S8. Self-determination.
> L1. International law.
> L2. *Ius ad bellum.*
> L3. *Ius in bello.*
> L4. Collective security.
> L5. Economic sanctions (under specified circumstances).
> L6. The diplomatic system.
> M1. Modernisation.
> M2. Economic cooperation.
> D1. Democratic institutions within states.
> D2. Human rights.[73]

Frost's treatment of these 'settled norms' begins to show that the 'goods' of the modern state domain of discourse, or indeed of any system of international relations, are not in fact as timeless as they first appear. Frost argues that:

> I shall regard a norm as settled where it is generally recognised that any argument denying the norm (or which appears to override that norm) requires special justification. Where I claim that a norm is settled I am not claiming that most people (or states) do in fact obey that norm. ... For example, that many states infringe the norm prohibiting one state interfering in the domestic affairs of another state does not undermine my contention that non-interference is a settled norm of the modern state domain of discourse.[74]

The first step in Frost's procedure for looking into the background justification for the modern state domain of discourse is to start with what everybody knows. This search reveals certain guiding *concepts* that are themselves capable of being understood in many different ways. It also avoids making (*a priori*) any strong claims about the 'necessary role of the state' or the 'ethical superiority of universal human rights', claims that would become the focus of a renewed epistemological critique by postmodernists or critical theorists. Nevertheless it is also quite clear that there is an important 'tension' between those goods that concern sovereignty and those that concern the rights of individual persons.[75] This tension is captured by the cosmopolitan/communitarian debate. Acknowledging that the postmodern critique of the traditional justification of statism or internationalism has some substance cannot lead to our ignoring the vital issue. When actions premised on norms of non-intervention clash with actions premised on norms of universal individual rights we have to find a way to answer the pressing questions that this clash generates. We cannot ignore the important political issues because we are unsure of the epistemological foundations of our argument. As Frost notes given the diversity of norms governing international relations today, 'it may be argued that the primary question for a normative theory of international relations is *whether* the system of sovereign states is a justifiable way of organising the government of the world'. Indeed this question has exercised many recent commentators. Given the pressing and controversial nature of this (and related) questions a successful political theory requires a critical edge that can acknowledge dissensus in international relations theory but still answer the hard questions arising from this fact. States, individuals and institutions hold a variety of opposing views on questions of international justice. How do we determine which views contribute most to international justice whilst rejecting bad foundationalism?

The key to this theoretical practice is finding a method by which one can discriminate between competing conceptions of international justice without falling foul of the charges of political or philosophical idealisation.[76] What is most striking about Frost's approach to international relations theory is the way he treats divergent understandings of the role of norms rather than uniform covering laws or 'facts' to outline contemporary tensions. Essentially this allows him to include a variety of political and ethical points of view in the first stage of his analysis while focusing upon the key issues in international relations. The reasons people give in defence of human rights, or global distributive justice, or for privileging sovereign rights vary dramatically and it is understanding and critically assessing these reasons that give an analysis of international relations its vitality. It is important to note that different reasons given in support of (for example) human rights can often require strikingly different international actions or portray a very different conception of the political direction of the international community. It is clear, for example, that the stronger liberal-cosmopolitan claims that seek to impose the full UN version of human rights as the core of any future international venture conflict with many accounts of the value that should be accorded to individual human agents. Feminists, communitarians, and many whose cultural heritage simply differs from that of western Europe all have something to add to the debate.[77] The outcome of this discussion will certainly have to privilege a particular understanding of human rights if it is to have any critical force. It therefore seems right to ask that the reasons we ask people to act against their convictions or to at least dilute their aspirations be clear and open to critical scrutiny. International justice is extremely high on the agenda of world politics. We therefore need the critical ammunition to assess the various claims made concerning the content of international ethics and the direction and mandate of the international community.

Following up on this line of reasoning Brown argues that normative theory, particularly the cosmopolitan/communitarian distinction, offers a more incisive angle of study than some of the core distinctions found in traditional international theory.

> The main point about these traditions is that they ground international relations theory within the wider projects of philosophy; they offer different and competing accounts of the way in which things 'international' are conceived and constituted within a wider understanding of how things hang together.[78]

Undoubtedly cosmopolitans are more 'transformationalist' than communitarians but this is not what really distinguishes them. The supporting justifications for 'Democratisation' and 'Modernisation' norms are philosophically distinct from those underpinning 'Sovereignty'. The philosophical support for human rights, for example, is typically individualistic, deontological and cosmopolitan. The philosophical support for sovereignty is often realist or communitarian. The major concerns of international relations theory are tied in with the cosmopolitan/communitarian debate. The claims of transformationalists, sceptics, postmodernists, poststructuralists, and critical theorists stand or fall on the strength of the normative buttresses that shore up their claims that we need/no longer need the sovereign state at the centre of international theory. To open out the cosmopolitan/communitarian debate is simply to explore the basic principles of international relations.

Constructing political theory: narrowing the focus

The cosmopolitan/communitarian distinction really begins to fill out the detail of the many positions taken in the current debates over international relations. Examining the sorts of reasons people give in defence of non-interventionist policies or in urging a greater policing of transnational human rights thus seems to offer the perfect starting point for an assessment of the key questions. However, in order to begin this process we need to begin to fill out our thumbnail sketch of the cosmopolitan/communitarian distinction.

Both Brown and Thompson point out that cosmopolitanism is never exclusively used in terms that strictly adhere to its philological roots. Politically and philosophically it is perfectly consistent to hold a cosmopolitan perspective but to reject a political vision of *cosmopolis*, a universal or world state. Cosmopolitans, argues Thompson, 'will reject the proposal for a world state if it seems to them that there are more costs than benefits as far as the promotion of individual rights or the maximisation of individual welfare is concerned'.[79] Cosmopolitanism is consistent with Kantianisms, utilitarianisms and various Marxisms; the distinction still leaves everything to be argued for while defining a general attitude towards international justice. Similarly communitarianism is a category that can support many forms of philosophy. Hegelians, relativists, realists (in the truly classical sense) can all be considered communitarians on Brown's desegregated use of the term. It is central to my argument that to be a communitarian, on this reading of the term, is not to cut oneself off from debates concerning justice in international relations. To do so would, in any case, make an exploration of international relations theory irrelevant to the elusive 'real world' of international politics. There is no satisfactory argument that proves definitively that principles of justice must arise from cosmopolitan assumptions.

For these distinctions to be useful they must be applied to the debates that surround substantive issues in international relations and in order to do this it is necessary to focus our attention on a less general aspect of the cosmopolitan/communitarian debate. Taking the basic framework of the cosmopolitan/communitarian distinction it is possible (and necessary) to examine the controversies between those cosmopolitans and communitarians who attempt to develop broadly 'secular' or constructivist principles of justice for the international arena. The focus on liberal theories of international ethics is unavoidable. The most contentious issues in international relations, the roles of the modern state and of human rights were developed within a period of liberal hegemony and continue to be discussed within the confines of a discourse broadly defined by that period of history. The 'modern state domain of discourse', as Frost terms it, justifies or condemns the state and its attached concepts and practices in terms that are historically liberal but currently agreed to be the correct focus for these justifications or criticisms of contemporary practice. The broad, if general, consensus upon the normative map of international relations gives this discourse (at least temporary) legitimacy. Nevertheless it is important to note that this legitimacy does not stem from the liberal heritage of this discourse and this is where the notion of a 'secular' (in Frost's terminology) or constructivist liberalism plays an important role. While the general outline of the cosmopolitan/communitarian debate (particularly in its liberal form) connects with the issues of contemporary international relations, the methodological and epistemological foundations drawn from its historical and philosophical origin are often subject to the criticisms outlined above. Taking the historical origin of contemporary discourse first it is clear that to accept uncritically the validity of a liberal discourse would be to assume the foundational and normative validity of the period of liberal hegemony in international politics. Such an assumption could only lead to a political conservatism, an endorsement of the *status quo*. Similarly (and taking the philosophical origin of liberal discourse) to accept uncritically the foundations of much liberal thought merely because liberal politics and language forms a large part of contemporary debate would lead to the implicit acceptance of metaphysical and moral assumptions that can and have been shown to be false or problematic. In short it would be to adopt a conceptual conservatism.[80] Highlighting these potential difficulties forms the bedrock of the critical projects of those thinkers examined above. For some postmodernists the recognition that some of the foundations of liberal discourse are illegitimate (in that they rely on unquestioned metaphysical assumptions or arbitrarily exclude sections of international society on unproven premises) leads to a call to renounce the liberal discourse in its entirety. However, given the general consensus that at least in part the 'modern state domain of discourse' (or a revised version of that discourse) has the potential to solve or mitigate some of the most pressing problems in international relations, it would seem reasonable only to reject those aspects of the debate that can be shown to rely upon illegitimate premises. It is this project that a critical and constructivist account of the cosmopolitan/communitarian distinction undertakes.

The postmodern position(s) rejected the validity of many cosmopolitan and communitarian theories on at least two interrelated grounds. The first of these relates to the epistemological and methodological problems associated with assuming the foundational necessity of certain political arrangements. Some communitarian theories, for example, assume that the state is the primary agent or unit of analysis in international relations. Ashley's critique of this position offers a useful tool here. Similarly certain cosmopolitan theories assume that the human species is the primary focus of moral or political analysis and this is equally problematic. For example, Marxian cosmopolitanism rules out the possibility that workers in different parts of the world may have different interests due to the assumptions and foundational role of concepts such as class or species being.[81] Likewise some versions of Kantian cosmopolitanism assume *a priori* the value of a federation of republican states or more radically a universal kingdom of ends because of the foundational assumption of the value of individual autonomy.[82] The general postmodern position that such strategies are to be disallowed unless the underlying assumptions can be deconstructed often merges with the second reason that postmodernism rejects the validity of many positions within the cosmopolitan/communitarian distinction. Here the critique of the assumption of the foundational status of dubious metaphysical and empirical assumptions about the nature of ethics and politics merges with a kind of moral scepticism. The repeated failure of enlightenment theories to prove their philosophical and moral premises leads to the denial that we can have knowledge about moral matters at all and thereafter to the claim that the political and theoretical strategies developed from enlightenment thought are doomed from the outset. In some cases scepticism about the possibility of moral knowledge stems not only from our apparent inability to prove all our premises but also from the claim that there can be no objective moral and political facts.

> Moral sceptics do not claim that although there might be moral facts, we cannot, for some reason, acquire knowledge of them. They claim, rather, that we have no moral knowledge because there are no moral facts to be discovered. Or else they claim that insofar as there are moral facts, they are not the sorts of facts that ground objective, or universally valid, moral truths. For example, they might construe them as relativistic facts about the conformity or non-conformity of one's behaviour with the social conven-

> tions of one's society. Thus epistemological moral scepticism is rooted in *ontological* moral scepticism.[83]

Many of these criticisms appear well focused. Any theory of international relations must argue for the continued validity or rejection of the state as the central unit of analysis. These theories must also be prepared to defend the epistemological and ontological assumptions they make in doing so. The cosmopolitans and communitarians that now take centre stage in this book do precisely this. They are critical, in the sense that they examine closely the structure and form of their arguments to ensure they do not fall foul of the first of the criticisms outlined above, and they are constructivist, in that they argue that it is still possible to give sense to moral and political judgments without making questionable assumptions about the nature of moral and political reality. This critical and constructivist normative theory gets its political relevance from its engagement with the most pressing issues in international relations (modelled in the cosmopolitan/communitarian distinction) and its theoretical relevance from its engagement with the problems of political and philosophical justification.

Conclusion: constructivism as a special case in the cosmopolitan/communitarian debate

If the theories I put forward as examples of constructivist international relations theory can fulfil the criterion outlined above then my claim that the cosmopolitan/communitarian debate captures the tensions that adjoin the empirical changes and the corresponding theoretical justifications in contemporary international politics is justified. Constructivism or 'secular liberalism' models the attempt by some liberal thinkers to base their ethical theory upon non-controversial assumptions. Non-controversial, that is, in terms of some of the methodological criticisms thrown up in the individualist/communitarian debate and wider debates concerning foundationalism and modernity. The examples offered here show that thinkers from both sides of the cosmopolitan/communitarian divide claim to have secularised principles of international justice that they claim are consistent with liberal aspirations. It is this aspect of the debate that must now hold our attention. The four central thinkers examined in this book are all self-consciously wary of relying on methodological foundations that would have been accepted almost without question less than a century ago. O'Neill and Frost specifically claim to have modernised Kantian and Hegelian philosophy respectively. In 'taking seriously the idea of a critique of reason' O'Neill seeks to save Kant from what is considered to be,

> a metaphysically preposterous account of the basis of freedom. ... [and to] set Kant's ethics in the context of his own accounts of reason, action and freedom, to argue that these should not be read as a metaphysical

extravaganza and to show that his ethical theory is neither pointlessly empty or relentlessly nasty.[84]

Initially O'Neill thought to reinterpret Kantian metaphysics so as to appeal to a modern audience and this is the project in *Constructions of Reason*. Subsequently, however, O'Neill has sought to divorce Kantian political principles from their metaphysical foundation and this is the project of *Towards Justice and Virtue*. Her principal claim is that the contemporary circumstances of justice and injustice (interconnectedness) require that we recognise universal obligations to humanity. This conclusion, O'Neill claims, is not shored up by dubious metaphysics or partisan moral principles. Similarly Frost, whose developmental communitarianism is pitted against O'Neill's cosmopolitanism, bids to secularise Hegel by divorcing Hegel's political philosophy from his metaphysics claiming that, '[c]onstitutive theory does not require of us that we either understand or accept Hegel's metaphysical system.'[85] For Frost, understanding how we are constituted as individuals within the framework of our social institutions and the 'settled norms' of international society (qua Hegel) rules out many understandings of human rights without requiring that the resulting theory be viewed as the next progression of world spirit. The other two examples of developmental communitarianism take a similar tack. The prime motivating factor that prompted Rawls to restate his liberalism in *Political Liberalism* was the desire to confront the issue of ethical pluralism and to spell out the fact that the foundation of liberalism is not what he calls 'comprehensive',[86] that it is 'political and not metaphysical'. Similarly Walzer's intellectual battle with the problem of universality in political theory results in the fascinating claim that any universal international ethics must stem from current political developments. All four thinkers are ostensibly concerned with the same sets of problems that arise from international relations and all four are interested in vindicating their claims to justice in international relations theory while keeping a wary eye on their justificatory procedure. Yet the claims that Walzer, Frost and O'Neill make on international justice on the back of their secular justifications differ quite radically. The differences are so distinct and in some cases so polarised as to make the cosmopolitan/communitarian distinction a very useful starting point from which to analyse their claims.

In the context of Brown's formulation of the cosmopolitan/communitarian distinction, and in particular in the context of this book, it is important to note at the outset as Brown does that, 'cosmopolitanism is a universalist principle but not all universalist principles are cosmopolitan'.[87] In many ways the theory advanced in the following chapters is a detailed working out of this point. All of the thinkers examined here focus on some understanding of universal ethics but this is neither to assume an answer to a contentious question in international relations theory nor to deny that there are essential differences between the types of philosophy being offered for scrutiny. The dominant tradition in normative theory is cosmopolitanism. As a tradition it argues, following (and in some cases incorporating) postmodernism and critical theory that the historical practice of treating the state or community as the final arbiter in matters of international theory and policy has been the chief cause of many problems in world politics. Cosmopolitans then go on to suggest that international relations theory must shift its focus to a conception of individual agency or moral worth and in doing so raise the concept of human rights to a controlling position. However in the following chapters it will become clear that cosmopolitanism may not be able to live up to the requirements of constructivism. In being seen to fail this standard it is vital that cosmopolitanism relinquishes the moral and political high ground to developmental communitarianism, a reworked liberal theory that can take account of the empirical developments and the theoretical intricacies that this first chapter has shown to be necessary to any understanding of international relations theory.

Notes and references

1 Some historians point to earlier treaties including Augsberg (1555) that led up to the treaty of Westphalia while others, including M. Wight go even further back to 1494 and the invasion of Italy by France. Wight's reasoning is that it was at this time that the European powers adopted Italian power politics (M. Wight, *Power Politics*, Leicester University Press, 1978, p. 30), however it was not until the end of the Thirty Years War that the majority of the principles were considered the norm.
2 See, for examples, A. Magrew (ed.), *The Transformation of Democracy?: Globalisation and Territorial Democracy*, Polity Press, 1997; D. Held, *Democracy and the Global Order: From the Modern State to Cosmopolitan Governance*, Polity Press, 1995 and L. Gross, 'The Peace of Westphalia 1648–1948', in R. Falk and W.F. Hanreider (eds), *International Law and Organization*, Lippincott, 1968.
3 McGrew, *The Transformation of Democracy?*, p. 6.
4 Held, *Democracy and the Global Order*, chapters 5 and 6.
5 McGrew, *The Transformation of Democracy?*, p. 7.
6 Held, *Democracy and the Global Order*, p. 135.
7 M. Williams, 'Rethinking Sovereignty' in E. Kofman and G. Youngs (eds), *Globalization: Theory and Practice*, London, Pinter, 1996, p. 115.
8 Williams, 'Rethinking Sovereignty', p. 116.
9 McGrew, *The Transformation of Democracy?*, p. 9.
10 See chapter 5.
11 See chapter 6.
12 See chapter 7.
13 See chapter 4.
14 C. Brown, *International Relations Theory: New Normative Approaches*, New York, London, Harvester Wheatsheaf, 1992, p. 8.
15 See M. Hoffman, 'Critical Theory and the Inter-Paradigm Debate', *Millennium*, Vol. 16, No. 2, Summer 1987, p. 231.
16 Brown, *International Relations Theory*, p. 12.
17 A. Linklater, 'The Achievements of Critical Theory', in S. Smith, K. Booth and M. Zalewski (eds), *International Theory: Positivism and Beyond*, Cambridge, Cambridge University Press, 1996, p. 279.
18 See for example M. Hoffman, 'Critical Theory and the Interparadigm Debate', *Millennium*, Vol. 16, No. 2, Summer 1987, p. 231. A. Linklater, *Beyond Realism and Marxism: Critical Theory and International Relations*, Macmillan, 1990. R. Cox, 'Social Forces, States and World Orders: Beyond International Relations Theory', *Millennium*, Vol. 10, No. 2, 1981, p. 128.

19 See R. Ashley, 'Untying the Sovereign State: A Double Reading of the Anarchy Problematique', *Millennium*, Vol. 17, No. 2, Summer 1988, p. 227. R. Rorty, 'Human Rights, Rationality and Sentimentality' in S. Shute and S. Hurley (eds), *On Human Rights*, Basic Books, 1993, p. 112 and J. Der Derian and M. Shapiro (eds), *International/Intertextual Relations: Postmodern Readings of World Politics*, Lexington Books, Maxwell Macmillan International, 1989.

20 For example, what is now thought of as the erroneous assumption that state-sovereignty was an unchallengeable fact of international politics is often cited as a principal cause of international conflict and injustice.

21 V. Spike Peterson, 'Shifting Ground(s): Epistemological and Territorial Remapping in the Context of Globalisation(s)', in E. Kofman and G. Youngs (eds), *Globalization: Theory and Practice*, London, Pinter, 1996, p. 15.

22 For this reason the brief note on critical theory (which predates postmodernism) appears after my discussion of the work of some representative postmodernists.

23 C. Brown, 'Critical Theory and Postmodernism in International Relations', in A. Groom and M. Light (eds), *Contemporary International Relations: A Guide to Theory*, Pinter Publishers, 1994, p. 61. See also R. Ashley, 'Living on Border Lines: Man, Poststructuralism and War', in Der Derian, J. and Shapiro, M. (eds), *International/Intertextual Relations: Postmodern Readings in World Politics*, Basingstoke, Lexington Books, Maxwell Macmillan International, 1989, p. 261.

24 Ashley, 'Anarchy Problematique', p. 230.

25 Ashley, 'Anarchy Problematique', p. 230.

26 Ashley, 'Anarchy Problematique', pp. 230–231.

27 Der Derian and Shapiro, *International/Intertextual*, p. xiv.

28 Ashley, 'Anarchy Problematique', p. 232.

29 Ashley, 'Anarchy Problematique', p. 233 see also p. 254.

30 Ashley, 'Anarchy Problematique', p. 254.

31 See for example R. Walker, *Inside/Outside: International Relations as Political Theory*, Cambridge University Press, 1993. J. Der Derian, 'A Reinterpretation of Realism: Genealogy, Semiology, Dromology', in J. Der Derian (ed.), *International Theory: Critical Investigations*, Macmillan, 1995, p. 363.

32 R. Detevak, 'Postmodernism', in S. Burchill, A. Linklater *et al.*, *Theories of International Relations*, London, Macmillan, 1996, p. 201.

33 See for example R. Ashley and R. Walker, 'Speaking the Language of Exile: Dissidence in International Studies', *International Studies Quarterly*, Vol. 34, No. 3, 1990, pp. 259–417.

34 Ashley and Walker, 'Speaking the Language of Exile', p. 395 cited Detevak, 'Postmodernism', p. 205.

35 Brown, 'Critical Theory and Postmodernism', p. 62.

36 Ashley, 'The Achievements of Post-Structuralism', in Smith, Booth and Zalewski (eds), *International Theory*, p. 253.

37 Ashley, 'The Achievements of Post-Structuralism', p. 253.

38 R. Rorty, *Philosophy and the Mirror of Nature*, Blackwell, 1980, p. 315.

39 Brown, *International Relations Theory*, p. 205.

40 See particularly R. Rorty, *Contingency, Irony and Solidarity*, Cambridge University Press, 1989 and R. Rorty, 'Human Rights, Rationality and Sentimentality' for expressions of Rorty's liberalism.

41 M. Cochran, 'Postmodernism, Ethics and International Relations Theory', *Millennium*, Vol. 25, No. 1, 1996, p. 33.

42 R. Rorty, 'Method, Social Science and Social Hope; Ungrounded Hope, Dewey vs Foucault', in *The Consequences of Pragmatism*, Harvester Press, 1982, p. 208.

43 Rorty, *Contingency, Irony and Solidarity*, p. 73.

44 Rorty, *The Consequences of Pragmatism*, p. 155. for a full description of the 'powers' of the liberal Ironist, which for reasons of space cannot be examined here, see Rorty, *Contingency, Irony and Solidarity*, particularly p. 73.
45 Rorty, 'Human Rights', p. 112.
46 Rorty, 'Human Rights', p. 119.
47 Rorty, 'Human Rights', p. 123.
48 Rorty, 'Human Rights', p. 122.
49 Cochran, 'Postmodern Ethics', p. 33. quotation from Rorty, 'On Ethnocentrism: A Reply to Clifford Geertz', *Michigan Quarterly Review*, Vol. 25, No. 3, 1986, p. 533.
50 Rorty, *Contingency, Irony, and Solidarity*, p. 84.
51 Rorty, 'Human Rights', p. 132.
52 Rorty, 'Thugs and Theorists: A Reply to Bernstein', *Political Theory*, Vol. 15, No. 4, 1987, p. 564.
53 R. Bernstein, *The New Constellation: The Ethical-Political Horizons of Modernity/postmodernity*, Polity Press, 1991, p. 278.
54 Bernstein, *The New Constellation*, p. 284.
55 C. Guignon and D. Hiley, 'Biting the Bullet: Rorty on Private and Public Morality', in A. Malachowski (ed.), *Reading Rorty: Critical Responses to Philosophy and the Mirror of Nature and Beyond*, Blackwell, 1990, pp. 360–361.
56 Rorty, *Contingency, Irony, and Solidarity*, p. 87.
57 See Cochran, 'Postmodernism, Ethics', p. 51.
58 K. Wain, 'Strong Poets and Utopia: Rorty's Liberalism, Dewey, and Democracy', *Political Studies*, Vol. 41, No. 3, 1993, p. 404.
59 S. Smith, 'Positivism and Beyond', in Smith, Booth and Zalewski (eds), *International Theory*, p. 38.
60 W.E. Connolly, 'Identity and Difference in Global Politics' in Der Derian and Shapiro (eds), *International/Intertextual*, p. 337.
61 Connolly, 'Identity and Difference', pp. 331–332.
62 Connolly, 'Identity and Difference', p. 333.
63 S. Smith, 'The Self Images of a Discipline: A Genealogy of International Relations Theory', in S. Smith and K. Booth (eds), *International Relations Theory Today*, Polity Press, 1995, p. 9.
64 Brown, *International Relations Theory*, p. 13.
65 To attempt to do any more here would be to explore a series of issues tangential to the goal of this thesis.
66 A. Linklater, 'The Question of the Next Stage in International Relations Theory: A Critical Theoretical Point of View', *Millennium*, 1992, Vol. 21, No. 1, p. 92.
67 Linklater, 'The Achievements of Critical Theory', p. 279.
68 By 'enlightenment project' I mean no more than a general belief in the power and developmental potential of rational change, a desire to create theory rather than critique all rationality.
69 Brown, 'Critical Theory and Postmodernism', p. 59.
70 Detevak, 'Critical Theory', p. 173.
71 Detevak, 'Incomplete States: Theories and Practices of Statecraft', in MacMillan and Linklater (eds), *Boundaries in Question*, p. 33.
72 Frost, *Ethics*, p. 79. A similar, although less detailed, starting point can be found in S. Brown, *International Relations in a Changing Global System: Toward a Theory of the World Polity*, Westview Press, 1996, p. 2.
73 Frost, *Ethics*, pp. 111–112.
74 Frost, *Ethics*, p. 105.
75 Frost, *Ethics*, p. 137.
76 Idealisation in political theory is a fairly clear concept the detail of which is usefully worked out in O'Neill's work. See chapter 4.

77 See for example R. Falk, 'A Half-Century of Human Rights', *Australian Journal of International Affairs*, Vol. 52, No. 3, 1998, pp. 255–272 and K.B. Hadjor, 'Whose Human Rights?', *Journal of African and Asian Studies*, Vol. 33, No. 4, 1998, pp. 359–368. Also Julie Peters and Andrea Wolper (eds), *Women's Rights, Human Rights: International Feminist Perspectives*, London, New York, Routledge, 1995.
78 Brown, *International Relations Theory*, p. 83.
79 Thompson, *Justice and World Order: A Philosophical Inquiry*, London, Routledge, 1992, p. 105. see also Brown, *International Relations Theory*, p. 13.
80 See E. Gellner, *Words and Things*, London, Gollancz, 1959, p. 44 cited Frost, *Ethics*, p. 102.
81 Cf. Brown, *International Relations Theory*, p. 45.
82 See chapter 2 for a further discussion of Kantianism.
83 R. Milo, 'Scepticism and Moral Justification', *The Monist*, Vol. 76, 1993, p. 381
84 O. O'Neill, *Constructions of Reason*, preface, p. ix. See also chapters 2 and 4 below.
85 Frost, *Ethics*, p. 143. See also chapter 5 below.
86 Cf. Rawls, *PL*, p. xvi and chapter 7 below.
87 Brown, *International Relations Theory*, p. 24.

2 Cosmopolitanism and critical cosmopolitanism

In order to introduce the thought of O'Neill, Frost, Walzer and Rawls and in particular those elements of their work that are fundamental to the discourse that this study sets out to examine, I intend to situate each thinker in the intellectual context of the cosmopolitan/communitarian distinction as outlined in the previous chapter. The important development here is that there is a narrowing of focus. This study is not concerned with the cosmopolitan/communitarian debate as a whole but with that area of thought that can be described as secular, or constructivist, liberalism. This focus is particularly interesting because while the distinctions between Kantian or Marxist cosmopolitanism and the communitarianism of Hegel or Rousseau are particularly clear and well charted by Brown, the dispute between contemporary liberal cosmopolitanism and liberal communitarianism is neither clear nor frequently charted. This shortcoming perpetuates the dominance of cosmopolitanism and obscures the potentially more fruitful tradition of developmental communitarianism. While cosmopolitan thinkers claim that their liberalism is the only viable way in which to model the development of the normative map of international relations, I intend to show that this commonplace assumption is far from secure. This challenge to current theory stems from a necessary re-examination of the limits of liberal principles of justice generated by the 'restricted' justifications available to the modern liberal. This examination is here conducted in terms of a debate between constructivist and developmental communitarians and constructivist cosmopolitans. To reiterate some points made earlier: The focus on normative discourse within the constructivist liberal tradition does not assume any particular conclusion to the debates concerning philosophical foundationalism, modernity and postmodernity. Rather it is intended to highlight an aspect of the liberal tradition that O'Neill, Frost, Walzer and Rawls can be seen to represent. The fascinating aspect of this tradition is that claims to have modified their philosophical predicates (in the light of criticisms of enlightenment metaphysics or empirical inaccuracy) have not led to a substantial shift in the normative and political principles generated by the ethical theories of these constructivist liberals. Walzer claims that the most 'liberal' principle we can expect in international relations theory is expressed in the 'moral minimum' yet both O'Neill and Frost (albeit for different reasons) claim that a substantive theory of human rights can, and must, be built into any understanding of contemporary international relations. It is this distinction (and similar contrasts) that requires of us that we treat the discourse between these thinkers as a special aspect of the cosmopolitan/communitarian debate.

I wish to start with an examination of the cosmopolitan arguments primarily because it is commonly assumed that any argument urging the liberalisation of international politics (or, more generally, any ethically progressive argument) is cosmopolitan. To explain further: All three representatives of the cosmopolitan position claim the moral high ground in contemporary liberal international relations theory. Beitz, for example, argues that the ideas expressed by cosmopolitan liberalism have been 'expressed in more than one ethical tradition in the west. ... Today it is a common element in virtually all forms of western liberalism as well as in most plausible ethical doctrines associated with conservatism and social democracy. We are (almost) all cosmopolitans now.'[1] The inference here is plain. Beitz argues that any ethically plausible, or liberal, theory is cosmopolitan. If this is truly to be the case it necessitates a widening of the scope of cosmopolitanism to such an extent that it becomes a catch-all description with no critical force. Not only is this undesirable but the descriptions of cosmopolitanism offered by Beitz, Pogge and O'Neill simply do not 'catch-all', they exclude quite obviously many forms of communitarian theory including developmental communitarianism. The commonplace assumption that follows from this is that those types of theory that do not fit the description of cosmopolitanism are neither ethically plausible nor liberal in aspiration, a position that is both unsustainable and impairs the development of liberal international relations theory.

That the majority of liberal international relations theory coheres with cosmopolitanism is beyond question. It is certainly easier, in many ways, to identify those thinkers chosen as examples of this tradition as cosmopolitans than it is to identify Frost, Walzer and Rawls as communitarians. In part this is due to the absolute dominance of cosmopolitanism in liberal international relations theory. In the case of the cosmopolitan theorists offered as examples of the tradition, all three adopt the title themselves and set themselves up in opposition to realism and communitarianism. That these thinkers accurately model a liberal-cosmopolitan approach to international relations is not disputed. What is contested is the description of the international relations theory of Frost, Walzer and Rawls as cosmopolitan and beyond that the description of all plausible liberal international relations theory as cosmopolitan. A rigorous understanding of the form and content of contemporary cosmopolitan theory leads, I argue, to the recognition that despite the emphasis upon conceptions of international law, human rights, international equality and the 'crime' of aggression found in the work of Frost, Walzer and Rawls, we are better placed to understand their distinctive contributions to liberal international relations theory if we separate their work from that of cosmopolitanism and focus on certain aspects of their liberalism that distinguish them as developmental communitarians. For example, Rawls' method is, he argues, Kantian. Nevertheless he shows four differences between 'Kant's moral constructivism' and 'the political constructivism of justice as Fairness.'[2] Later, in the 1999 version of *The Law of Peoples*, Rawls explicitly distances himself from cosmopolitanism in what will be seen as his most norm-governed or communitarian writing to date. The methodological issues that Rawls' position raises permeate the normative debate that international studies should be concerned with. The Kantianism of O'Neill is outraged by Rawls' methodological liaison with 'relativism', the Kantianism of Beitz and Pogge is astounded by the normative conclusions that Rawls draws from his position, and yet Rawls maintains that all political liberalism is doing is limiting the comprehensive nature of Kant's moral theory by appealing only to those aspects of that theory relevant to the political. In other words Rawls attempts to model the appropriate limits of 'liberal' international justice and in doing so distances his theory from cosmopolitanism. Rawls' argument that 'Political Liberalism must, of course, reject Kant's constitutive autonomy; yet his moral constructivism can endorse political constructivism as far as it goes'[3] will introduce us to this aspect of the liberal, methodological debate in chapters 3 and 7 below. The force of this claim depends, I shall maintain, upon the recognition of the importance of the way in which their communitarianism constructs an account of international ethics. The separation of developmental communitarianism from gradualist cosmopolitanism can be seen to form a vital part of a pertinent understanding of contemporary international relations theory.

Kantian philosophy and cosmopolitan conclusions

Despite the dominance of the cosmopolitan position there is still some confusion about its core principles and arguments. In particular the moral predicates and the political project of cosmopolitanism are often confused in the introductory literature. Scruton's *A Dictionary of Political Thought* is as guilty as any in defining cosmopolitanism in the following manner.

> Its greatest advocate in modern times has been Kant, whose prescription for 'perpetual peace' involves the generation of an international government obedient to the conception, incipient in the thinking of every moral agent, of a 'kingdom of ends' in which everything is as it ought to be, and ought to be as it is.[4]

This entry is troubling both as a description of cosmopolitanism and of Kant's *Perpetual Peace*.[5] The idea that Kant requires a kind of universal government that acts as a 'universal kingdom of ends' stems from a confusion of Kant's political and moral theory. It is important that the distinction is made as merging the two obscures the way in which the political project of cosmopolitanism relies upon the moral ideas that are developed out of Kant's transcendental idealism. The core of cosmopolitanism is not a vigorously defined political project but a concern for a particular type of moral agent – the autonomous individual. There are a number of political perspectives that stem from the Kantian moral project (something also obscured by this common rendering of 'cosmopolitanism' and that I go on to examine in the next section) but the shared heritage of cosmopolitanism is what holds it together as a tradition. It is also what marks developmental communitarianism off from this strand of liberal thought.

The formula of the universal kingdom of ends, cited by Scruton, is a much-maligned expression of what is possibly the best-known aspect of Kant's ethical writing, 'the categorical Imperative'.[6] The categorical imperative is an expression of practical reason, an expression of moral principle that is necessary in itself (i.e.: necessary to the idea of morality itself without reference to an end). Moral philosophy up until Kant, so Kant argued, had simply been concerned with 'hypothetical imperatives' (end-orientated maxims of action), which, Kant argued, could only be rules of skill or councils of prudence. However, for Kant 'nothing but the *idea of the law* in itself ... can constitute that pre-eminent good which we call moral, a good which is already present in the person acting on this idea and has not to be awaited merely from the result'.[7]

The categorical imperative states the universality of the moral law. It is the basis of all morality, independent of the world as it appears. The categorical imperative originally appears in the 'formula of the universal law', '*Act only on that Maxim through which you can at the same time will that it should become a universal law.*'[8] The formula of the kingdom of ends is, Kant argues, another expression of the moral law. Putting aside scholarly debate over whether any of the other formulations of the categorical imperative are consistent with the first formulation, the formula of the kingdom of ends is said to be concerned both with the form and the matter of the moral law. Thus Kant writes '*So act as if you were through your maxims a law making member of a kingdom of ends.*'[9] In this formulation of the categorical imperative the form of the moral law (its universality) and the matter of the moral law (the necessary idea of autonomy[10]) are combined to create the kingdom of ends. The basic idea is that all human beings as reasoning agents must act on principles that all other human beings could accept regardless of political, cultural or geographical differences. Such differences are morally irrelevant. The kingdom of ends is necessarily universal in scope, combining the autonomy of all rational agents as legislators of the universal law. Yet for Kant this 'kingdom of ends' is only an ideal of a moral community and can serve only as a regulative ideal. The 'as if' in Kant's formulation is meant to act as an analogical argument to introduce a maxim of regulative judgment.[11] Put crudely: to act morally is to act from pure principles of moral reason (practical reason) with no view to an end. An agent can use the idea of a universal kingdom of ends to test his or her action (or maxim) against the principles of the moral law which at its most basic is the idea that all human beings must be free to act autonomously, on their own will. No moral action can hamper the potential to act of another individual. Thus an exacting conception of what it is to be a moral agent is built into the basis of Kantian theory. These arguments represent a drastically abridged version of some of Kant's moral philosophy but Kant was under no illusion concerning the possible political outcome of his project. While these arguments do underwrite some of Kant's political theory, cosmopolitanism, in the form of a universal government, is not predicated directly upon this argument about morality.

To explain: In the *Metaphysics of Morals* Kant puts forward an idea of moral progress that begins with a necessary move out of the state of nature:

> it still lies *a priori* in the rational Idea of such a condition … that before a public lawful condition is established, individual men, peoples, and states can never be secure against violence. … So unless it wants to renounce any concepts of Right, the first thing it has to resolve upon is the principle that it must leave the state of nature.[12]

Immediately prior to this Kant argues that: 'since the earth's surface is not unlimited but closed, the concepts of the Right of a state and of a Right of nations lead inevitably to the Idea of a *Right for all nations (Ius Gentium)* or *cosmopolitan right (Ius Cosmopoliticum)*'.[13]

The move of an individual from a state of nature to civil society is a moral imperative. It is necessary to the very *idea* of justice. Similarly, one might assume, given that the state of nature between sovereign states is 'a condition that one ought to leave in order to enter a lawful condition',[14] it would be necessary to extend civil society until it is universal thus realising the kingdom of ends as a political ideal. However, in *Perpetual Peace* Kant states that:

> [n]or can one say of nations as regards their rights what one can say concerning the natural rights of men in a state of lawlessness, to wit, that 'they should abandon this state' (for as nations they already have an internal, legal constitution and therefore have outgrown the compulsion to subject themselves to another legal constitution that is subject to someone else's concept of right).[15]

He goes on to espouse a version of *Ius Cosmopoliticum* that is 'limited to conditions of universal hospitality'.[16] The vital distinction, which the merging of Kant's moral and political theory obscures, arises from Kant's concern with the conditions of both internal freedom (autonomy) – something he deals within his moral philosophy – and external (or political) freedom – something he deals with in his political theory. Understanding morality is a very different proposition to thinking about the correct ordering of political or international society. While Kant (and most contemporary cosmopolitans) remain committed to the moral ideal of the autonomous individual it is clear from his political theory that protecting the freedom of individuals from tyrannical government requires that our international aspirations are limited. Nevertheless it is still possible to argue from a Kantian argument concerning individual freedom that the bounded, territorial nation-state or a communitarian privileging of the shared norms of local culture cannot deal adequately with the moral imperative to treat all individuals as autonomous. Indeed this moral cosmopolitanism forms an important part (perhaps the most important part) of the contemporary cosmopolitan tradition. In order to analyse the cosmopolitan arguments it is necessary to see how they get to the moral position that insists on this focus on the individual agent. In general, contemporary cosmopolitans seek to distance themselves from Kant's metaphysical system. Recognising that this moral argument is separate from the political argument thus gives us a useful starting point from which to judge the validity, or otherwise, of their claims. We can focus on the separate claims that the individual agent should be given priority over the community and then on the relation between this claim and the political project that is built around it.

Despite the fact that moral and political cosmopolitanism do not necessarily derive from the same argument it is true to say that most contemporary cosmopolitans do prescribe a more global vision of transnational politics. It is therefore important to understand the pattern that this argument takes. It is clear, I think, that Kant's primary reason for limiting *Ius Cosmopoliticum* to universal hospitality seems to be that this is all we can have if we are to acknowledge that politics represents a bastion between freedom and potential tyranny. Indeed he builds upon this idea writing,

> But as to the external relations among nations, it cannot be expected that a nation will give up its constitution, even if despotic (which is the stronger in relation to foreign enemies), so long as it risks the danger of being overrun by other nations; consequently it is permissible to delay the intention to implement improvements until a better opportunity arises.[17]

This introduces the second claim commonly made by cosmopolitanism; that, given the 'better opportunity' that contemporary political interdependence provides, the requisite conditions for realising a greater form of *Ius Cosmopoliticum* are now in place. For Kant there was no doubt that history should theoretically proceed to a full instantiation of his ideal. Indeed in a note to the preceding quotation he argued that

> [t]hese are permissive laws of reason: to allow a condition of public right afflicted with injustice to continue until everything is either of itself or through peaceful means ripe for complete transformation. … Revolutions brought about by nature itself will not find excuses for still greater oppression, but will use revolution as a call of nature to create a lawful constitution based on principles of freedom, for only this fundamental reform is enduring.[18]

Yet the reasoning employed to get to this conclusion is also part of Kant's transcendental idealism, his metaphysical system and as such represents an unacceptable justificatory strategy in contemporary theory. By this I mean that Kant's metaphysic, which purports to show the constitution of the order of values and that they are known *a priori*, rests on contestable philosophical and theological assumptions that remain unproven (and possibly unprovable). While the metaphysical debates continue (indeed their duration invites the inference that these debates are essentially contestable) one way in which this difficulty is bypassed in the current literature is to revise the premises of the argument so that they are constructivist rather than metaphysical. In the words of a neo-Kantian constructivist:

> Constructivism in ethics ... is in the first instance a claim that their principles are not established by metaphysical arguments, or discovered in the world, but that they must be constructed on the basis of plausible (*one might add justifiable*), no doubt abstract, assumptions.[19]

Taking this tack does not automatically solve the problem. The basis of constructivist political theory (for neo-Kantians and others) is the desire to sidestep the convoluted arguments of foundationalist political theory. Dropping claims that purport to show that one particular ethical tradition is true and all the others false does not mean we have to make unsupported claims about ethics. The critique of foundationalism, whether directed from postmodernism or critical theory, only targets those enlightenment theories that build elaborate political schemes upon questionable foundations. Constructivist political theory seeks to avoid such criticism by searching for an alternative method of justification. It seeks to show that its prescriptions are demonstrable or 'vindicable' before those agents for whom that stretch of reasoning is supposed to be compelling. The task that contemporary political theory has set itself is to show, in the abstract, what sorts of ethical and political programmes would (or could) be adopted by the actors in international politics. We may not be able to agree on the ultimate nature of morality, or the number of angels that can dance on the head of a pin, but by turning ethical questions into political ones we can, at least, begin a fresh conversation about the direction that our fledgling international community should take.

The general recognition that pure Kantianism leaves certain fundamental premises unproven and is thus unsatisfactory has had an effect on contemporary cosmopolitanism in international relations theory. Most interestingly the two claims noted above tend to be run together. The idea that *some* conception of autonomy is the proper subject of ethical reflection is not disputed. Cosmopolitan thinkers now argue that (a) communitarian strategies fail to deal adequately with the notion of autonomy, (b) that the requisite conditions for a fuller notion of *Ius Cosmopoliticum* are existent, and therefore that (c) the political programmes of a revised Kantian cosmopolitanism (which can still use the individualist conception of autonomy) are now better placed to develop international relations. All this must be proven. Any theory that does not make the necessary arguments to shore up its claims must be treated with extreme caution and many versions of contemporary cosmopolitanism fail to present all the necessary evidence. Cosmopolitan as a tradition makes both political and ethical claims and often runs them together. One particularly important example of this is to be found in the claim that principles of justice should be universal in form and in scope; that is that such principles must derive from universalisable ethical premises and be applicable to all individuals regardless of political boundaries. This claim stands in opposition to a wide variety of plausible arguments in international theory. Of immediate relevance here is the relativist/realist counterclaim that there is no proof that the whole world could (or should) share the same ethical principles or the communitarian claim that the basic arguments that underpin this typically cosmopolitan claim assume wrongly that all individuals however situated could (or should) be brought to share the same principles of political ethics. Both these responses have a very respectable pedigree and both conclude that the political world built on top of cosmopolitan ideals would be dangerously unstable (and in the case of the communitarians that it would also be morally vacuous). It is up to contemporary cosmopolitans to make the predicates to their arguments secure, to show (without making questionable or highly contested assumptions) that the conception of individual agency, or the idea of universal applicability that they take from Kant can be applied to contemporary international politics; that liberal cosmopolitanism really is the way forward.

Contemporary liberal cosmopolitanism

In order to maintain the focus of my argument it is important to examine just those representative aspects of cosmopolitanism that challenge the claims to liberalism of developmental communitarianism. To this end the following sections will develop the cosmopolitan challenge to the idea of developmental communitarianism through the work of three thinkers, Pogge, Beitz and O'Neill. All three self-professed cosmopolitans develop a conception of international justice that rests on a gradualist political agenda based on a 'moral cosmopolitanism' developed to challenge the communitarian assumptions of Rawls and likeminded thinkers. For example, Pogge's exploration of Rawls' domestic political theory led to a series of exceptionally well-informed critiques of Rawls' international relations theory post *Theory of Justice* (*TJ*) and subsequently post 'LOP'.[20] Similarly the well-known *Political Theory and International Relations*[21] of Beitz heralded many articles directly related to the cosmopolitan/communitarian debate often criticising communitarians such as Walzer and liberals such as Rawls from a cosmopolitan point of view.[22] The work of O'Neill, on the other hand, plays a more significant role in the structure of my argument. Not only does O'Neill criticise Rawls, Walzer and communitarianism from a moral cosmopolitan point of view, she criticises them (and by extension developmental communitarianism) from a rigorously constructivist cosmopolitan point of view. That is, from a cosmopolitan position that has attempted to modify its position to take account of the justificatory problems that beset the conventional development of cosmopolitanism.

When looking at the cosmopolitanism of the three representatives of this tradition one thing to note is that all three thinkers are developing a moral cosmopolitanism in favour of what Pogge calls 'legal cosmopolitanism' and what

Beitz calls 'institutional cosmopolitanism'.[23] That is, they develop a series of cosmopolitan arguments that do not necessarily posit universal world government as their ultimate goal. The basic presuppositions of Beitz and Pogge are the same and taking both authors as an introduction to contemporary liberal cosmopolitanism offers good examples of what constitutes cosmopolitanism as a tradition of thought. It is worth quoting Pogge's description at some length as it begins to outline some of the more subtle distinctions between cosmopolitan liberalism and communitarian liberalism.

> Three elements are shared by all cosmopolitan positions. First *individualism*: the ultimate units of concern are human beings, or persons – rather than, say, family lines, tribes, ethnic, cultural or religious communities, nations, or states. The latter may be units of concern only indirectly, in virtue of their individual members or citizens. Second *universality*: the status of ultimate unit of concern attaches to every living human being equally. ... Third, *generality*: this special status has global force. Persons are ultimate units of concern for everyone – not only for their fellow compatriots, fellow religionists, or such like.[24]

Pogge goes on to outline three types of cosmopolitan theory, but these three aspects are, he maintains, present in all three. As a basic description of cosmopolitan values it coheres with the description offered by Beitz that argues that cosmopolitanism is 'inclusive and non-perspectival'[25] and both argue that different (and subsequently non-liberal) viewpoints are thus partial or lack appropriate moral generality. These three aspects of cosmopolitanism stem from the Kantian reasoning outlined above and it is important that Pogge and Beitz be seen to justify their position in a manner acceptable to contemporary international relations theory.

For Beitz institutional cosmopolitanism is that form of cosmopolitanism that seeks the instantiation of a world government whereas moral cosmopolitanism is merely a label for a family of doctrines that share a common view about ethical justification defined by an 'impartial egalitarianism'.[26] Beitz even goes so far as to suggest that some communitarian values can play a role in cosmopolitan political debate because some 'unambiguously cosmopolitan values such as international peace may best be served in a system in which there is a convention of respect for the autonomous domestic jurisdiction of states'.[27] Despite the obviously outrageous inference that international peace is solely a cosmopolitan value it serves our purpose here to try and reach the kernel of Beitz's argument because it is certainly not the case that Beitz wishes to back away from the central tenets of cosmopolitanism or to blur any distinction that is central to the cosmopolitan/communitarian debate. Beitz's admissions to communitarianism are, as Brown rightly points out, rather confusing given his criticisms of non-interventionist policy in *Political Theory and International Relations* and his Kantian account of moral personality in 'Cosmopolitan Ideals and National Sentiment'.[28] However the admissions he makes are not as great as they first appear. For Beitz communitarian ideals can play two types of role in practical judgment, the first is the 'common notion that compatriots should take priority in foreign policy decision making' and the second is that 'communitarian values can be treated as inputs to an impartial deliberative process – as values to be weighed against all the other values at stake in a choice.'[29] For Beitz the first method of using communitarian values is as illegitimate as it is partial. The second mode of reasoning is however legitimate from the cosmopolitan perspective. This may well be the case but, given the way Beitz formulates the requirements of this deliberative process, it is not communitarianism. Indeed as Beitz argues a little later in the same article,

> we would be justified in recognising an entitlement to statehood for a communal group only if doing so was not only best from the point of view of the group but also best overall. As we shall see this significantly qualifies the responsiveness of cosmopolitanism to communitarian values.[30]

Beitz, in limiting the political claims of the cosmopolitan lobby has, he believes, made all the necessary concessions to a plausible or liberal communitarianism that would allow them to co-opt his plan for international justice. Any communitarian who could do so would, it seems, be capable of crossing the philosophical floor to the cosmopolitan side. Beitz's moral position is quite consistent with the paucity of the concessions he offers to communitarianism and he is thus one of the most strident critics of the work of Rawls and Walzer offered in this work. Beitz, despite the apparent concessions he makes to communitarianism, maintains the most important distinction of the cosmopolitan/communitarian debate. Beitz does not allow the priority of community or polity over universal and individualist ethics even under the unstable and often warlike conditions of an international system characterised by ethical and political pluralism. He retains the Kantian ideal of an autonomous individual as moral agent and gives it supreme authority over all other conceptions of agency. Pogge takes Beitz's basic position and modifies it further allowing us to see clearly how far cosmopolitanism is prepared to go to accommodate the most disruptive force in international ethics – international politics.

The three types of cosmopolitanism outlined by Pogge are developed via a distinction drawn between legal and moral cosmopolitanism. Legal cosmopolitanism (institutional cosmopolitanism for Beitz) can be dispensed with immediately. It is that type of ethical/political programme that is committed to a concrete political ideal of a universal society.[31] Moral cosmopolitanism, although compatible with legal cosmopolitanism, is further divided, suggests Pogge, into interactional and institutional cosmopolitanism. Interactional cosmopolitanism is said to posit certain fundamental principles of *ethics* where institutional cosmopolitanism posits principles of *justice*.

> Interactional cosmopolitanism assigns direct responsibility for the fulfilment of human rights to other (individual and collective) agents, whereas institu-

> tional cosmopolitanism assigns such responsibility to institutional schemes. On the latter view, the responsibility of persons is then indirect – a shared responsibility for the justice of any practices that one supports: one ought not to participate in an unjust institutional scheme (one that violates human rights) without making reasonable efforts to aid its victims and to promote institutional reform.[32]

While both of these forms of cosmopolitanism may be combined, the self-professed institutional approach of Pogge offers a more subtle approach to contemporary international relations theory than the other forms could. To explain:

> On the interactional view, human rights impose constraints on conduct, while on the institutional view they impose constraints upon shared practices. the latter approach has two straightforward limitations. First, its applicability is contingent, in that human rights are activated only through the emergence of social institutions. … Secondly, the cosmopolitanism of the institutional approach is contingent as well, in that the global moral force of human rights is activated only through the emergence of a global scheme of social institutions.[33]

Here Pogge can be shown to be approaching the subject of human rights (at least in part) in a manner similar to the approach of Rawls in 'LOP' and this is why his challenge is so important. Pogge argues that this idea of 'a rather minimal conception of human rights' viewed through institutional cosmopolitanism is compatible with the Kantian notion of our moral obligation to create a comprehensive institutional scheme,[34] that the two limitations do not violate the cosmopolitan condition of generality yet that his view leads to a more plausible overall morality.

Pogge offers what he sees as a 'broadly consequentialist' variant of institutional cosmopolitanism. Without developing a comprehensive notion of international human or economic rights that one might expect from a purely Kantian cosmopolitanism, Pogge develops his theory arguing that

> [t]he institutional view … broadens the circle of those who share responsibility for certain deprivations and abuses. … We are asked to be concerned about human rights violations not simply insofar as they exist at all, but only insofar as they are produced by social institutions in which we are significant participants.[35]

The central point being made here is not that the character of human rights is (in the first instance at least) local and particular, a claim that would certainly engage the interest of the developmental communitarianism featured in this work. While this would seem to be a plausible interpretation of this (and previous) statements, Pogge's development of institutional as opposed to legal and interactional cosmopolitanism has done far more than remain loyal to the principle of generality as the second half of the previous quotation begins to show.

> Our negative duty not to cooperate in the imposition of unjust practices, together with our continuing participation in an unjust institutional scheme, triggers obligations to promote feasible reforms of this scheme that would enhance the fulfilment of human rights.[36]

The principal foundation of Pogge's cosmopolitanism, hinted at here and developed more forcefully in his discussion of global economic justice and vertical sovereignty, is interdependence and it is this that triggers our dormant Kantian obligation to generate a social world founded on reasonable moral institutions.

It is the way in which we accrue these obligations to all other human agents that interests me here. My concern is that if Pogge, as a representative of cosmopolitanism, cannot tell a compelling story about how these arise then, at best, he gives the actors in international politics no reason to engage in progressive ethical debate and, at worst, reverts to merely asserting the ethical superiority of those states that have, by dint of military power, come to dominate global politics. This is not the way to build a just international community. It also obscures a developing tradition within liberal political theory that has the wherewithal both to give accessible reasons for acting ethically in international politics and to develop principles that suit the new world order.

For Pogge, an awful lot rests on the claim that the circumstances of justice (globalisation, relative scarcity and other contingent, but permanent, features of international politics) have developed to a stage where cosmopolitan ethics offer the only principles that can justly and effectively order world politics. The idea that the development of universal principles of justice is linked to the development of the international community does play a vital role in the ideas of the developmental communitarians. However, as a strategy of Pogge's institutional cosmopolitanism, this claim seems overstretched. Indeed the four italicised reasons Pogge puts forward to support his claims to cosmopolitanism '*peace/security ... reducing oppression ... global economic justice ... Ecology*' are supported by a thoroughgoing cosmopolitan claim, 'the human right to political participation'.[37] This right is not a group right but belongs to each individual as the right to equal opportunity, it is a democratic right that insists that political units of power smaller than 'humanity' are justified in acting 'if and only if its benefits (laws passed in an undemocratic manner or violating human rights are not applied) outweigh its costs (unobjectionable laws are blocked in violation of the political rights of the larger unit). ... further ... commonalities of language, religion, ethnicity, or history are strictly irrelevant'.[38] These are assumptions that communitarian thinkers, even developmental communitarian or liberal communitarian theorists must question. For commonalities of language or history and so on are not subordinate to human rights, acting as a contingent basis for the institutions which enact such rights. They play an active role in creating these rights and perhaps more importantly in developing the universal validity of such rights. Community, it is argued by the communitarians, is both history *and* justification and human rights are contingent upon that justification, not just for their actualisation or instantiation but also for their existence. The principal tension here is between Pogge's position that claims that all individuals (conceived of as Kantian moral agents) have *a priori* a set of rights that guarantee the Kantian precondition of morality (autonomy) and the position adopted by the developmental communitarians that suggests that we can have no preconceived conception of agency that we impose upon world politics but that we must find an appropriate conception of agency from within the practices of international interaction and develop an appropriate set of rights etc. from there. The arguments for both positions have to be made explicit and tested.

The difficulties inherent in putting forward a cosmopolitan position can be illustrated by looking more carefully at the basic arguments of Pogge's position.[39] The three principal tenets that Pogge argues that cosmopolitanism must hold a categorical allegiance to are: (1) individuality, (2) universality and (3) generality.[40]

This claim is linked to the secondary claim concerning the attainment of the requisite conditions for a fuller notion of *Ius Cosmopoliticum*, the claim that interdependence triggers our Kantian obligations to humanity.[41] The central point to note here is that these two claims are not just linked but that, if we are to give up unprovable metaphysical assertions in favour of an openly justifiable theory, the three principles as a statement of cosmopolitan ethics *rely* upon the second claim and that this fact significantly affects the force of the argument to cosmopolitanism. The three principles are not undisputed methodological starting points in ethics. In contemporary theory Frost's reworking of the Hegelian notion of the constitutive theory of individuality, Walzer's claim that communally developed conceptions of freedom defend us from the excesses of formalism, and Rawls' claim that only a theory of political autonomy rather than the Kantian notion of constitutive autonomy is viable all stand against Pogge's thesis.[42] The counterclaims of Frost, Walzer and Rawls do not, of course, prove that Pogge is wrong but if Pogge's theory is not to rely upon unproven or metaphysical premises all his assumptions must be open to scrutiny. In avoiding foundationalist arguments it seems more than likely that allegiance to Pogge's cosmopolitan justice cannot be categorical in the Kantian sense. Rather it must be hypothetical, that is contingent upon arguments concerning the political institutions necessary to provide principles of justice for the relevant circumstances of justice – i.e. on the argument that the requisite conditions for a greater *Ius Cosmopoliticum* are in place. My claim here is that it is not acceptable just to assume radical forms of principles 1, 2 and 3 that combine to claim both universal form and scope for the argument that all individuals everywhere must be treated equally on every moral issue (as the first principle of morality itself). For this to hold we must add arguments that tell us that contemporary political conditions require a more universalist approach to international justice and that the principles of Kantian cosmopolitanism provide the most relevant framework for working out the best approach. These arguments rely on claims concerning moral and political interconnectedness that were explored in the first chapter. The means–ends reasoning employed here is implicitly adopted by Pogge in his shift from interactional cosmopolitanism (which worked out principles of ethics) to institutional cosmopolitanism (which works out principles of justice). Here our moral and political obligations are not given by the notion of moral personality but by our participation in politics – the circumstances of justice and injustice. We are interconnected politically, through our actions, rather than as a consequence of any synthetic *a priori* judgments concerning the noumenal self. Thus our allegiance to principles 1,2 and 3, the generic features of cosmopolitanism, must be hypothetical (relying upon means–ends reasoning) rather than categorical (relying upon the first principles of morality) and this considerably weakens or alters the cosmopolitan case. It weakens the case in two ways. Firstly Pogge's ethical theory is contingent upon evidence concerning the actual interconnectedness of agents in world politics. It will be recalled from the previous chapter that both the empirical and the theoretical claims made in support of interdependence and globalisation are heavily contested. Secondly (and because the evidence is so contested) Pogge finds himself arguing not for the necessity of liberal-cosmopolitan ethics but asserting the benefits of cosmopolitanism in international relations, something that he contrasts with the style and content of Rawls' theory of international justice.[43] The power of cosmopolitanism, usually thought to stem from the structure of the moral arguments, has been abandoned by Pogge (and necessarily so) but in replacing that power with mere 'assertive liberalism' and highly contested claims about the current state of international politics Pogge significantly reduces the attractiveness of cosmopolitanism. There is a very significant change of emphasis in the structure of Pogge's cosmopolitanism. Earlier versions argue that cosmopolitanism is the only acceptable ethico-political position in international relations theory. Pogge's assertive liberalism is an argument suggesting that while the universalisation of liberalism is not a moral necessity, it can be seen (from a liberal perspective at least) as an attractive political proposition for present-day international relations. A successful argument of the first type might well be convincing but an argument of the second type does not supply all the necessary tools to be authoritative unless it can show that contrary to current practice an individualist account of agency is both possible and desirable and able to solve some of the pressing problems of world politics.

Pogge's political project could, if these necessary arguments were made, offer a stern challenge to developmental communitarianism. Many communitarians with liberal sympathies, Rawls, Walzer, Frost and Rorty all want to see human rights play a greater role in international relations but their awareness of the contingency of this desire leads them to be wary of cosmopolitan claims, even the adjusted claims of Pogge's institutional cosmopolitanism. Ultimately Pogge's institutional cosmopolitanism needs a universal morality, even if it is a universal morality that we must work towards. His project is to continue, in reaction to Rawls, the work he began in *Realizing Rawls*. To go further than *TJ*, and more lately 'LOP', and to argue for 'the great importance, and the possibility, of working toward an international community that is well ordered, at least in the sense of sharing a kernel of political morality together with a categorical allegiance to it'.[44] The question that Pogge's institutional cosmopolitanism asks of developmental communitarianism is 'how liberal can you be while retaining your doubts about this goal?' It is significant that Pogge, in defining a familiar liberal element of global liberalism, the idea 'that a conception of social justice must take persons as the ultimate units of concern' can argue that 'Rawls gives a fairly representative statement of this tenet. ... The same idea receives at least nominal endorsement from Michael Walzer, perhaps the most vocal liberal advocate of state's rights'[45] although the justifications for their arguments differ sharply from those of Pogge. Both Pogge and Beitz present their cosmopolitanism as a challenge to the liberal aspirations of Rawls and other liberal communitarians, their claim is that anything less than the refined and to some extent diluted institutional and moral cosmopolitanism they offer is simply not liberal. Yet while I concur with Pogge that both Rawls and Walzer do use the idea of social and international justice that he attributes to them, what is absolutely vital about this fact is that Rawls and Walzer (and to a more limited extent Frost) justify their position in a totally different (and more successful) manner than the cosmopolitans. In seeking a new and more secure justification for international ethics the developmental communitarians abandon the first principles of moral cosmopolitanism and construct a more appropriate theory of international justice. While this tradition necessarily falls short of the three principles of cosmopolitanism that Pogge clings to it has a far more powerful argument because it modifies both the justification and conclusion so that it does not have to rely upon heavily contested assumptions or bold assertions.

There is however one variant of cosmopolitanism that attempts to make precisely the same move as developmental communitarianism without abandoning the three basic tenets of cosmopolitanism. O'Neill's critical and constructivist cosmopolitanism makes an explicit attempt to overcome the shortcomings of contemporary cosmopolitanism and it is therefore necessary to offer a preliminary examination of this possibility.

Critical and constructivist cosmopolitanism

While it is interesting and profitable to examine the cosmopolitan theory of international ethics and politics offered by Beitz and Pogge, it is even more pertinent to examine the cosmopolitan thesis offered by a secular liberal willing to construct (rather than discovering or triggering qua Beitz and Pogge) a Kantian liberalism. As with Beitz and Pogge, O'Neill engages directly with the cosmopolitan/communitarian debate but O'Neill attempts to put a forceful case for cosmopolitanism by constructing the arguments necessary to the conclusions reached by Beitz and Pogge. O'Neill's critical cosmopolitanism recognises that these arguments have to be made if the appropriate justifications of cosmopolitan principles of international justice are to have any degree of plausibility and then proceeds to do so. In doing the necessary groundwork for a contemporary cosmopolitanism O'Neill offers the best example of the cosmopolitan-liberal claim to moral and political authority in international relations theory. Because of this her position is fully examined in chapter 4 but here it is necessary to indicate the direction her argument takes and to show how the constructivist project begins to fill in the gaps at the base of current thinking about international relations.

Merely to suggest that O'Neill engages with the cosmopolitan/communitarian debate would be to understate her relation to the argument of this study. Her insistence that global, egalitarian principles of justice can be applied to international relations has been unflinching even during her progressive secularisation of Kantian-liberalism. In *TJV*, O'Neill's most recent and most secular work, she argues that a

> rather stringent conception of universalisability as the core of practical reasoning is the Kantian kernel of the book's argument. … that justice and virtue need not be rivals, and that a rigorous conception of reasoning about action will allow us to construct substantive accounts of both without the need to establish any metaphysics of the person, or of the Good.[46]

Here justice is viewed in terms of universalist claims against the state and other political institutions and virtue in terms of particularist claims about the good life and the ethos of men and women in the community. O'Neill attempts to reunite these two features of our political vocabulary that have become separated in the modern age. For O'Neill ethical universalists who follow on from Plato and ethical particularists who follow on from Aristotle have both had to confront modernity and the crisis of foundationalism and have become 'unanchored'.[47]

> Most writing on justice has remained faithful to universalist and to increasingly cosmopolitan aspirations – but has hoped to jump ship when metaphysical certainties foundered and to load old appeals firmly onto minimal appeals to reason. Most writing on Virtue has repudiated universalist ambitions, yet continues to use the old ethical vocabulary that relied on supposed metaphysical or religious certainties to endorse received habits, conventional excellences and prized commitments. The divergence of justice from virtue is not a matter of demonstrated difference: it has arisen because both are unanchored, and the two have drifted apart. Ultimately accounts of both domains of practical reason need to answer charges of arbitrariness.[48]

O'Neill's task is to critique both cosmopolitanism and communitarianism and to unite the two under secular but universal principles of practical reason. In doing so O'Neill constructs a critical conception of practical reason that develops ethical principles for international relations theory that are cosmopolitan in both scope and content. Furthermore her theory purports to show that communitarian assumptions are not necessary even in a liberalism developed for the modern age. In developing her thesis O'Neill challenges developmental communitarianism on its own terms, recognises the paucity of many contemporary defences of cosmopolitanism yet continues to pursue her own cosmopolitan project. The full force of the challenge to the secular liberalism of the developmental communitarians is further revealed in a brief sketch of the direction O'Neill's argument takes.

For O'Neill the scope of justice is determined by the assumptions that agents are committed to when they act in circumstances where justice can be an issue rather than on a Kantian metaphysics of the person.

> Circumstances of justice are circumstances in which conflict between agents is possible – and may be avoidable, or at least regulatable, by institutions of justice. ... Where all three elements of the circumstances of justice – plurality, finitude and sharing a world – obtain, injustice can occur and issues of justice can always be raised.[49]

If justice is the mediation of conflict between a plurality of finite agents then the circumstances of justice are, O'Neill argues, not limited by state boundaries or communal boundaries or ethnic boundaries: 'We trade, we broadcast, we travel, we negotiate. For practical purposes we are already committed to viewing both nearby and distant and unknown others as agent like ourselves.'[50]

In working out this position, the idea of interconnectedness, O'Neill appears to make precisely those arguments I suggested must be a feature of a viable contemporary Kantianism in the previous sections. While (as both Pogge and Beitz argued) political communities and institutions may be useful for the administration of cosmopolitan/liberal justice they are purely contingent upon justice. For O'Neill, 'the internationalist commitments and implications of liberalism are damaged if they are vindicated by reference to an aspect of the *Sittlichkeit* of a specific tradition.'[51] In developing a secular appeal to a Kantian *Moralität* O'Neill recognises that some elements of the communitarian critique of liberalism are relevant. In particular she argues (*contra* Pogge) that we cannot simply universalise western liberal practices but that we must construct a universally accessible account of international justice. The idea of accessibility at work here is vital as it is the criterion by which we can judge the scope of the ethical theory that can be supported by the interconnected agents in world politics. O'Neill also argues that while some cosmopolitan accounts rely upon predicates accessible only to a few Kantians, not all Kantian accounts of justice suffer from this failing. The principal criticism of cosmopolitan ethics – that the theory relies upon an unproven and widely inaccessible account of the moral and political agent (what O'Neill terms an idealised account of agency) – is a very powerful one. Yet O'Neill claims that some criticisms of liberalism's 'abstract' reasoning about autonomy is premised on an unsustainable linkage of the idea of abstraction with the idea of idealisation. This argument, central to all stages of O'Neill's work (and further developed in chapter 4) argues that communitarians and other critics of liberalism are correct to criticise idealised accounts of political morality but that her conception of a secular liberal methodology that incorporates abstraction does not fall into the same category.

> Idealization requires abstraction but they are not the same thing. … When we idealize we add a predicate to a theory, and the theory applies only when that predicate is satisfied. Abstract but nonidealized accounts of agents [that omit certain predicates] can apply to agents of diverse *sittlichkeit*, idealized accounts … not merely do not refer to the varying historical and cultural characteristics of particular agents but apply only to idealized, hypothetical agents whose cognitive and volitional features may be missing in all actual human agents.[52]

These two vital features of O'Neill's secular liberalism, the claim that universal principles of action must be the focus of justice and that an abstract account of agency (without the features that have lead many contemporary thinkers to reject such an account) can inform the cosmopolitan scope of justice, combine to form a stern challenge to the relative apprehension of developmental communitarianism. Her argument sets out to 'develop institutions and practices which effectively limit and prevent injury to all who fall within the scope of ethical consideration – on whichever side of various borders their lives are led'.[53] Her rejection of Kantian metaphysics and idealised accounts of agency also brings her project closer to the secular liberalism offered by developmental communitarianism. Therefore O'Neill's claim that 'it is beside the point to complain that an abstract liberal account of justice fails to take community seriously enough, since it is predicated on the view that in modern times a serious conception of justice cannot presuppose community'[54] is both a challenge to communitarianism and sets a standard against which any claim to have developed a contemporary liberalism must be measured. It sets a standard because the tradition of thought that I have called developmental communitarianism argues that because an abstract account of individual agency is unsustainable on empirical and theoretical grounds any account of international justice has to review its premises, construct a more politically oriented account of agency and thus modify the demands that a universally accessible account of agency can make on international politics. If O'Neill can sustain her argument and thus supply the framework for a cosmopolitan account of justice then the claim that cosmopolitanism should be thought of as the high point of liberal international relations theory becomes more uncomplicated to defend. For this reason chapter 4 examines O'Neill's claims in detail, ultimately showing their shortcomings, before I go on to construct the tradition of developmental communitarianism.

Concluding remarks

The cosmopolitan challenge to developmental communitarianism is no straw man. In showing that Kant's theory and Kantian theories have to be modified, and have been modified, in an attempt to meet those standards of justification appropriate to international relations theory the cosmopolitan perspective remains a real and important contender in international ethics. The emphasis placed upon the cosmopolitan position is particularly important to the liberal aspect of the cosmopolitan/communitarian debate, as it is that heritage that is traditionally associated with liberalism in international relations theory. As far as liberal ethical theories in international relations are concerned the cosmopolitans join with O'Neill in arguing that the 'myopia of communitarian and kindred positions offers little insight'[55] yet this common response to communitarian claims does not even begin to acknowledge the importance of the developmental communitarian position. Before exploring the claims of O'Neill's constructivist cosmopolitan in detail I wish to outline the developmental communitarian response to the crisis in traditional cosmopolitanism. This allows us to examine the counterclaims of a tradition developed in opposition to the cosmopolitan theorists and completes the sketch of the relevant (but often obscured) strategies of the contemporary debate in liberal international theory. O'Neill's attempt to recover cosmopolitanism from its critics is not the only response to the empirical and theoretical developments in world politics. Indeed the communitarian camp has been one of the primary beneficiaries of the current changes. In acknowledging the problems inherent in relying upon foundational or metaphysical justifications or inaccessible accounts of agency many realists and not a few disaffected cosmopolitans have turned to communitarianism in attempts to rethink the role of the political community or to reground theories of justice. However just as cosmopolitanism has been affected by current developments in world politics so has communitarianism. For this reason the next chapter focuses only on developmental communitarianism, that aspect of communitarian thought that has confronted, and attempted to overcome the pitfalls of, contemporary international relations theory. In subsequent chapters I examine in detail the merits and failures of some of the most interesting arguments presented in this debate and demonstrate that developmental communitarianism offers the more promising insight into contemporary international relations theory.

Notes and references

1 Beltz, 'Cosmopolitan liberalism', p. 125.
2 Rawls, *PL*, Lecture III, §2, p. 99.
3 Rawls, *PL*, Lecture III, §2, p. 100.
4 R. Scruton, *A Dictionary of Political Thought*, Pan Books in association with Macmillan Press, 1982. The use of the dictionary here is purely illustrative of a wider understanding of the 'stereotyped' interpretation.
5 I. Kant, *Perpetual Peace and Other Essays on Politics, History, and Morals*, trans. T. Humphrey, Hacket Publishing Co., 1983, p. 107.
6 See particularly I. Kant, *The Moral Law: Kant's Groundwork of the Metaphysic of Morals*, trans. H.J. Paton, Routledge, 1991.
7 Kant, *The Moral Law*, pp. 66–67.
8 Ibid.
9 Kant, *The Moral Law*, p. 95.

10 The idea of autonomy is, Kant argues, 'the supreme condition of the will's conformity with universal practical reason. (see 'The formula of Autonomy' in Kant, *The Moral Law*, p. 93). Unless all rational beings are free to enact the moral law the categorical imperative, on a matter of simple logic, cannot be universal.
11 H. Caygill, *A Kant Dictionary*, Blackwell, 1995, p. 86.
12 Kant, *The Metaphysics of Morals: Metaphysical First Principles of the Doctrine of Right*, trans. M. Gregor, Cambridge University Press, 1991, §44, p. 124.
13 Kant, *Metaphysics of Morals*, Part I, §43, p. 123.
14 Kant, *Metaphysics of Morals*, Part I, §61, p. 156.
15 Kant, *Perpetual Peace*, §§355/356, p. 116.
16 Kant, *Perpetual Peace*, Third definitive article, p. 118.
17 Kant, *Perpetual Peace*, Appendix I, p. 129.
18 Ibid.
19 O'Neill, *TJV*, p. 45; italics mine.
20 See for example T. Pogge, *Realizing Rawls*, Ithica and London, Cornell University Press, 1989. also T. Pogge, 'An Egalitarian Law of Peoples', *Philosophy and Public Affairs*, Vol. 23, No. 3, Summer 1994, pp. 195–225.
21 C. Beitz, *Political Theory and International Relations*, Princeton, Princeton University press, 1979.
22 See for selective example C. Beitz, 'Bounded Morality: Justice and the State in World Politics', *International Organisation*, Vol. 33, No. 3, summer 1979, pp. 405–424 on Walzer. C. Beitz, 'Cosmopolitan Ideals and National Sentiment' *The Journal of Philosophy*, Vol. 80, No. 10, October 1983, pp. 591–600 on Rawls and C. Beitz, 'Cosmopolitan Liberalism and the States System', in Brown (ed.), *Political Restructuring*, p. 123.
23 See Beitz, 'Cosmopolitan Liberalism', p. 125. Pogge 'Cosmopolitanism and Sovereignty', *Ethics*, Vol. 103, October 1992, p. 49. and O'Neill 'Justice and Boundaries', in Brown (ed.) *Political Restructuring*, p. 70.
24 Pogge, 'Cosmopolitanism and Sovereignty', p. 48.
25 Beitz, 'Cosmopolitan Liberalism', p. 124.
26 Beitz, 'Cosmopolitan Liberalism', p. 126.
27 Beitz, 'Cosmopolitan Liberalism', p. 129.
28 Cf. Brown, *International Relations Theory*, pp. 175–177.
29 Beitz 'Cosmopolitan Liberalism', p. 129.
30 Beitz, 'Cosmopolitan Liberalism', p. 133.
31 Pogge, 'Cosmopolitanism and Sovereignty', p. 49. Beitz, 'Cosmopolitan Liberalism', p. 124.
32 Pogge, 'Cosmopolitanism and Sovereignty', p. 50. It is interesting to note that Pogge suggests that the Rawls of *TJ* combines interactional and institutional cosmopolitanism. See chapter 7 for an example of how far Rawls' thought is currently removed from any variety of cosmopolitanism.
33 Pogge, 'Cosmopolitanism and Sovereignty', pp. 50–51.
34 Pogge, 'Cosmopolitanism and Sovereignty', note 8, p. 51.
35 Pogge, 'Cosmopolitanism and Sovereignty', p. 52.
36 Ibid.
37 Pogge, 'Cosmopolitanism and Sovereignty', p. 64 see also note 29.
38 Pogge, 'Cosmopolitanism and Sovereignty', p. 68.
39 I also believe that the following arguments hold for Beitz's cosmopolitanism.
40 Pogge, 'Cosmopolitanism and Sovereignty', p. 48 and p. 68.
41 Pogge, 'Cosmopolitanism and Sovereignty', pp. 50–51.
42 These ideas are developed and fleshed out in subsequent chapters. One point here is that my interpretation of Walzer's position differs sharply with the one Pogge offers in 'Cosmopolitanism and Sovereignty', p. 74.
43 Cf. Pogge, 'An Egalitarian Law of Peoples', passim.

44 Pogge, *Realizing Rawls*, p. 216.
45 Pogge, 'Liberalism and Global Justice: Hoffman and Nardin on Morality in International Affairs', *Philosophy and Public Affairs*, Vol. 15, No.1, 1986, p. 69, note.4.
46 O'Neill, *TJV*, p. 6.
47 O'Neill, *TJV*, chapter 1, pp. 13 and 36.
48 O'Neill, *TJV*, p. 37.
49 O'Neill, 'Justice and Boundaries', pp. 82–83. See also chapter 4.
50 O'Neill, 'Justice and Boundaries', p. 83.
51 O'Neill, 'Ethical Reasoning', p. 709.
52 O'Neill, 'Ethical Reasoning', p. 712.
53 O'Neill, *TJV*, p. 5.
54 O'Neill, 'Ethical Reasoning', p. 714.
55 O'Neill, 'Justice and Boundaries', p. 70.

3 Developmental communitarianism

Liberal ambitions, secular approaches

The principal claims of this book are (a) that critical cosmopolitanism, while circumventing the problems associated with much foundational cosmopolitanism, cannot support the ethical and political programme it wishes to defend and (b) that the international ethics of developmental communitarianism can overcome the criticisms of liberal international relations theory and, by virtue of their communitarian (or norm-oriented and constructivist) method, still posit a viable liberal approach to international ethics and politics. The case to be made depends upon the arguments made in the following four chapters. Here, in order to introduce the idea that it is the developmental communitarian method of Frost, Walzer and Rawls that gives them the edge in this debate, it is necessary to construct the tradition of developmental communitarianism. I intend to show the divergence in methodological and philosophical outlooks between developmental communitarianism and cosmopolitanism, to begin to outline the general method of developmental communitarianism and to show that each of the three thinkers examined shares enough ground with the others to warrant the construction of the developmental communitarian tradition.

It is not my intention to begin with a general survey of communitarian international relations theory. I accept here the principal criticisms levelled against traditional communitarianism but argue that Frost, Walzer and Rawls do not rely upon theoretical strategies that are discredited by these criticisms. The principal criticisms of communitarianism are:

1 That communitarianism leads necessarily to moral relativism.
2 That this relativism leads necessarily to a reindorsement of the *status quo* in international politics, and
3 That such a position relies upon a discredited ontological argument that posits the foundational status of the community or state.

All three of these criticisms are linked and often merged in contemporary theory. Charges (1) and (2), if proven, would be accepted as damaging to the communitarian case in the light of evidence relating to interconnectedness/interdependence and the contemporary circumstances of justice examined in chapter 1. The success of arguments (1) and (2) have often depended upon the arguments in support of criticism (3). A foundational attachment to the idea of the sovereign state or the *a priori* constituency of humanity was shown to be problematic in chapter 2. Essentialist claims concerning the foundational status of the state or community are, in much communitarian writing, allied to criticisms of universalist or individualist ethics, more generally of abstraction in political philosophy. However such a strategy would leave communitarians at the mercy of precisely the same arguments that are used to critique the foundations of traditional cosmopolitan thought. Simply replacing one ontologically dubious argument concerning the foundations of ethics with another is not a satisfactory approach. The examples of developmental communitarianism offered here are given precisely because they do not take this tack. Given the problems inherent in justifying contested foundations in international ethical theory Frost, Walzer and Rawls all argue (in opposition to O'Neill) that an account of international justice that takes the developing international community as its starting point is more readily defensible and still able to get beyond the *status quo*. The relevant facts about contemporary international relations do not have foundational status but do limit the practice of methodological abstraction. The counterclaim, an example of which is offered in O'Neill's critique of Rawls in chapter 4, is that the limits communitarians place on abstraction in international political philosophy still idealise, or illegitimately privilege, the role of the state or community. For communitarianism to be seen as justifiable this argument must be shown to be false.

First, however, some preliminary remarks on terminology. I have chosen to label Frost, Walzer and Rawls as developmental communitarians because I believe it necessary (for the advancement of liberal international relations theory) to point out how far removed the justifications of their liberal ideas are from those of liberal cosmopolitanism. Frost, Walzer and Rawls all use conceptions of human rights and develop theories of international justice which suggest (if the current literature is to be believed) that they could be included within the cosmopolitan tradition. However the way these thinkers develop or construct their position is what makes their contribution to contemporary international relations theory so important. In responding to empirical and theoretical developments in world politics these theorists have attempted to reconstruct a viable basis for their liberalism and in doing so have acknowledged that they also have to adjust their liberal conclusions. In order to account for political and cultural diversity and ethical pluralism these theorists argue that it is not possible to develop an accessible international liberalism that begins with a cosmopolitan account of the rights-bearing individual. Rather, all three theorists begin from a construction of an international political community interconnected through a states system. For this reason, and working within Brown's construction of the cosmopolitan/communitarian debate, these theorists are labelled communitarian. The principles that this generates are similar in focus but narrower in scope than those generated by cosmopolitanism but are, I maintain, far more secure. Many critics who acknowledge this either argue that the ensuing theory is not liberal or that any remnants of a liberal theory have been arrived at illegitimately. These conclusions are perpetuated by the fallacy that cosmopolitanism is the sole guardian of liberalism in international relations theory. If this were the case then liberalism is in serious trouble. The communitarian premises of the work of Frost, Walzer and Rawls lend their theories a buttress against the problems examined in chapters 1 and 2. Their modified liberal conclusions do fall short of the three cardinal principles of cosmopolitanism outlined in the previous chapter but such modifications are necessary if liberalism is to retain theoretical respectability in contemporary world politics. Liberal conclusions must wait upon their proof and, I shall argue, only developmental communitarianism supplies an appropriate proof. While the principles generated by this tradition fall short of cosmopolitanism they nevertheless surpass the conclusions traditionally associated with communitarianism, hence the need for a modified nomenclature. Without abandoning their communitarian premises Walzer and Rawls both show the potential within current international political practice for the development of certain liberal principles. Hence 'developmental communitarianism'. Developmental communitarianism as a tradition is developed to show that the liberal aspirations of Rawls, among other thinkers, are neither myopic nor one dimensional but simply a realistic approach to understanding liberal political concerns in contemporary international relations.

A realist or a realistic theory of human rights?

One thing that certainly links the three theorists whom I use to define the tradition of developmental communitarianism is the confusion that surrounds the interpretation of their work. No one, it seems, knows quite how to pigeonhole them. While this is true of all three theorists it is particularly true of Walzer. In some interpretations Walzer is viewed as a rather confused communitarian whose liberal sympathies (worn boldly on his sleeve in the form of his allegiance to universal rights to life and liberty) are not related to his particularism. Conversely, Walzer is sometimes viewed as a failed just war theorist whose work is, when you get right down to it, as realist as the self-proclaimed amoralists of that school. Both of these interpretations are wrong. To be sure, it has taken Walzer some considerable time to fully work out his position. But the time has been well spent and Walzer has produced a subtle and unified theory.

The charge of realism, or relativism, is one that is never very far away from the communitarians. Its genesis is the mistaken belief that anything short of a cosmopolitan commitment to universal principles of justice opens the floodgate and allows a tide of amoral, pragmatist *realpolitik* to overwhelm international justice. The tension between pragmatism and ethics in the work of the developmental communitarians can be clearly seen if we look at one example of the view that Walzer is merely a realist. Janna Thompson, writing about Walzer's early just war theory, argues that his introductory critique and rejection of the realism of Thucydides does not amount to a rejection of realism per se as 'what separates Thucydides' world from Walzer's world are mere contingencies.'[1]

Walzer, who in this work is treated as communitarian (although it might seem that he rejects the description)[2] argues that the realist case is simply '*inter arma silent leges*: in time of war the law is silent'.[3] Taking 'The Melian Dialogue' in Thucydides' *History of the Peloponnesian War* as an archetype, Walzer takes issue with the theory that underlies the dialogue. The Melians, in Thucydides *History*, had remained neutral in the war between Athens and Sparta (unlike the other island peoples) until Athens had attacked their lands. While Melos was small to the point of tactical insignificance the example it set to the other islanders 'necessitated' direct action.[4] The meeting between the two sides and the narrative that ends in the eventual capture of Melos and the slaughter of all men of military age has, Walzer argues, one central message. Walzer quotes from Jaeger's *Paideia: The Ideals of Greek Culture*, 'the principle of force forms a realm of its own, distinct and separate from the laws of the moral life'[5] but Thucydides' own words are equally strong as he argues that in war 'the standard of justice depends on the equality of power to compel and that in fact the strong do what they have the power to do and the weak accept what they have to accept' thus compelling the Melians to leave any substantive claims to justice from their case.[6] The slaughter of the Melians and the argument that precedes it is explained in reference to necessity.[7] The Athenians had no choice but to ignore the Melians' pleas of justice, to do otherwise would be to court disaster.[8] Despite Thucydides account of the debate, Walzer points out that '[w]e have no account of the Athenian decision to attack Melos or of the decision (which may have been taken at the same time) to kill and enslave its people'.[9] Basically Walzer's primary aim in examining the realism of Thucydides is to argue that any account of international relations that makes its case based on the necessitous relations engendered by the politics of power is seriously flawed. Walzer's case is that 'this account of the "necessities" of international politics ignores the political decision making process in which matters of war and foreign policy are debated'.[10] His specific reasoning is that

> [t]he Athenians shared a moral vocabulary, shared it with the people of Mytilene and Melos; and allowing for cultural differences, they share it with us too. They had no difficulty, and we have none, in understanding the claim of the Melian magistrates that the invasion of their island was unjust. It is in applying the agreed-upon words to actual cases that we come to disagree.[11]

That the Athenians could share with us a moral vocabulary that is relevant to a discussion of justice and international relations is a fascinating claim in itself. That this claim is put forward by a thinker considered to be a communitarian, or whose thought is considered to be separated from the realism of Thucydides only by contingency is, from the point of view of the present argument, equally fascinating. Thompson's point is that for all Walzer's assurances that the conflicting parties share a moral vocabulary, when it comes to laying out his view of international justice the shared moral vocabulary of the Athenians and

Melians may well have still been subverted in the face of purely political reasoning. In the case of Walzer, Thompson argues,

> [s]ince laws can always be violated and agreements broken, the threat of aggression and violence always hovers in the background of international relations even in periods of relative peace. How much room there is for pursuing justice will depend on how overt, persistent and serious these threats become.[12]

There is certainly an element of truth in Thompson's contention that Walzer shares some conceptual ground with realism. However she has seriously underestimated the importance of Walzer's project of social criticism, of the suggestion that there can be shared moral language and that political decision making utilises such language. In short Thompson, among others, underestimates the importance and relevance of his developmental communitarianism. Indeed the ethical message of liberal communitarianism has been widely overlooked and many commentators on international relations theory prefer to look to the communitarians' relationship with realism rather than the issues of justice and ethics with which they engage. Even a cursory examination of the boundaries of developmental communitarianism begins to show that the dynamic interplay of international ethics and international politics is precisely what marks the tradition out as a vitally important voice in the current conversation.

The moral claims that Walzer puts forward, and their relation to communitarianism, are examined in detail below. However, the idea that a self-proclaimed proponent of just war theory may be thought of as continuing the realist line in the political theory of international relations *and* as playing a vital role in the liberal debates surrounding international ethics is relevant to this section as it is the perceived tension between these two aspirations that has led to the widespread dismissal of communitarian claims to have something to add to the liberal debate in international ethics. Walzer's just war theory allied to the exposition of his moral theory in *Thick and Thin: Moral Arguments at Home and Abroad* make a mockery of the sharp contrast between the politics of morality and the politics of necessity whilst recognising the importance of both aspects of international relations. The argument that all international theory has some normative content does not prejudge questions of how states should act in war or how we should conceive of international justice, if indeed there can be said to be any such thing. Indeed the cosmopolitan/communitarian framework is a direct reminder of this. As Brown notes

> [t]he 'realist' critique of international justice deploys some powerful arguments; nonetheless, it need not delay us for long, because some of these arguments can be met without too much difficulty, others can be incorpo-

> rated in a different kind of discourse, while yet others simply act to bring about a closure in ways we are not obliged to accept.[13]

Walzer's just war theory, along with many other communitarian thinkers, falls under the second of these categories. For Walzer, notions of justice appropriate to the international sphere are significantly different to those appropriate to the domestic sphere – the former being 'thin' or 'minimalist', the latter being 'thick' or 'maximalist'.[14] The thin account of ethics is not sufficient to guide international politics, while universal in scope it depends on particularistic sovereign states both for its construction and its realisation. This dependency of ethics upon politics incorporates an account both of ethical development and of how politics must deal with such ethical development. Such a dependency does not preclude, Walzer argues, a universal theory of rights from playing a role in international politics but it does insist that ethical uncertainty (a well-regarded symptom of Walzer's ethical communitarianism) defer to political sensitivity. For example, in *Spheres of Justice* (*SJ*) Walzer tells us that

> two rights (life and liberty) seem to account for the moral judgments that we most commonly make in time of war. They do real work. … Men and women do have rights beyond life and liberty, but these do not follow from our common humanity; they follow from a shared conception of social goods; they are local and particular in character.[15]

These elusive rights to life and liberty have been a point of focus for Walzer's critics since the publication of *JUW* and *Spheres of Justice*. Yet in *Thick and Thin*, a book that really fills the philosophical gaps of *JUW*, Walzer goes on to develop his position, arguing that

> minimalist meanings are embedded in the maximal morality, expressed in the same idiom, sharing the same (historical/cultural/religious/political) orientation. Minimalism is liberated from its embeddedness and appears independently, in varying degrees of thinness, only in the course of a personal or social crisis or a political confrontation.[16]

When situated within a full exegesis of Walzer's reworking of just war theory and his later development of his moral theory this quotation really outlines the direction that Walzer's developmental communitarian method takes. Walzer's principal point is that ethics and morality develop (or are constructed) politically, through the lives we share and the understandings we develop as interconnected agents. For Walzer it is not possible to sustain an argument that suggests that all individuals everywhere share a universal morality that structures their everyday existence. The plurality of existent communities have a myriad of ethical beliefs that have developed historically and which are very often non-negotiable. Here Walzer does not deny an emerging interconnectedness between agents in international politics but he does deny that there is, or that under contemporary conditions that there could be, a connection of cosmopolitan form and scope. The emerging structure of interconnectedness has led to the development of a reiterated moral minimum (a universal ethics) but because the agents of international politics do not share (and cannot at present be legitimately brought to share) a maximalist understanding of what is vital to their historical/cultural/religious/political lives, this moral minimum is very thin and serves only to allow us to recognise that some element of political morality is being violated. This recognition does not, or does not yet, provide a platform for a political restructuring that would mirror the cosmopolitan project. Walzer's rejection of cosmopolitanism is twofold. Firstly he believes that their moral project is not supported by the current structure of international politics and ethics (and thus that cosmopolitans fail to meet the requirements of constructivism). Secondly, and following on from this, he believes that their political project is illegitimate. Because of the transient 'thinness' of universal ethics, international politics, argues Walzer, holds as its highest principles propositions of territorial integrity and non-intervention, propositions scorned by many liberals as inhibiting moral universalism and focusing upon the wrong moral agent,[17] as continuing a fruitless, realist line of thought. However for Walzer the language of international relations *is* normative, morality plays a large part in our international relations. His outlook is related to that of the realists. The sovereign state (understood in a multi-dimensional way) is the primary agent in world politics and its first duty is particularistic, to protect its citizens. Nevertheless it is more effective to treat Walzer as a developmental communitarian than a realist. Communitarian because his grasp of the history of international politics leads him to believe that the politics of necessity and the politics of morality develop, in the first instance at least, within the political community. Developmental because his grasp of the historicity of his subject matter allows him to recognise that concepts such as those of the nation-state, or of national security are not beyond dispute or development and that international political morality is being constructed through our political interaction. The idea that a 'realist' theory of international politics could argue that 'if principles determine decisions, decisions in turn modify and refine principles: this is the way that both law and morality change over time'[18] and even allow that some universal ethical values could play an important role in international relations is what gives the cosmopolitan/communitarian debate its vitality.

Despite his opposition to cosmopolitanism Walzer believes that he is adding to the tradition of liberal political philosophy. This contention must be taken very seriously. Walzer's contribution to liberal international relations theory cannot be truly evaluated if his work is labelled realist, treated as simple communitarianism (and thus as opposed to liberal thought) or simply added to the periphery of cosmopolitan thought. When the cosmopolitan/communitarian distinction is applied to liberal international relations theory it generates a far more important debate than current theoretical divisions recognise. Thinkers from both sides of the debate, that is the liberal-communitarian thinkers and the liberal-cosmopolitan thinkers, are engaged in a debate from which we can learn much about the problems and the potential of liberal international ethics and politics. My construction of a developmental communitarian tradition is not intended to exhaust the cosmopolitan/communitarian distinction or liberal political theory. Rather it is constructed to remove the interpretative obstacles that stand in the way of a vital division in contemporary liberal international relations theory. Once these obstacles have been removed and the developmental communitarian tradition has been constructed, my final argument, that developmental and constructivist communitarian theories provide the most secure justifications for contemporary liberal international theory and that they do so in a significantly different way to traditional liberal theory, can be made.

Secular Hegelianism as developmental communitarianism

A more ambitious proponent of developmental communitarianism, Mervyn Frost, adds further to the need to distinguish between cosmopolitans and communitarians within liberal international relations theory. In this book Frost is taken as an example of developmental communitarianism. Like Walzer, he explicitly disassociates himself from the description 'communitarian' but unlike Walzer he bases his theory of international relations on a specifically Hegelian account of individuality, the 'constitutive theory of individuality'.[19] Like Walzer's developmental communitarianism, the purpose of Frost's project is to develop the 'liberal' discourse of human rights while offering a secular theory and his approach is communitarian in that it looks initially to the development of values within the modern society of states for answers. For Frost, the constitutive theory of individuality forms the most suitable and coherent background justification for the 'settled norms' that we share in our international dealings and can thus be used to as a reference point to help us solve some particularly hard cases in interstate relations. A full examination of this position appears below (see chapter 5) for now our focus must be why, when both Walzer and Frost differ in theoretical style, and when both explicitly reject the term 'communitarian', would we benefit from treating these thinkers as communitarians and oppose their ideas to those we place in the cosmopolitan tradition?

An interesting way of looking at this question is to approach it by looking at the way in which those we wish to ascribe to our constructed tradition view the debate they are taking part in. Frost's position is interesting. He argues that his subject matter is normative in content in that the focus of his study, human actions (either individual or group) cannot be understood (although they can be observed) unless we engage in normative theory. Normative theory is itself inconceivable except within a context of shared understandings, that is within 'a domain of discourse'.[20] For Frost,

> all normative issues in world politics today refer, either directly or indirectly, to the state, inter-state relations and the role of individuals as citizens of states. If this is correct it is then possible to encapsulate all the several

> normative questions in the one central question: 'What in general is a good reason for action by or with regard to states?'[21]

In identifying what he terms the 'modern state domain of discourse' it would seem that Frost has indeed placed himself in the communitarian camp, if we define this tradition loosely as a tradition that either denies the opposition between the value of individuality and of citizenship or simply assigns importance to states as opposed to individuals.[22] Brown, who endorses constitutive theory as an alternative to liberal individualism but compatible with the political message of liberalism, explicitly endorses the characterisation.[23] However Frost, who employs different descriptive language, not only sets up his stall in opposition to those positions that we have no difficulty describing as cosmopolitan but also in opposition to communitarianism, in particular to Walzer's communitarianism.

Frost begins his defence of the claim that the current normative context in which we must view international relations is the 'modern state domain of discourse' by identifying and examining two principal objections to his position. The first of these positions is identified as 'the conflict of ideologies' objection, a position that maintains that

> there is no such area of agreement within which the difficult issues may be situated. On this view the most conspicuous feature of the domain of international relations is the lack of any such core consensus to serve as a basis from which to solve the more difficult cases, since the more difficult normative issues typically arise between peoples with radically opposed ideologies.[24]

This is essentially the realist or sceptic criticism, although it is broader than the conception of realism I outlined above. The second position, the 'natural law/community of humankind' objection is very similar to the cosmopolitan position. Thinkers who take this approach do not dispute that there is a substantial normative context but argue that 'it is not situated in the state centric practice, but in a more fundamental community, namely, the community of humankind'.[25] The way Frost deals with the first of these objections offers an interesting insight into the question of whether we should classify Frost as a communitarian at all and more relevantly whether we should link Frost and Walzer in this tradition as an important part of an understanding of contemporary international relations theory.

The majority of thinkers working within the cosmopolitan/communitarian debate and the discourse of international ethics acknowledge the impact (whether or not they believe its importance is warranted) of the realist/amoralist position in the philosophy of international relations. In order to begin the task of normative theorising Frost rejects the strict, or caricatured realist position arguing that 'the person or state who acted as a consistent amoralist would not be recognizable as a person or state properly so called'[26] and constructs the 'conflict of ideologies' position from a series of marginally more sophisticated arguments against the idea that there is a consensus in international affairs that allows us to solve its problems. This realist/sceptical tradition is constructed from at least three distinct positions. The first position is that of the American realist Hans Morgenthau. Morgenthau's position, argues Frost, is not the archrealist 'there can be no underlying consensus' but that since the end of the first world war such a consensus has eroded and that the international domain has descended into radically opposed 'irrational nationalisms and fanatical religious zealotry'.[27] The second of these 'distinct' positions is that of Walzer, who, writes Frost

> argues that in the modern world there is no political consensus; that in the modern world people do not experience a sense of political being with a single frame of reference. Instead people have divided political allegiances. His argument is against the applicability of the state centric view according to which a person's political being is conceived within a state centric frame of reference.[28]

This interpretation of Walzer, allied with Frost's lengthier exegesis of Walzer's international theory is problematic and leads Frost to distance himself both from Walzer and the communitarian position. However, before looking more closely at this aspect of Frost's argument it is interesting to note that the next distinct tradition he places in the conflict of ideologies approach to international relations theory is his rendering of communitarianism. The 'pluralist perspective' and its close cousin, communitarianism stem, Frost maintains, from the idea, elaborated by B. Paskins and M. Dockrill in *The Ethics of War* and quoted by Frost, that 'the contemporary world is living with the aftermath of what Nietzsche termed "the death of god," that is, the collapse of all consensus on an authoritative political, social, moral and political order'.[29] Because of the lack of an overarching consensus, and presumably if we follow Nietzsche's reasoning because of the impossibility and indeed undesirability of such an overarching consensus, all we can hope for is a radical form of pluralism, or communitarianism that argues, writes Frost quoting from C. Wright Mills, that 'in the end, if the end comes, we just have to beat those who disagree with us over the head'.[30] Despite the amusing prose, albeit borrowed, one must take issue with Frost's construction of the tradition. Firstly his construction of the tradition is too rigid. Frost's response to the conflict of ideologies approach is that

> parties to the disputes in international affairs do not normally confront one another in this mutually uncomprehending way. They rather tend to confront one another in the context of well established practice. Their disputes are situated within a common state centric domain of discourse.[31]

There are two distinct points being made here. The second point that can be dealt with first is the idea that the 'modern state domain of discourse' is the established context for problem solving in international relations. This point limits discussion of international problems to a context-dependent frame of reference and specifies that context in direct opposition to what Frost terms the 'natural law/community of human kind approach', an approach also known as cosmopolitanism. For Frost the distinction between his approach and this method differ in

> the portrayal it gives of the basic community from which argument must proceed. It claims that there is a moral community of humankind which it conceives to be in some way independent of the modernizing inter-state practice, whereas I consider just that modernizing state system as providing the idiom within which normative argument takes place.[32]

The argument is not that there is no context-dependent consensus about right action in international relations but that the cosmopolitans have not identified it correctly. Frost goes on to identify and take issue with a related view, the idea that problems in the international sphere, understood here as occurring within the modern state domain of discourse, can only be resolved from a wider perspective. It is sufficient here to recognise that Frost rejects both positions although not as comprehensively as he rejects his version of the amoralism of the 'conflict of ideologies' approach. However the first point that Frost makes, that his theory differs from communitarianism, and particularly Walzer's position, over whether there is an arena for moral discourse at all is immediately relevant to my argument. If sustainable, Frost's claim would refute the very basis of the distinction that this work rests upon.

Frost has set his position up in opposition to three approaches to international ethics. The least controversial is scepticism, a position that has been dealt with in previous chapters. Frost also opposes his position to cosmopolitanism and the idea that a state-oriented approach and a cosmopolitan approach should be opposed is happily endorsed. The other position, rejected here, is that Frost's position is antithetical to pluralism and communitarianism. This argument is formed in the first point made by Frost in response to the 'conflict of ideologies' approach (above). Frost maintains that pluralists and communitarians (simply classified as communitarians in this work) argue that parties to international affairs confront each other with no shared context, no consensus about how they are to solve any problems that arise. Furthermore they argue that the ideological framework within which these parties operate prevents such a consensus arising. This characterisation of a tradition of thought is far too strict. With Walzer serving as our example, as his work does for both Frost's work and the present study, it is possible to show both that the communitarian position admits more to the notion of development in international understanding than Frost allows and that Frost shares conceptual ground with this tradition.

There are two principal objections to Frost's account of Walzer's international theory. The first focuses on the notion that there is no normative context for the mediation of disputes in international affairs, the second on the claim that Walzer's theory is in the contract/consent tradition of political thought.[33] The first of these claims is rather odd, considering that Frost, later in his book, goes on to examine the six propositions of Walzer's 'legalist paradigm' and argues that

> [t]he key point in all of this is that there is a settled norm in international society that infringements of the territorial and political sovereignty are *prima facie* wrong. Any state attempting such an act is taken to be guilty of a wrong unless some special justification can be provided.[34]

Here Walzer provides the normative framework that Frost complains is lacking in his work and thus Frost must concede that the ground between Walzer's position and his own is much less than the conceptual gulf suggested by his earlier analysis. Both Frost and Walzer base their account of international ethics on what Frost calls 'settled norms' or what Walzer terms 'reiterative universals' (see chapters 5 and 6 below). The central difference is that Frost believes he is licensed to cite seventeen 'settled norms'[35] where Walzer believes that very few substantial conceptions of the 'moral minimum' are shared over any lengthy period of time. Nevertheless if Frost and Walzer can be seen to present theories that are different in degree rather than in kind then developmental communitarianism as an intellectual framework for understanding a form of ethical theory may begin to gain some substance. The second point is more complex. Frost distances his position from that of Walzer's because his 'constitutive theory of individuality' forms a background justification for his list of settled norms in a totally different way from that of Walzer. Or so he seems to believe.

Frost distances his position from that of Walzer because he believes Walzer's thought to be in the social contract tradition of political theory, a fact that would privilege a nonsensical (for Frost and other constitutive theorists) idea of the pre-social, rights-holding individual. The opposition here, if put very simplistically, is between an argument that suggests that the community shapes the individual versus an argument that suggests that a conception of individual-as-agent shapes a concept of rights and regulates the form of the 'just' community. While framed in a rather basic manner this opposition can be seen as one of the fundamental divisions within the individualist/communitarian debate in mainstream political theory. The introduction to one of the seminal introductory texts to this debate shows that

> [b]oth communitarian and individualist theories begin with the image of the individual. But the former claims that there are social attachments which determine the self and thus individuals are constituted by the community of which they are a part. In that sense the individualist image of the self is ontologically false. Individualists also fail to see that this community is not

> necessarily a voluntary one, and that the social attachments which determine the self are not necessarily chosen ones.[36]

The methodological/ontological argument leads directly into the normative argument. For example, if we are to base our notion of justice on an understanding of the nature of community, justice must focus (in the first instance at least) on the common good; if we found justice on the notion of the pre-social, rights-holding individual the justice must look to those individuals. This individualist/communitarian debate plays an important role in the cosmopolitan/communitarian debate and if Frost can oppose his position to that of Walzer then both the cosmopolitan/communitarian divide (as constructed in this study) and the examples used to highlight the most vital issues arising from this construction must be discounted as false. Fortunately, for my argument, Frost's position here is untenable. There is plenty of evidence in *JUW*, to back up Frost's case. Indeed he cites much of it in support of his claim and particularly focuses on the elusive rights to life and liberty that entailed 'the right of men and women to build a common life and to risk their individual lives only when they freely choose to do so'.[37] These 'rights', that were the focus of much of the criticism of the particularist claims of Walzer's earlier work also form the staple of Frost's cause as he argues that '[t]he string of quotations ... clearly illustrates Walzer's belief that the state's authority is derived from the consent of the governed and that the state's sovereign right to engage in war is thus based, finally, on individual rights'.[38]

This interpretation of Walzer's theory, and the problems that this generates (for Frost's account of international relations) is based on a misunderstanding of the background justification (to use Frost's language) that Walzer provides for his theory. Liberal ideas of human rights, of the necessity of individual consent, of what Walzer terms his idea of a 'thin universal', or 'minimal' morality, are not pre-social but develop over time and out of our communal existence. Rather than exhaust this argument, and pre-empt a more detailed discussion (below) it is worth quoting at some length from Walzer's 'background justification'.

> I have in the past suggested the image of a core morality differently elaborated in different cultures. ... But ... these descriptions suggest mistakenly that the starting point for the development of morality is the same in every case. Men and Women everywhere begin with some common idea or principle or set of ideas and principles, which they then work up in many different ways. They start thin, as it were, and thicken with age, as if in accordance with our deepest intuition about what it means to develop or mature. But our intuition is wrong here. Morality is thick from the beginning, culturally integrated, fully resonant, and it reveals itself thinly only on special occasions, when moral language is turned to specific purposes.[39]

Our 'thin moral sense', our adopted language of human rights (protected, in Walzer's view, only by the rights of sovereign states) is constructed, over time and in explicit opposition to a new or unfamiliar normative problem, it is not foundational. This is a point Frost comes very close to noting as he writes 'I do not intend to examine these now. I merely wish to point out that there is in his theory a strong sense in which a state's rights are not derived from individual contract/consent but are prior to it.'[40]

While Frost had access to *Thick and Thin*, indeed he cites it on occasion, he did not make full use of it. If he had he would find, in Walzer's work, a theory compatible with his own in that 'it takes seriously the truth that when we reason about normative issues we do so from within a standpoint defined by specific institutions such as the state, and the interstate system'.[41] This is not to suggest that the works of Walzer and Frost are completely compatible but to suggest that they share enough ground that they can be appropriately situated within a communitarian framework in the context of the cosmopolitan/communitarian framework and my more specific argument.

If Walzer and Frost can be said to share the distinction of being labelled 'communitarians' can they also share the term 'developmental communitarians'. In the context of the present argument it is important that they do as my purpose is not to highlight well-documented stereotypes but to show the dynamic effect that the cosmopolitan/communitarian debate has had on liberal discourse on international ethics. It is not the purpose of this chapter to rehearse the argument of later chapters and so rather than focus solely on Frost's account of 'constitutive theory' the present remarks will be limited to a more general discussion of Hegelian thought.

It is almost inconceivable to think in terms of an Hegelian philosophy that is not historically sensitive. Hegel's understanding of his philosophical enterprise was to elaborate and identify the 'spirit of an age', a passage, known to all students of the history of political thought, sums this up perfectly: 'When philosophy paints its grey on grey, a shape of life has grown old, and it cannot be rejuvenated, but only recognised, by the grey on grey of philosophy; the owl of Minerva begins its flight only with onset of dusk.'[42]

This methodological stand is not inherently conservative. Pelczynski sums up Hegel's meaning succinctly, writing:

> while the philosopher must try to grasp concepts which are 'actualized', 'operative', or 'living', one must not assume that concepts are rational simply because they possess this character. This is where the 'plain man' and the philosopher often part company. If serfdom, slavery, and the subjugation of women, have been accepted in society for centuries, the ordinary folk tend to see nothing wrong in them. The philosopher, on the other hand, may more easily perceive that they are basically incompatible with the ideals of equality or freedom which the society professes and which pervade all other aspects of ethical life.[43]

Both history and historicity are important to the Hegelian/idealist tradition of thought. The writings of two contemporary Hegelian thinkers, C. Brown and

J. Charvet confirm this. C. Brown adopts a constitutive approach explicitly to introduce a 'dynamic of change',[44] Charvet, also writing within the intellectual framework of the cosmopolitan/communitarian debate, argues that 'whether we start, ethically speaking, from individuals or states, there may still be an important, if subordinate place, for the other type of ethical entity'.[45] The question that Frost, and other Hegelian thinkers must face is how far they can proceed with their argument once philosophical history makes way for a more secular approach and that is the aspect of Frost's work that will occupy us in chapter 5.

The character of the 'developmental' aspect of communitarianism that I set out to uncover is precisely that which searches for the force of human rights discourse in the work of Frost and Rawls or the moral minimum in Walzer, while attempting to account for the empirical and theoretical problems that we experience in international relations. The particular normative problems generated by the secularisation of liberal philosophy, the refusal to rely on Hegelian or Kantian metaphysics, does not divorce us conceptually from the projects that Kant or Hegel had in mind and this is something that Frost firmly believes in. Secular Hegelianism, it would seem, is conceptually much closer to Walzer's methodological position than has previously been admitted. In the work of Walzer and Frost we can discern two attempts to create principles of justice for the international political arena while starting from broadly particularist assumptions. The dynamism within the Hegelian position and within the wider communitarian position, the idea of a developing area of consensus within the international sphere found in the work of Walzer, Frost and, I will argue, Rawls, make the title 'developmental communitarian' both appropriate and important. However, in order to complete an argument in favour of examining one aspect of the current liberal debate in international relations theory in terms of a dialogue between developmental communitarianism and cosmopolitanism, it is necessary to examine the reactions engendered by one manifestly liberal position that seems to contrast (albeit in subtle but important ways) with the positions occupied by cosmopolitanism.

Rawls and developmental communitarianism

My primary reason for characterising Rawls' work as developmental and communitarian lies in my contention that we should take very seriously indeed Rawls' claim to have constructed principles of domestic and international justice that necessarily fall short of the Kantian principles he associated his early work with.[46] As with the work of Walzer and Frost the method adopted in Rawls' *PL* and 'LOP' leads to the adoption of broadly liberal principles of international justice as a conclusion deduced from the circumstances of justice and the ability of agents (suitably understood) to achieve a consensus upon these principles. Against foundational liberal cosmopolitanism Rawls argues that we cannot specify in advance an ideal conception of the agent and associated principles of justice and against constructivist cosmopolitanism Rawls argues that we cannot at present abstract to an idea of a pre-political rights-bearing agent. My principal claim, introduced here and defended in response to O'Neill's critique of Rawls in chapter 4 and in my exegesis of Rawls' theory in chapter 7, is that Rawls shares conceptual ground with both Frost and Walzer and transcends the developmental communitarianism of both theorists.

It is not, of course, completely original to claim that the new Rawls is a communitarian thinker. Schwarzenbach in 'Rawls, Hegel and Communitarianism'[47] makes a strong case that suggests that Rawls' work resembles what Frost terms secular Hegelianism. Similarly Alejarndro attempts to defend Rawls from Sandel's communitarian critique by placing both thinkers in the communitarian tradition.[48] However it is more usual, particularly in the field of international ethics to see Rawls' work referred to as liberal and cosmopolitan. Both Beitz and Pogge, two of the most prominent critics of Rawls' international relations theory, portray Rawls as a theorist who does not understand the international implications of his liberalism.[49] Even O'Neill who cites Rawls' 'Justice as Fairness: Political not Metaphysical'[50] as Rawls' 'most nearly communitarian writing'[51] uses Rawls as proof that the universalist message and internationalist commitments of liberalism are being eroded.[52] I intend to explore my interpretation of Rawls within a full exposition of his international relations theory and this must wait until chapter 7. Here I wish to introduce Rawls' own claims to have moved away from the neo-Kantian tradition, Pogge's criticism that Rawls is in danger of becoming illiberal, O'Neill's claims that Rawls either relies too heavily on metaphysical liberalism or upon foundational statism, and to introduce the idea that Rawls has indeed moved to the idea of a constructivist communitarianism outlined in relation to the work of Walzer and Frost. All of these themes will be reintroduced in the context of an exegesis of Rawls' theory. The principal aim here is to show that the definite move towards constructivist and developmental communitarianism is not illiberal and that Rawls can be shown to share conceptual ground with the other two thinkers I have ascribed to this tradition of thought.

Rawls is famous for having led a steady (and explicit) retreat away from the tenets of Kantian political theory. By the time he gave first expression to his idea of a 'Law of Peoples'[53] Rawls had already highlighted the ways in which his Kant-inspired political philosophy differed from Kant's own view. In particular he noted four differences between Kant's moral constructivism and the political constructivism of justice as fairness that made his theory 'political rather than metaphysical'.[54] In making this argument Rawls found that he was required to abandon what he terms Kant's theory of 'constitutive autonomy' in favour of what he terms 'doctrinal autonomy'. This is a very significant move and impacts heavily on Rawls' conception of international justice. The distinction that Rawls draws between Kant's constitutive autonomy and his own theory of doctrinal autonomy stems from the different aims of Kant's philosophical investigations and Rawls' own. Kant's doctrine of autonomy has, Rawls points out,'a regulative role for all of life'. In Rawls' terms:

> Constitutive autonomy says that the so-called independent order of values does not constitute itself but is constituted by the activity, actual or ideal, of practical (human) reason itself. I believe this, or something like it is Kant's view. His constructivism is deeper and goes to the very existence and constitution of the order of values. This is part of his transcendental idealism.[55]

Rawls' political constructivism is, of course, less ambitious. It seeks to avoid making 'comprehensive' claims about the order of values. Rather, it gets its force from the fact that it is justifiable before the relevant parties in world politics. In effect this is what contemporary political theory (O'Neill included) has settled for. In separating his constructivism from Kant's 'deeper' and comprehensive approach Rawls notes that 'the full significance of a constructivist political conception lies in its connection with the fact of reasonable pluralism'.[56] An acknowledgment of the importance of this 'fact' requires the recognition that agents cannot be brought to agree upon any moral authority or the order of values. The constructivist concern to avoid imposing such order requires, in turn, that the in-built universalism and individualism of constitutive autonomy is replaced by 'doctrinal', 'political' or 'reasonable' autonomy. The goal of doctrinal autonomy is the working out of fair terms of social cooperation, rather than the working out of the order of values. The idea of autonomy that Rawls' constructivism aspires to is simply autonomy from the various comprehensive doctrines that make up the moral and social fabric of our political world. In laying out the theoretical basis of doctrinal autonomy, Rawls argues that the constructivist must ally a thin conception of practical reason to a normative framework that gives full weight to the autonomy of 'appropriate conceptions of society and the person'.[57] Doctrinal autonomy is said to protect the autonomy of the agents by refusing to privilege any particular view of moral authority and tempering abstract theorising by drawing on the normative framework of international politics achieves this goal. While this ensures that all agents could endorse the principles of justice, and so ensures that Rawls' theory is universal, it also ensures that constructivist liberalism cannot endorse cosmopolitanism.

For Rawls 'there is no relevant subject, politically speaking, for which we lack principles and standards to judge'.[58]The Law of Peoples is universal in reach in that it gives principles for all politically relevant subjects in world politics. It gains this universality by drawing on the norms of international society (the background conditions of world politics) – something that Rawls contrasts with the Kantian method of deducing the universality of the moral law from practical reason.[59] However, achieving this universality requires that we reject cosmopolitanism. In Rawls' *Political Liberalism*, 'the conceptions of society and the person', or in 'The Law of Peoples' the 'background conditions of international society' dictate the outcome, or content, of practical reason.[60] Political constructivism has to face the fact that not all agents in world politics believe in individuated politics or ethics. The principal idea here is that a constructivist theory may not include a notion of agency as a predicate to its thesis unless that notion of agency is found in the public political culture (or background conditions) of the political arena that is being examined. In Rawls' international relations theory it is the background conditions of world politics that limit the cosmopolitan practice of methodological abstraction and oblige us to focus on the claims of peoples and their governments rather than a Kantian conception of the autonomous individual.[61] In sum, the way in which it is still possible to think universally about ethical matters requires that we water down cosmopolitanism, to focus on the agency of Peoples, rather than persons, and to limit severely the claims of human rights and distributive justice. For Rawls then, the fact that we cannot assume (with Kant) that individuals are autonomous under the moral law does not mean we have to drop the idea that ethics should be universalisable. We do, however, have to alter our view of what principles should be universalised.

The quasi-communitarian focus on international society (rather than a cosmopolitan focus on individual agency) leads theorists, such as O'Neill, to argue that Rawls' neo-Kantianism has no ethical or political potential. This is so because, in moving to a non-comprehensive theory, Rawls makes his account of practical reason and his account of international ethics hostage to the prevailing norms of international society. The use of the phrase 'practical reason' in 'LOP' is (as Rawls has recently acknowledged) misleading.[62] Principles of justice are not in any sense deduced from principles of practical reason except insofar as such principles follow from their ability to convince those agents who currently make up international society. O'Neill aims to improve upon Rawls' theory by developing a much stronger account of practical reason which, while still constructivist, can lead to cosmopolitanism. In setting out her own theory O'Neill picks up on this point. O'Neill writes,

> [t]he more guarded constructivism that I shall outline follows Rawls in that it does not look for the vindication of ethical principles in metaphysical argument, or in discoveries about the world. It differs from the one Rawls has developed in two ways. In the first place it assumes only an abstract, hence non-idealizing and banal, account of agents and of conditions of action. Secondly, it aims to articulate and to vindicate a conception of practical reason without appeal either to unvindicated ideals or to unvindicated particularities.[63]

O'Neill's principal criticism of Rawls' constructivism is that he relies so heavily upon the norms of contemporary society, which govern the outcome of any process of practical reasoning, that his theory simply avoids relying upon metaphysical claims by endorsing the relevant *status quo*.[64] O'Neill, working from within the same theoretical constraints, believes that Rawls has sold himself, liberalism and neo-Kantianism short. This debate will occupy our attention in the next chapter.

Pogge, like many liberal theorists, is outraged by Rawls' retreat from liberal internationalism. In fact he goes as far as to say that Rawls simply misunderstands the role of liberalism in world politics. In his critique of Rawls' international relations theory, Pogge argues that the following statements represent a liberal and non-liberal stand respectively.

1′ A liberal society must leave room for certain non-liberal communities and lifestyles.
2′ It would be illiberal to impose liberal institutions on a society that contains many persons who do not share our liberal values.[65]

These statements, said to represent the argument in the domestic case, show that Rawls would accept (1′) and reject (2′) because 'while our society can contain many different kinds of communities, associations, and conceptions of the good, some liberal in character and some not, it can be structured or organised in only one way.'[66] When constructing principles of justice for a well-ordered liberal society in *PL* I believe that Rawls would indeed do as Pogge suggests. The essential point to note however is that in international relations theory Rawls would not reject (2′) because the political culture of the international sphere simply does not license the belief that a strongly liberal global order is an appropriate political mechanism with which to administer international justice. Rawls, like Walzer and Frost, argues that the only place we can begin our theory of international relations is by taking account of the background conditions of international society, of the idea of interconnectedness. In Rawls' view the international community is significantly different in structure, content and in the demands it places upon association from a historically liberal democratic and bounded state and this, he believes, necessitates different political constructions. Rawls' constructivism thus takes a similar starting point to the reiterative universalism of Walzer and Frost's 'modern-state-domain of discourse'. In contrast to foundationalist cosmopolitanism,

> a constructivist view such as justice as fairness ... do[es] not begin from universal first principles having authority in all cases. ... Rather, [principles of justice] are constructed by way of a reasonable procedure in which rational parties adopt principles of justice for each kind of subject as it arises ... its authority rests on the principles and conceptions of practical reason, but always on these as suitably adjusted to different subjects as they arise in sequence; and always assuming that these principles are endorsed on due reflection by the reasonable agents to whom the corresponding principles apply.[67]

Rawls does not believe (as O'Neill does) that the background conditions of a cosmopolitan world order exist. While O'Neill criticises Rawls heavily for his stance here it is perfectly reasonable, indeed, so I shall argue, more reasonable than the vision of interconnectedness with which O'Neill predicates her cosmopolitanism. For Rawls,

> a further reason for proceeding thus is that peoples as corporate bodies organized by their governments now exist in some form all over the world. Historically speaking, all principles and standards proposed for the law of peoples must, to be feasible, prove acceptable to the considered and reflective public opinion of peoples and their governments.[68]

Rawls does not abandon his liberal convictions, as Pogge would have it, but argues (quite consistently) that there are no (non-comprehensive or non-foundational) grounds for believing that a strong form of Kantian-liberalism is just in this instance. Here Rawls' emphasis on a dynamic political consensus avoids the 'greater international conflict' in the area of human rights engendered by Pogge's 'more assertive liberalism' and other cosmopolitan theories of human rights (see chapter 7). Pogge's 'categorical allegiance' to liberal principles of justice examined in chapter 2 does not allow him the room to argue that if the international arena is not liberal the form of international justice should not be strongly liberal. Rawls' method allows him to argue that the principles a liberal could agree to and the rights it is reasonable to expect a more heterogeneous group of agents to agree to are different and that this is a consequence of relying only on realistic and accessible theoretical strategies. A clear example here is the reasoning Rawls attributes to a liberal acceptance of human rights in a brief article in *Dissent* and the reasoning he provides for the inclusion of a shortened list of human rights acceptable to the parties in 'LOP' (see chapter 7).[69] Rawls' stand here gives rise to criticisms of relativism, just as the position taken by Walzer gives rise to such criticism. Jones and Pogge argue that Rawls risks 'tolerating too much' in seeking to construct political principles of justice rather than comprehensively liberal principles of justice.[70] O'Neill argues forcefully that norm-governed practical reasoning is not suited to the ethical demands placed upon us all by the international sphere.[71] Even those critics who believe that Rawls has moved from the liberal to the communitarian camp argue that he unduly restricts the laws of international cooperation.[72] Pogge's insistence upon categorical allegiance to liberal principles does not, in my view, constitute the only form of liberalism. While Rawls' theory is not foundationally liberal it is certainly not illiberal. Rather Rawls argues that moving from an *a priori* attachment to Kant's constitutive theory of autonomy (a view which argues that all human beings – regardless of political or historical situation – must be viewed as having a particular moral personality) to a constructed account of political autonomy (which argues that given the circumstances of justice – reasonable pluralism – and the problems with various forms of foundationalism we must admit a diversity of moral positions and thus a desegregated conception of moral personality) is a necessary historical progression of liberalism.[73] Paden puts the general argument well:

> in 'The Law of Peoples', Rawls can be understood as advancing an argument to show that even if liberals and communitarians can't live in the same

> society, they can still agree on certain (liberal) principles of justice to govern international relations.[74]

The most relevant problem at this stage of an exegesis of Rawls must be whether or not this strategy could be accurately called (developmental) communitarianism. Paden while accepting Barry's argument that Rawls is attempting to assuage the communitarian tradition argues that Rawls is not communitarian enough.[75] O'Neill goes still further arguing that Rawls is generalising from a liberal conception of the state rather than any communitarian understanding of community and is thus an idealising liberal.[76] I will deal with O'Neill's position at length in the next chapter, here it is sufficient to assert that I believe O'Neill to be wrong. However a brief discussion of the idea that Rawls is methodologically communitarian should serve to conclude this preliminary sketch of the developmental communitarian tradition.

In agreeing with O'Neill (on the cosmopolitan side) and Walzer and Frost (on the communitarian side) that principles of politics and ethics must be constructed rather than discovered or assumed, Rawls is committed to a rejection of foundational liberalism and communitarianism. The distinction between cosmopolitanism and communitarianism drawn here rests partly on the starting point chosen by each tradition. While traditional cosmopolitan and communitarian positions would debate the virtues of taking existent communities or abstract general principles as their starting point in terms of the foundations of ethics, the debate that still rages between constructivist theorists hinges on what information we can legitimately retrieve from political life without adding to that information or supporting it by resorting to discredited moral or political assumptions and strategies. O'Neill's constructivist cosmopolitanism argues that we do have grounds for abstracting a concept of moral agency and then generalising that concept as a universal critical and cosmopolitan ideal. Rawls and Walzer, and to a more limited extent Frost, contest this arguing that politics and the political borders we use both to limit and protect or instantiate our moral understandings place serious limitations upon how far we can abstract to a cosmopolitan notion of the individual. Indeed, argue the developmental communitarians, the obvious heterogeneity of global cultures means that we must construct principles of justice for international politics alone and ensure that the heterogeneity of global culture is left intact insofar as the peoples of international society wish it to be so. The idea here is that international politics is a sphere of interaction which does not always intrude into domestic political or personal life. Furthermore the developmental communitarians do not attach any foundational value to the heterogeneity of the international sphere. It is simply a fact, and insofar as this fact does not conflict with the legitimate aims of international relations we have no reason to question its validity. This does not imply that all cultures and points of view are legitimate. Indeed this method leads the developmental communitarians to conclude that some expressions of political and social culture are not permissible or tolerable in international politics. Furthermore all of the theorists I examine argue that some form of universal ethics is essential to international relations. The two principles that Rawls argues lead to this conclusion are the twin virtues of tolerance and freedom. To suggest that this is either illiberal or too liberal is to miss the most important point in his work.

Concluding remarks

Developmental communitarianism is thus a signifier for a type of constructivist theory that stands in opposition to traditional liberal cosmopolitanism and to constructivist liberal cosmopolitanism. In opposing foundational cosmopolitanism, O'Neill's critical cosmopolitanism and the developmental communitarianism of Frost, Walzer and Rawls outline the limits of liberal theory in contemporary political philosophy. Liberal theorists may not 'idealise' or add dubious predicates to their theory in order to ensure that liberal principles appear legitimate (O'Neill). Liberal theorists may not start theorising from 'outside of the cave' (Walzer), or from outside the relevant domain of discourse (Frost), or by assuming in advance the legitimacy of comprehensively liberal principles (Rawls). Liberal theorists are not entitled to develop liberal principles of international (or cosmopolitan) justice at all until they have shown that such principles can be (or are) constructed under the contemporary circumstances of justice or prevailing conditions of international interconnectedness. The burden of the present chapter has been to introduce the ways in which those thinkers I have labelled developmental communitarians differ significantly from the constructivism offered by O'Neill. The principal area of disagreement between them focuses on the correct method for modelling interconnectedness in international relations and their competing claims to have legitimately developed principles of justice compatible with this model. This is the debate that the final parts of this study will concentrate upon. O'Neill's work stands as the paradigm of constructivist cosmopolitanism. Against O'Neill, Frost, Walzer and Rawls all share the belief that the political and geographical space that the human race has used to give its ethical and political customs and practices meaning and safety are morally or politically relevant. In this they share enough ground to be labelled communitarian in order to distinguish them from foundational and constructivist cosmopolitanism. Their arguments to this conclusion are, I shall contend, more secure than any variant of liberal cosmopolitanism. From here they all demonstrate a developmental, yet still constructivist, approach to the real problems of international relations. The claim that I believe follows from the construction of the tradition of developmental communitarianism is simply this: liberalism does have important implications for the possibility of international politics but unless that liberalism is constructed along developmental communitarian lines it is in danger of being theoretically unjustifiable and of producing unjust and politically dangerous principles and policies.

Turning now to an exegesis of four constructivist liberal theorists, one cosmopolitan and three communitarian, I intend to demonstrate the philosophical and political difficulties in developing a liberal cosmopolitanism for the modern age and the benefits of an increased understanding of developmental communitarianism. The principal burden of this third part of my argument is to show that beyond cosmopolitanism is a liberal tradition that does not simply hide its philosophical inadequacies behind historical contingency but that makes the most successful argument to necessarily revised or reworked liberal principles of international justice. The developmental communitarians are often accused of shrinking from their liberal convictions and again this is due in part to the rival claims of cosmopolitanism. Yet despite the power and meticulous nature of what is perhaps the most rigorous exposition of contemporary cosmopolitanism, that of O'Neill, it will become clear that her thoroughgoing liberal principles are not suited to the political conditions of international relations. Once even the best example of constructivist cosmopolitanism has been shown to be wanting the full force and potential scope of the liberalism of the developmental communitarians has to be scrutinised. This route offers the best, and possibly the only, way forward in liberal international relations theory.

Notes and references

1 J. Thompson, *Justice and World Order: A Philosophical Inquiry*, London, Routledge, 1992, p. 3.
2 See chapter 6. Also M. Walzer, 'The Communitarian Critique of Liberalism', *Political Theory*, Vol. 18, No. 1, February 1990, p. 7.
3 Walzer, *JUW*, p. 3.
4 D. Greene, *Greek Political Theory*, University of Chicago Press, 1967, Part I.
5 Walzer, *JUW*, p. 7.
6 Thucydides, *History of the Peloponnesian War*, trans. Warner, Penguin Books, 1954, bk 5, p. 402.
7 Walzer, *JUW*, pp. 7 and 8.
8 J. Thompson, *Justice and World Order*, p. 2. See also Thucydides, *History*, bk 5, p. 405.
9 Walzer, *JUW*, p. 9.
10 Thompson, *Justice and World Order*, p. 2.
11 Walzer, *JUW*, pp. 11–12.
12 Thompson, *Justice and World Order*, p. 3.
13 C. Brown, 'International Social Justice', in D. Boucher and P. Kelly (eds), *Perspectives on Social Justice*, London, Routledge, 1998, p. 4.
14 M. Walzer, *Thick and Thin: Moral Arguments at Home and Abroad*, University of Notre Dame Press, 1994. See also *JUW* although this message is somewhat obscured here. See chapter 6 below.
15 M. Walzer, *Spheres of Justice: A Defence of Pluralism and Equality*, Blackwell, 1983, p. xv.
16 Walzer, *Thick and Thin*, p. 3.
17 Walzer, *JUW*, pp. 61–62.
18 Cf. M. Walzer, 'Political Decision Making and Political Education', in Richter (ed.), *Political Theory and Political Education*, Princeton University Press, 1980. Here Walzer is specifically contrasting his position with that of the realists.
19 M. Frost, *Ethics in International Relations: A Constitutive Theory*, Cambridge University Press, 1996.
20 Frost, *Ethics*, p. 78.
21 Frost, *Ethics*, p. 79.
22 Cf. C. Brown, *International Relations Theory: New Normative Approaches*, New York, London, Harvester Wheatsheaf, 1992, p. 12.

23 C. Brown, 'The Ethics of Political Restructuring in Europe: The Perspective of Constitutive Theory.', in C. Brown (ed.), *Political Restructuring in Europe: Ethical Perspectives*, Routledge, 1994, pp. 166–167.
24 M. Frost, *Ethics and International Relations: A Constitutive Theory*, Cambridge, Cambridge University Press, 1996, p. 80.
25 Ibid.
26 Frost, *Ethics*, p. 47.
27 Frost, *Ethics*, p. 81.
28 Ibid.
29 B. Paskins and M. Dockrill, *The Ethics of War*, Duckworth, 1979, p. 102 cited Frost, *Ethics*, p. 81.
30 C. Wright Mills, *The Sociological Imagination*, Oxford University Press, 1959, p. 77 cited Frost, *Ethics*, p. 82.
31 Frost, *Ethics*, p. 82.
32 Frost, *Ethics*, p. 85.
33 Frost, *Ethics*, p. 131. It might also be noted that these two criticisms of Walzer's work are mutually exclusive. No thinker can argue (1) that there is no shared context for working out normative theory and (2) that all politics is to be conducted within contract theory or in light of certain inalienable individual rights. Position (2) is simply the claim that there is a foundational (or constructed) normative framework.
34 Frost, *Ethics*, p. 132. The legalist paradigm is examined further in chapter 6 below.
35 See Frost, *Ethics*, pp. 111–112 and chapters 2 and 7.
36 S. Avineri and A. de-Shalit (eds), *Communitarianism and Individualism*, Oxford, Oxford University Press, 1992, p. 3.
37 Walzer, *JUW*, p. 61 cited Frost, *Ethics*, p. 131.
38 Frost, *Ethics*, p. 131.
39 Walzer, *Thick and Thin*, p. 4.
40 Frost, *Ethics*, p. 135.
41 Frost, *Ethics*, p. 141.
42 G.W.F Hegel, *Elements of the Philosophy of Right*, A. Wood (ed.), Cambridge Texts in the History of Political Thought, Cambridge University Press, 1991, preface, p. 23.
43 *Hegel's Political Writings*, trans. T.M. Knox, introductory essay by Z. Pelczynski, Oxford University Press, 1964, pp. 114–115.
44 Brown, 'The Ethics of Political Restructuring', p. 170.
45 J. Charvet, 'Contractarianism and International Political Theory', in D. Boucher and P. Kelly (eds), *The Social Contract from Hobbes to Rawls*, Routledge, 1994, p. 175.
46 See particularly Rawls, *TJ*, §40 and compare with *PL*, Lecture III, §2.
47 S. Schwarzenbach, 'Rawls, Hegel, and Communitarianism', *Political Theory*, Vol. 19, No. 4, November 1991, pp. 539–571.
48 R. Alejarndro, 'Rawls' Communitarianism', *Canadian Journal of Philosophy*, Vol. 23, No. 1, 1993, pp. 75–100.
49 See particularly Pogge, 'Cosmopolitanism and Sovereignty', p. 50; Pogge 'An Egalitarian Law of Peoples', p. 195 and Beitz, 'Cosmopolitan Liberalism', p. 123.
50 Rawls, 'Justice as Fairness: Political not Metaphysical', *Philosophy and Public Affairs*, Vol. 14, 1985, pp. 223–251.
51 O. O'Neill, 'Transnational Justice', in D. Held (ed.), *Political Theory Today*, Polity Press, 1991, chapter 11.
52 See chapter 4.
53 J. Rawls, 'The Law of Peoples', in Shute and Hurley (eds), *On Human Rights: The Oxford Amnesty Lectures*, Basic Books, 1993.
54 Rawls, *PL*, p. 99 and Lecture III, passim.
55 Rawls, *PL*, p. 99.
56 Rawls, *PL*, p. 90.
57 Rawls, *PL*, p. 98.

58 Rawls, 'LOP', p. 86.
59 Rawls, 'LOP', §12.2
60 Cf. Rawls, *Political Liberalism*, p. 108.
61 Rawls, 'LOP', pp. 46 and 50. See also *PL*, Lecture VII.
62 Rawls, *The Law of Peoples*, Harvard University Press, 1999, p. 86.
63 O'Neill, *TJV*, p. 48.
64 O'Neill, *TJV*, p. 46.
65 Pogge, 'An Egalitarian Law of Peoples', p. 217.
66 Ibid.
67 Rawls, 'LOP', p. 46. See also *PL*, Lecture VII.
68 Rawls, 'LOP', p. 50.
69 Cf. Rawls, '50 Years after Hiroshima', *Dissent*, Summer, 1995, p. 324 and Rawls, 'LOP', passim. See chapter 7 below.
70 E.g. P. Jones, 'International Human Rights: Philosophical or Political?' in S. Caney, D. George, and P. Jones (eds), *National Rights, International Obligations*, Westview Press, 1996.
71 O'Neill, *TJV*, p. 51. See also chapter 4 below.
72 See for example R. Paden, 'Reconstructing Rawls' Law of Peoples', *Ethics and International Affairs*, Vol. 11, 1997, p. 231.
73 Rawls, *PL*, Lecture III.
74 Paden, 'Reconstructing Rawls's Law of Peoples', p. 223.
75 Paden is here accepting the argument in B. Barry, 'John Rawls and the Search for Stability' *Ethics*, Vol. 105, 1995, pp. 904–5. See Paden, 'Reconstructing Rawls' Law of Peoples', pp. 223 and 231.
76 See chapter 4 below.

4 Critical constructivism

Onora O'Neill on moral and institutional cosmopolitanism

Onora O'Neill's place in the structure of this argument offers two vital insights. As a constructivist her work directly engages with the political and philosophical context in which questions concerning international justice are addressed by those thinkers that I have termed developmental communitarians. Her particular brand of constructivism joins with Walzer, Frost and Rawls in offering a genuine response to the critique of foundationalism and to the seemingly irreconcilable facts of pluralism and interdependence. As a cosmopolitan constructivist O'Neill's work challenges and provides a foil for the communitarian constructivism that this part of my argument sets out to examine and, ultimately, to promote. O'Neill's general position argues that not only is a constructivist theoretical approach necessary to contemporary international relations theory but that a cosmopolitan constructivist approach is necessary. Constructivist cosmopolitanism is thought of as the high-watermark of contemporary international relations theory. It comprises both the latest and most sustainable form of theoretical justification and the most popular liberal theory of international justice. For O'Neill the basis of communitarian constructivism seeks to provide an account of justice and virtue (predominantly virtue) that needs no metaphysically substantiated accounts of the good. It is the attempt 'to see the basic norms and commitments of a society, or of a life, as the bedrock for practical reasoning: authoritative practical reasoning for a given society or individual appeals to their constitutive norms, characters or senses of identity'.[1] Throughout her work O'Neill explores what she sees as both the ethical costs and theoretical limitations of such an enterprise. O'Neill's focus is formed by her constructivist cosmopolitanism and the underlying principles that license this focus can, and do, speak volumes to the debates that form a vital part of international relations theory today. All the thinkers in the following chapters attempt to provide justifiable principles of ethics that are applicable to the expanding scope of inter- or transnational politics. With traditional human rights discourse under constant attack for being restrictively liberal in orientation and the Westphalian system of international politics under attack for being unable to deal with the expanded circumstances of justice and injustice, the outcome of the debate between constructivist cosmopolitans and constructivist communitarians should have a marked significance for international relations theory.

The principles that O'Neill generates capture the logic of constructivist cosmopolitanism. Her argument (and those of other cosmopolitanism thinkers attempting to find universally justifiable principles) focuses upon the logic of moral argument itself and the notion of 'connectedness' (to use O'Neill's term) or interconnectedness (see chapter 1) or the 'relevantly similar' (see my discussion of Mackie's exposition of the logic of universality below). These are the core ideas that have to be examined when we make ethical statements about world politics. The principal idea is that principles of ethics must be universalisable across the domain of all concerned parties. The cosmopolitans argue that the restricted domain of ethics offered by non-cosmopolitanism thinkers ignores this basic requirement. The advantage of presenting O'Neill as the major exponent of constructivist cosmopolitanism is clear. O'Neill, more than anyone else, has written widely on constructivism, cosmopolitanism *and* international relations. O'Neill's critique of foundationalism and of particularism and the subsequent construction of universal, yet politically orientated, principles of obligation offers the prime example of a philosophically rigorous constructivist cosmopolitanism. While the use of O'Neill's work as the sole example of cosmopolitanism might seem to provide a (numerically) unbalanced account of constructivist cosmopolitanism (given the three accounts of communitarian approaches to international relations theory offered below) this is quite simply a matter of focus. It is the purpose of this book to explore the largely ignored depths of constructivist and developmental communitarianism. Given the powerful counter-intuitive appeal of cosmopolitanism in international relations theory, it is necessary only to offer a rigorous test of such accounts of international justice by offering a philosophically and politically valid alternative in the cosmopolitan mode. If the developmental communitarianism displayed in the following chapters can be shown to evade the criticisms offered in O'Neill's critique of non-cosmopolitan constructivism, if it can offer relevant criticisms of her moral and institutional cosmopolitanism, and if it can make a pertinent contribution to the philosophical and political issues surrounding questions of international justice then the substantive goals of my argument will have been met. Given the relatively recent application of constructivist approaches to political and international theory it is hardly surprising that there is no great mass of literature on the subject. Nevertheless the power and meticulous nature of O'Neill's work should assuage most doubts. O'Neill's cosmopolitanism is no straw opponent. In many ways a constructivist, and hence justifiable, cosmopolitanism is the grail of liberal political theory. If it could be shown that there was a unified ethical theory that all the peoples of the world could sign up to and that it would be plainly unreasonable to refuse to do so then it would be possible to list the rules that a global community should conform to. However, the intuitive appeal of cosmopolitanism conceals the hegemonic steamroller of liberal dominance in world politics. If we are to base a genuinely international community on accessible principles of ethics then we cannot ignore the objections of non-liberal peoples. Yet it is equally clear that we cannot allow the hubbub of different political and ethical cultures to drown out the possibility of shared principles without which we can have no community at all. This chapter is designed to test the liberal claim that cosmopolitan principles could be shared, without ethical cost, by the peoples of the world. The arguments are complex and abstract but get to the heart of the central issues in world politics today, the central question of which is simply: 'what ethical principles can we use to structure the development of a truly international community?'

In order to meet its goal this chapter must offer as full an exegesis of O'Neill's work as possible while showing its relation to the developmental communitarian project. To this end this chapter will examine O'Neill's two-step approach to what she terms her 'critical constructivism'.[2] While O'Neill's theory has been developing over a number of years and a number of publications, this chapter will take her recent *Towards Justice and Virtue* (*TJV*) as the definitive text through which to understand her cosmopolitanism. This is not simply a matter of chronology. O'Neill's 'Maverick Kantianism' has developed through a number of books and articles but principally through *Faces of Hunger* (*FH*) (1986), *Constructions of Reason* (*CR*) (1989) and *TJV* (1996).[3] In developing her *moral* cosmopolitanism, the first step in her argument, O'Neill has slowly divorced her brand of secular Kantianism from its enlightenment origins. While O'Neill is adamant that the standard criticisms of Kantian, deontological reasoning (that it is too abstract and thus smacks of empty formalism) are wide of the mark and that the standard uses of Kantian ethics are similarly inaccurate, her project has been to vindicate a practical, critical, constructivist and non-foundational understanding of the place of the categorical imperative in our moral lives.[4] The choice facing international relations theory is between 'standards of reason that can govern both practice and theory, and disorientated consciousness'[5] and this is a theme continued in later work. Where *TJV* has the advantage is in making a more explicit connection between O'Neill's position and other contemporary philosophical accounts of the political world. An interpretation of Kant that suggests that his conception of practical reason is itself constructed (the major burden of section 1 of *CR*) is fascinating in itself, but it is even more relevant when considered in contrast to the other contenders in this debate.

In constructing a critical account of practical reason O'Neill initially develops an account of the *focus* and *scope* of ethics. In developing her position O'Neill provides the theoretical premises of constructivist cosmopolitanism. A brief and relatively uncritical exegesis of this aspect of her work, highlighting those considerations most pertinent to the structure of this book, is all I intend to offer in the first part of this chapter. The second step in O'Neill's project is to offer an account of the *structure* and *content* of ethical reasoning. The political programme of cosmopolitanism is both undetermined and malleable. This property is vital, argue the cosmopolitans, because politics must be free to adapt to the circumstances of justice and injustice, to the changing face of international relations. More determinate theories, such as those offered by particularists or realists, often rely upon principles that are not sustainable when confronted by such change. Thus the focus and scope of ethical theory (the argument for moral cosmopolitanism) is thought to be more important than its substantive content (the argument for institutional cosmopolitanism). While the implications of O'Neill's cosmopolitanism are always international, a brief exegesis of the second step in her argument will also focus on her explicit engagement with problems of international justice found particularly in *FH*, but also in a number of more recent articles and contributed chapters.[6] The third part of this chapter will then examine some potential problems in O'Neill's line of argument. Here I will be focusing particularly on O'Neill's claim that principles of ethics must have both universal form and cosmopolitan scope. This fascinating merger of the philosophical and political requirements of ethics may well, I argue, be the weak link in the flow of O'Neill's argument through which the viability of developmental communitarianism emerges. Towards the end of this chapter (as a final critique of cosmopolitanism and as preface to the chapters dealing specifically with developmental communitarianism) I examine O'Neill's criticisms of Walzer and Rawls. In failing to make her case against the work of these two authors who stand as prime examples of the type of political philosophy I believe is required by the current circumstances of international relations, O'Neill invites a re-examination of what I believe can be termed the developmental communitarian method.

Constructing practical reason: moral cosmopolitanism, focus and scope

For O'Neill the constructivist projects share a common aim. As O'Neill describes it:

> Constructivism is in the end no more, but also no less, than an attempt to work towards a result that is neither unattainable for those whose lives are both led using the categories and norms of restricted milieu and connected to those of others with differing categories and norms, nor unsustainable for what they could become. It may be thought of rather prosaically as starting from available materials (rather than from ideal inventory of unavailable materials).[7]

This, I believe, is a particularly good account of the constructivist project, one that can be applied to the work of Frost, Walzer and Rawls as well as to the work of O'Neill, and exploring the basis of this claim really offers an insight into the final claim of this study. O'Neill insists that a viable theory must take account of the widening scope of justice *and* focus only on non-idealised agents and agencies in world politics, something that is not (in most international relations theory and particularly not in the work of Walzer and Rawls) the case at present. If O'Neill can produce a theory that establishes and transcends the inadequacy of particularist varieties of international relations theory while demonstrating the need for (and remaining within) the appropriate boundaries of constructivist political theory then the appeal of developmental communitarianism will be significantly weakened.

Focus

O'Neill's initial thought is to examine the appropriate philosophical focus and the philosophically and politically relevant scope of her subject matter. A brief and relatively straightforward exegesis of this aspect of her work will serve to highlight the basis for O'Neill's cosmopolitanism. This rather abstract starting point engages immediately, although at a higher theoretical level, with those issues outlined as a focus for international relations theory in earlier chapters. Many interpretations and theories of international relations have been shown to include illegitimate assumptions as a major premise of their argument. The assumption that the nation-state has a necessary or foundational place in the analysis in world politics is one clear example highlighted by the poststructuralist or postmodernist literature. In engaging with questions concerning the type of reasoning we may legitimately use in constructing justifiable theories of justice O'Neill ensures from the outset that no illegitimate or tenuous premises are included in our argument, premises that may exclude (or include) agents from (or in) the theory of justice without sound reasons. Thus the first steps in O'Neill's argument engage with one of the basic themes of this book: that despite acknowledged problems in traditional political and international theory constructivist theory can provide acceptable descriptions of and prescriptions concerning international justice. O'Neill's seemingly abstract exploration of practical reason is simply outlining acceptable, and therefore constructivist, strategies for reasoning about international relations.

O'Neill argues that it is vital that we develop intelligible and abstract principles of action that can avoid the problems of relativism and idealisation. Here relativism and idealisation are key notions in understanding the failure of much traditional international relations theory. The main conclusions from her brief survey of contemporary thought are that communitarian theories based, for example, on particularist relativism or norm-oriented practical reason (which, it appears, amount to the same thing) cannot adequately provide for the modern circumstances of justice and that much cosmopolitan, or universalist, writing appears arbitrary in that it relies upon idealised starting points. The problem of relativism and particularism and its relation with the modern circumstances of justice is pretty clear (at least as a pattern of argument). The principal claim is that if interdependence is a fact then neither relativism nor particularism can hold as a basis for principles of international justice. The problem of idealisation in moral theory is also pretty clear although the distinction between abstraction and idealisation that O'Neill wishes to highlight may be less so. The issue, O'Neill argues, is that two very different problems in ethical theory are often merged in criticism of abstract theory. O'Neill has written about this problem at length and in many places and here it is worth quoting her at length.

> Some complaints that ethical reasoning is too abstract object mainly to reliance upon abstract views of agents. ... Abstract ethical and political theories, it is said, make assumptions about agency which are not satisfied by human agents. The theories fail because they ignore the social and historical

> features that are constitutive of human agency, and assume capacities for reasoning and choosing which human agents simply lack.
>
> The target of this line of criticism is not, however, just abstraction. The objection is not just that much (too much) that is true of human agents is *omitted* in some accounts of agents, but that much (too much) that is false of human agents is *added*. Descriptions of agents in much post-enlightenment ethical and political theory are often *idealized*; they are satisfied only by hypothetical agents whose cognitive and volitional capacities human beings lack.[8]

Idealisation, a charge O'Neill associates particularly with Rawls (see below), is obviously an illegitimate strategy in ethical and political theory. Any idealised theory would rely upon false predicates. Genuine abstraction however does no such thing. Furthermore, we are told, abstract reasoning is more suited to contemporary international relations theory than all forms of particularism, historicism and communitarianism. In attempting to vindicate an account of reason that can be used in constructing justice for the modern world O'Neill develops an elementary requirement for an appropriate account of reason.

> For anything to count as practical reasoning it should, in particular, *at least aim to be followable by others for whom it is to count as reasoning*. Ways of organizing action that fail this minimal standard can hardly count as reasoned. Those who organise action and thinking about action in ways which they take to be followable by some of those who are to follow, even be convinced by, their claims offer those others no reasons. What they say or do will appear arbitrary to those others.[9]

O'Neill goes on to show that of the various conceptions of practical reasoning offered by universalist and particularist thinkers most do not meet even this basic standard. End-oriented reasoning, such as that used by 'platonist' thinkers who provide a conception of an objectively good teleology or *the* good, will appear arbitrary unless the appropriate metaphysics is universally validated. Instrumental reasoning (again end-oriented) will appear 'barefacedly' arbitrary to those who do not share the subjective conception of the goal of practical reason. Even act-oriented reasoning of the particularist variety (norm-oriented) would appear incomprehensible to 'outsiders' even when those 'outsiders' fall within the relevant sphere of action.[10] For O'Neill

> [a]lthough it is plausible enough that *some* stretches of practical reasoning have a *restricted* scope, in the sense that they are taken to be followable only by a restricted and homogenous audience, so are 'insiders' reasoning, not all practical reason can have such restricted scope. In the first place practical reasoning has to be followable not only by those directly addressed on a given occasion, but by wider groups. In reasoning, in justifying what we do, in criticizing what others do, we constantly appeal to a wider group, of whose boundaries we lack any definitive conception. Secondly we do not

> think that all those for whom thought or action is to be cogent will be closely similar to one another.[11]

In addressing the question of the appropriate focus of ethics O'Neill argues that '[a]ction could be guided (to some extent) by fixing the *ends* it is to achieve, the *source* from which it is to emerge, or the *form* it is to take'.[12] Despite the fact that most universalists have taken all three paths and that particularists tend to take the second route O'Neill argues that the form of action (and therefore principles of action) rather than the sources or results of action must be the primary focus of practical (hence ethical and political) reasoning. The focus of the particularists upon the sources of action can, O'Neill has argued, lead to a restrictive relativism that is ill suited to contemporary political reality. Similarly the would-be universalism of Rawls, who combines instrumental end-oriented reason (in the search for stability) with norm-oriented act-centred reasoning (in his grounding of such thought in liberal public political culture or a shared history of international law) risks arbitrariness. O'Neill's major claim is that both particularism and Rawlsian liberalism are accessible to too few agents to be of relevance when considering transnational justice. This claim is part of a vital contest. If O'Neill's claim is proven it not only makes my claim concerning the viability of developmental communitarianism unconvincing but it ultimately establishes her thesis. O'Neill's cosmopolitanism relies in part upon her arguments concerning the form of practical reason and subsequently upon her contention that non-cosmopolitan accounts of practical reason (principally those communitarian accounts of practical reason that draw on the norms of a given society) do not provide an accessible account of interconnectedness. On this reading of her argument the failure of both arguments requires the urgent re-examination of developmental communitarian accounts of international relations (see below).

The 'Kantian' or 'critical' conception of practical reason that O'Neill develops is neither end-oriented nor norm-oriented and so, argues O'Neill, is not as prone to inaccessibility in the way that the other conceptions of practical reason are. Essentially O'Neill's claim is that communal or political values that some agents believe their agency to rely upon are not morally justifiable if they are not universalisable across the range of relevant others. There are, O'Neill argues, two elementary senses in which principles are formally universal.

> The most elementary sense in which a principle may be said to be universal is … if it applies to or holds for all rather than merely for some cases in its domain. … The second sense … is that the range of beings is seen as extensive: the scope of principles is inclusive, perhaps (more-or-less) cosmopolitan.[13]

Of these formal features the first is relevant to O'Neill's case that the focus of ethical concern should be both universal and abstract. All those agents concerned must (potentially) be able to agree that the principles of practical reason adopted are relevant to them in their shared condition. This, it must be noted, does not tell us which agents are concerned by what problem in any particular domain. The second feature is yet to be proven relevant or inviting and forms part of O'Neill's account of the formal scope of ethical inquiry and thereafter of her account of the structure and content of ethics.[14] O'Neill argues forcefully against the idea that formal universality automatically underwrites a uniformity of requirement and leaves her account of the focus of ethics as a formal account of abstract and universal reason that leaves almost everything still to be determined. Formal universality cannot prescribe uniform action because in generating universal principles we leave plenty of room for those principles to be enacted across a plurality of cases.[15] However, rejecting the claim that universalism breeds uniformity does not lead to the opposite conclusion; that universality is an empty formalism. O'Neill's case, put simply, is that any stretch of reason that cannot appeal to all relevant agents and is therefore not universal in its domain cannot be called reasoned. Anything that does not meet this test is rejected and such rejection is not the consequence of an empty formalism.[16]

Thus far O'Neill believes that she has proven the following five points:

1 That action is the primary focus of all practical reasoning.
2 That action must be grasped under descriptions that are intelligible to all those who reason about it.
3 That the need for such a description does not rule out the use of abstract principles.
4 That universal principles, which abstract from many predicates, need not prescribe uniform action.
5 That there is no need to think that indeterminate principles of action cannot play a role in ethics.[17]

These points simply outline the criteria of practical reason and encounter certain widely held concerns about such formal principles. Accepting these points does not commit us to accepting cosmopolitanism. Furthermore O'Neill claims that there is nothing about starting from her principles of reason that threatens a virtuous and embedded political existence. If the account of the proper focus of ethics in *TJV* is simply a vehicle for discussing the requirements of ethical reasoning the task left for O'Neill is to account for the second type of universality she seeks. The idea of an abstract and inclusive conception of practical reason must be linked to the idea that such reason must have a more-or-less cosmopolitan scope. As O'Neill points out

> Some culturally specific practical principles, which many particularists find acceptable, are thought of as holding universally but only for quite particular and limited domains; others, which universalists maintain, such as the abstract principles of the Human Rights Movement and of contemporary work on justice, are presented as having the widest cosmopolitan scope. As we can see, universal principles are barely avoidable, and lead neither to

> dangerous rigorism nor vacuous formalism. However this conclusion not merely does not fix everything: it fixes remarkably little.[18]

and it is at this point that her work really seeks to challenge that of the developmental communitarians.

Scope

The move from a focus on universal principles (in the minimal sense) to an admission that such principles must function universally in the sense of covering more-or-less all agents is perhaps the keystone to O'Neill's cosmopolitan edifice. In accepting the first argument all we are committed to is acknowledging the fact that justifiable principles of practical reason (or ethics) are intelligible to and followable by all *relevant* agents. Both Walzer and Rawls generate principles that satisfy these requirements yet it is clear (below) that neither of these developmental communitarians would accept that formal universality of principle leads *ipso facto* to a more-or-less cosmopolitan universality of scope. Clearly there is still much work to be done.

In order to bypass the 'smouldering and inconclusive wrangles'[19] that surround questions concerning the scope of ethical concern O'Neill once again offers a formal account of how we must fix the proper scope of ethics.

> A practical way of fixing the scope of ethical consideration need not supply a complete account of who or what counts as agent, or as subject. It must, however, provide at least a procedure by which agents can work out to whom (or what) they must accord ethical standing, so view as falling within the scope of ethical consideration.[20]

From the basic question of ethics, 'what counts as giving justifiable reasons?' we get to the second basic question; 'to whom must we give such reasons?' For O'Neill there are three assumptions that structure all activity, assumptions which may or may not be present to the actors' consciousness. Despite the tendency of some particularist and universalist writing to deny or ignore these assumptions and despite the fact that complex personal and political struggles surround questions of the scope of ethics, there are three abstract yet interconnected aspects of action that O'Neill argues are particularly relevant.

> These are the assumptions *that there are others* (seen as *separate* from the agent); *that those others are nevertheless connected to the agent* (either or both can act on the other); and *that those others have limited but determinate powers*.[21]

These assumptions are termed plurality, connection and finitude respectively. Plurality, as a basic assumption, is hardly controversial. The idea that when we act we assume that there are distinct others whom we may affect, or whose activity may affect us, is a core element of the circumstance of justice and injustice.

Without a plurality of agents and agencies questions of ethics would not arise. The assumption of finitude is also non-controversial. In assuming plurality we almost automatically assume that those whom we might affect have important vulnerabilities and capabilities. It is, however, O'Neill's use of the idea of connection that offers most to her cosmopolitanism, as indeed the concept of interconnectedness was shown to be vital to the literature on interdependence and globalisation in chapter 1. It is here that the fact that we might affect others is posited as the beginning of our cosmopolitan obligation to take this into account when we act. In itself the assumption of connection is seemingly straightforward. Like the other assumptions it is a simple presupposition of activity. Denying the agency or existence of others, denying their vulnerability in the face of evidence to the contrary are obviously tendentious tactics in political philosophy. Similarly

> [j]ust as boundaries of ethical consideration can be manipulated by denying plurality and finitude that are implied by activity, so they can be manipulated by denying connection. This is sometimes done by depicting others as lacking the very connections which various activities assume.[22]

It is O'Neill's working out of the modal requirements of recognising connectedness that leads directly to her cosmopolitanism. Indeed, when directly addressing issues of international ethics, her initial remarks leave us in little doubt as to her intentions.

> For example, the division of the earth and its inhabitants into mutually exclusive, bounded groups by state boundaries has provided a powerful and systematic way of discounting or at least diminishing the ethical standing of 'foreigners' who live beyond 'our' frontiers, even by those whose activity is in fact premised on the view that those whom they purport to exclude are others to whom they are connected in varied ways. … [Yet] Whenever their activity assumes a plurality of finite and connected others, they are also committed to including those others within the scope of their ethical consideration.[23]

For O'Neill the fact that international political activity assumes that it will effect the agency of 'others' (in this case distant strangers) means that international justice must be cosmopolitan. The practical basis for constructing an account of the scope of ethical consideration based on the corrigible assumptions agents make when engaged in specific activities is that it fulfils the modal requirements of practical reason. In other words it is intelligible to and followable by *all* concerned. Other forms of reasoning either deny or invent facts about the world and cannot claim to be constructivist and thus as relevantly accessible. As O'Neill notes:

> Constructivism in ethics, it should now be clear, is not a novel philosophical method or procedure. To construct is only to reason with all possible solidity from *available* beginnings, using *available* and *followable* methods to reach *attainable* and *sustainable* conclusions for relevant audiences.[24]

For O'Neill if constructivism is necessary the question that remains is whether constructivism is necessarily cosmopolitanism in scope. Connection, O'Neill argues, is empirically universal as well as philosophically so. Any denial of connection can be shown to be either naïvely inaccurate or capriciously false.

> Agents who assume that certain others *will not* act on them, nor they on those others, often nevertheless base their activity on the view that those others *could* act on them. ... In the contemporary world, people act on quite strong assumptions even about the most distant strangers. ... Put more brutally, a background assumption of the most affluent lives is that state power will effectively keep most distant strangers more or less in their place and in their poverty.[25]

O'Neill's argument, to this point, is simple: in assuming plurality, connection and finitude we assume ethical responsibility. It is the form this responsibility takes that structures O'Neill's cosmopolitanism. We do not have to be politically or socially connected to all agents to assume an ethical connection. Any contraction of the idea of connection by the introduction of stronger and privileged communitarian notions of political connection or of realist notions of *raison d'état* have ethical and practical consequences which are not, O'Neill argues, acceptable. Walzer, when he assumes the importance of self-determination in the state, Rawls when he assumes the importance of reasonable political autonomy and Frost when he assumes the importance of the modern state domain of discourse are all denying a shared cosmopolitan responsibility. If the scope of ethical consideration is more-or-less cosmopolitan then the primary sphere of responsibility is, O'Neill argues, cosmopolitan.

For O'Neill we must assume that all agents are capable of suffering injury and in doing so assume a cosmopolitan obligation to rejecting injury. This conclusion is not, I believe, a necessary one. My principal reason for making this claim is that O'Neill omits too much of relevance to international justice. To put this point another way; an examination of O'Neill's argument leads to the conclusion that abstraction is just as problematic as idealisation. While the arguments to this conclusion are made in the following chapters, it is important to examine briefly the cosmopolitan edifice O'Neill places upon her discussion of the focus and scope of ethics. It is important both because it gives us a glimpse of O'Neill's political cosmopolitanism and also because my principal criticism of O'Neill's work is that the link between the two forms of universality she constructs (universal reason and universal politics) is weaker than she allows.

The structure and content of cosmopolitanism

For O'Neill

> once it is accepted as a basic requirement of practical reasoning that non-universalizable principles are to be rejected, this demand can lend authority to some stretches of instrumental and normative practical reasoning, and reveal the lack of authority of other stretches.[26]

Putting aside the theoretical, general argument to focus on O'Neill's account of the structure and content of ethics leads to a better understanding of the consequences of her cosmopolitanism for international relations theory. At this stage in her argument O'Neill has proven that practical reason must be universalisable (an idea that she notes is separate from the notion of cosmopolitan scope)[27] and in her attempt to provide structure and content for her cosmopolitan account of international relations theory O'Neill must attempt to link the argument in favour of universal theory to one concerning a more-or-less cosmopolitan politics.

O'Neill suggests that recognising the universality of plurality, connection and finitude (and thus of potential injury) leads to a universal and cosmopolitan categorical imperative to prevent injury. In this manner she assumes that what she terms the major premises of ethics (outlined in her work on the focus of ethics) are more important than the minor premises of ethics (political institutions and existent moral, political and ethical attitudes and practices). O'Neill makes no direct case for this and the force of her argument depends almost entirely upon her contention that neither Walzerian particularism nor Rawlsian idealism can produce theories or policies that are relevant to contemporary world politics.

For O'Neill '[the] procedure for establishing the scope of ethical consideration suggested that many significant demarcations, such as state and community boundaries, or the boundaries of private life, may not generally be legitimate limits to ethical consideration'.[28] This is not to deny the need for political structuring in world politics or to claim that a world state is a prerequisite if we are to live a truly ethical life. O'Neill recognises the political limits to ethics arguing that:

> in choosing between imperfect institutionalisations of the rejection of injury that are achievable at a given time and place some forms of injury will be *unavoidable* and hence not unjust. ... A requirement or commitment to reject injury must be expressed in action that does not avoidably injure in ways that are either *systematic* or *gratuitous*.[29]

This cogent argument has very significant connotations for the structure of international society and the conduct of world politics. In one of her more international relations oriented works O'Neill cashes out this line of argument.

> If these considerations are convincing, they may have very significant and complex implications for justifiable intervention in the case of human rights violations beyond state boundaries, for the justice of legislation that selectively restricts boundary crossing, whether for asylum, travel, migration, abode, work, settlement or to take up citizenship, and for the justice of an economic order predicated on transnational economic intervention which lacks both transnational powers of taxation and transnational institutions to relieve poverty.[30]

How do O'Neill's doubly modal requirements of practical reason invite this cosmopolitan outlook? There are two principal steps that lead O'Neill to this conclusion. The first is her claim that her construction of Kantian principles, or requirements of practical reason, reveal a series of obligations. The second is the further claim that these obligations attach to all agents and agencies connected by the domain of world politics.

The first claim in turn divides in two. Least important (for the purposes of this exposition) is the argument that the language of obligations is more useful than the language of rights. Her claim is that an emphasis on the obligations generated by the principles of practical reason captures more fully the requirements of ethics than does an emphasis on the rights such principles generate. This much is O'Neill's account of the structure of ethics. Of primary importance is the claim (that stems not from her account of the structure of ethics but from earlier claims relating to the logic of ethics) that a cosmopolitan range of obligations is imposed by the principles of practical reason. The cosmopolitan range of obligations is described as follows.

Types of duty or obligation

Universal

Perfect Held by all, owed to all; counterpart liberty rights; embodied above all in legal and economic systems.
Imperfect Held by all owed to none; no counterpart rights; embodied above all in character and expressed in varied situations

Special

Perfect Held by some owed to specified others; counterpart special rights; fixed by structure of specific transactions and relationships; can be distributed universally given appropriate institutions.
Imperfect Held by some owed to none; no counterpart rights; embodied in ethos of specific relationships and practices and in characters; often, but not exclusively, expressed in action within special relationships.[31]

These obligations are required, O'Neill argues, because inclusive principles of injury, neglect and indifference are not universalisable across the domain of connected others.[32] This much is captured by O'Neill's account of the focus and scope of ethics. The concepts doing most of the work here are connectedness and universality. Showing that we are connected to a plurality of finite others obliges us to take account of them when we act. This form of reasoning is accessible but not, O'Neill admits, motivationally sufficient. But accessibility, the fact that all *could* act upon such principles, is for O'Neill enough.

> Reasoning can be accessible even when it is not motivationally sufficient, but it must construe the problems faced in ways that strike its audience as relevant and must propose ethical standards, criteria and arguments which are accessible to them. If it relies on inaccessible starting points, ethical reasoning will seem to speak in alien and irrelevant categories or rely on some mythical 'universal' mode of moral discourse. Yet how is a heterogeneous audience to be addressed without a universal mode of ethical discourse? How can the widely scattered and socially and ideologically divided individuals, institutions and collectivities the risk and course of world hunger be addressed in ways that are accessible to all, or even widely accessible?[33]

O'Neill forgoes any discussion of motivation. It is, she maintains too confused an area of political philosophy. In order to effect her thesis she must show that all agents and agencies are connected (that the circumstances of justice are indeed cosmopolitan), that this requires that we take account of their ethical standing and thus (by inference) that other theories, those that limit the sphere of international activity, are irrelevant to world politics.[34]

Moving on to a brief discussion of the content of ethics allows us to see how O'Neill believes her theory could cash out in political terms. Her institutional cosmopolitanism relies absolutely upon her account of the proper scope of ethics (developed from her account of practical reason and the circumstances of justice) and this is something that allows her to be fairly indeterminate about the 'best' political arrangements.

> The (realistic) 'moral cosmopolitanism', to which the more-or-less cosmopolitan scope of ethical consideration that is in fact assumed by agents in the contemporary world points, does not show which determinate form of institutional cosmopolitanism is feasible or optimal for now, let alone best for all time. ... Both *global* and *less-than-global* thinking about justice makes quite realistic and down-to-earth demands. In each context the objective is to establish institutions and practices which (as far as possible) prevent and limit systematic or gratuitous injury.[35]

Because the circumstances of justice and injustice are directly related to the agency of individuals and collectivities the transformation of the powers of agents and agencies is a necessary feature of O'Neill's cosmopolitanism. The central thrust of O'Neill's argument here is that certain types of act that may be the source (or potential cure) of injustice take place only within a social context. She rightly points out that 'no individual acting alone can marry or get divorced, promise or contract, form or dissolve a partnership, sell or buy a commodity, or negotiate or break a treaty'[36] and properly suggests that on many occasions an inadequate institutional infrastructure causes and perpetuates injustice. However the conclusion that O'Neill repeatedly draws from this evidence is that 'given our present actual commitments and involvements in acting, we cannot then coherently argue that moral concern, and least of all that justice, stops either at boundaries of states, or at social boundaries of other sorts. Anyone who makes such a move in *our* world evidently shifts ground illegitimately'.[37] This conclusion has obvious implications for O'Neill's cosmopolitanism. For example it requires institutions that act on universal principles and rejects institutions that do not, particularly nation-states that operate on restricted principles of justice (by, for example, focusing (perhaps as a first priority) upon the human rights of fellow citizens). The argument is seemingly straightforward and convincing. There are however a number of missing steps concerning both the idea of connection and the requirements of universalisation (the more-or-less cosmopolitan scope of justice and the universal focus of justice respectively) that highlight a gap between the philosophical and political ideas evident in O'Neill's conclusion. It is to these problems that I turn now.

Universalisation and cosmopolitanism

For O'Neill 'once the legitimacy of treating actual state boundaries as limits to justice has been called into question, an appeal to sovereignty or to assumed lack of responsibilities to non-citizens cannot automatically outweigh an appeal to justice'.[38] But how has O'Neill called the legitimacy of such boundaries into question? Essentially she has done so by suggesting that the requirement that practical reason be universalisable *plus* the fact that we are connected to all other agents on a more-or-less cosmopolitan scale requires a cosmopolitan approach to international relations. These two arguments have to be fleshed out and examined if this conclusion is to be accepted. The first argument is primarily philosophical and can be easily developed by applying Mackie's questions concerning the status of ethics and universality to O'Neill's argument.[39] The second is primarily political and focuses on the way O'Neill uses the idea of connectedness. The requirement that practical reason be universalisable and the ensuing suggestion that all agents are universally ethically connected appear to combine to produce the force of O'Neill's argument. However her position here, I will suggest, is only sustainable (and then in a much weaker form) if she succeeds in showing that other approaches to international relations theory cannot take seriously the pressing issues that we face. Both these arguments are central to the success of liberal cosmopolitanism. If the philosophical primacy of cosmopolitan ethics is not proved necessary then the secondary claim that cosmopolitan ethics offers a better way of dealing with international problems than any non-cosmopolitan theory becomes vital. Indeed I believe that this is the direction that O'Neill's argument is forced to go. If however the subsequent political argument is seen to place too demanding a series of requirements upon international relations and non-cosmopolitan theories can be shown to make more accessible demands upon international society while still attacking the real problems of world politics then the case for adopting a revised liberal theory becomes exceptionally strong.

Taking issue with the philosophical requirement that practical reason be universalisable, the first of O'Neill's claims laid out at the beginning of this chapter, it is clear that O'Neill is suggesting that we must focus on what is morally relevant and discount those aspects of our lives that are arbitrary in some way. For O'Neill local and bounded traditions and practices are examples of such arbitrariness and fall far short of the requirement of practical reason because they cannot and do not take adequate account of all relevant and connected others. This follows, she maintains, from the logical structure of moral reasoning itself and not from some idealising liberal cosmopolitanism. I do not believe that this is the case. Following Mackie's seminal line of reasoning here is particularly enlightening. Mackie begins by posing the same question as O'Neill (albeit in a different form) but when exploring the logical structure of moral reasoning comes to a very different conclusion.

> Do the desires and especially the sufferings of other people, if known to me, constitute a reason for me to do something, if I can, or to try to do something to satisfy those desires or to relieve those sufferings? It would be natural to say that they constitute some reason; how strong a reason, how easily over-ruled by other considerations, may be a matter of dispute.[40]

For Mackie moral judgments are universalisable. Any truly moral statement concerning an action ('such and such is good or bad' etc.) is nonsensical if it cannot hold for other relevantly similar action. As Mackie notes the key to understanding the logic of morality is the idea of 'relevantly similar'[41] and he goes on to argue convincingly that there are three stages of universalisation that attempt to account for the 'relevantly similar'. It is worth quoting Mackie at some length here.

> There are, then, different kinds or stages of universalisation. In each of them a moral judgement is taken to carry with it a similar view about any relevantly similar case. But the first stage rules out as irrelevant only the numerical difference between one individual and another; the second stage rules out generic differences which one is tempted to regard as morally relevant only because of one's particular mental or physical qualities or condition, one's social status or resources; the third stage rules out differences which answer to particular tastes, preferences, values and ideals. It is at most the first stage … that is built into the meaning of moral language:

> the corresponding logical thesis about the second stage is more controversial, while that about the third stage would be plainly false.[42]

If this argument holds, and I believe it does,[43] then O'Neill is not merely expressing the 'doubly modal' requirements of ethics and therefore needs to support her thesis in a different way. O'Neill's claim is that particularist practices, value systems and politics are morally irrelevant, that the treatment of (for example) non-Muslims in a fundamentalist Muslim state and a liberal state are relevantly similar. This argument employs all three (subjective) stages of universalisation and while intuitively powerful it is, as Mackie points out, a liberal stance.[44] It relies upon means–ends reasoning to produce hypothetical imperatives rather than upon an analysis of the requirements of practical reason to produce categorical imperatives. In this it appears that O'Neill does not really transcend the arguments of Beitz and Pogge who (it will be recalled from chapter 2) I argued also relied upon hypothetical imperatives in arguing for their cosmopolitan theory. In the case of Beitz and Pogge their arguments were seen to be contingent upon the premise that the requisite conditions for a fuller *Ius Cosmopoliticum* are in place. The same must be said of O'Neill's argument. Her argument relies upon her case concerning connection and that issues of justice and virtue on a cosmopolitan scale are relevantly similar. O'Neill recognises that 'connection will peter out at differing boundaries for different agents and in activities of differing sorts in different circumstances'[45] and that there is a need to make the specific outcomes of our Kantian deliberations contextually accessible to those agents and agencies whose action is needed.[46] Nevertheless O'Neill remains adamant that

> [t]he segments of a full domain of ethical consideration can only be organized if *some* inclusive principles cover the entire scope of acknowledged ethical consideration … Hence those that lead their lives in the contemporary world will need at least some inclusive basic principles whose scope is more-or-less cosmopolitan.[47]

This much is not disputed either by the developmental communitarians who provide an alternative to cosmopolitanism or by Mackie. But O'Neill's fleshing out of her account of cosmopolitan obligations entails much more than this. An argument to this point does not, in itself, qualify as cosmopolitan. However, showing that the argument that ethics should be universal does not lead directly to cosmopolitanism is not necessarily destructive of cosmopolitanism. Particularly if O'Neill can successfully go on to make the second part of her case. The second stage of O'Neill's argument focuses on the contemporary circumstances of justice and injustice. Her case is that the contemporary circumstances of justice require inclusive ethical principles and that non-cosmopolitan reasoning cannot supply such principles. To be sure, recognising that O'Neill is not making claims based on the logic of morality itself may take something away from her argument. But if she can show that cosmopolitan principles are necessary anyway, then we will not have lost much in exposing what Mackie calls the fiction of the objectification of moral values and obligations.[48] The universalisability test (in conjunction with an account of the circumstances of justice) may still play a critical role in contemporary international relations theory.

In *TJV* the argument that cosmopolitanism is the only relevant ethical and political theory is supported by two arguments. The first, that the logic of morality itself requires cosmopolitanism, is not complete. It also relies upon the supplementary argument that no other form of practical reasoning and politics can cope with the circumstances of justice. If we accepted the first argument then this supplementary argument would serve only to outline the focus of ethics and to counter certain widely held difficulties with the idea of abstract practical reasoning. As we are not forced to accept the first argument the supplementary argument becomes one of prime importance. O'Neill claims that neither particularism nor Rawlsian liberalism can provide principles relevant to the modern circumstances of justice. Her principal claim is that the modes of existence they privilege are not accessible and cannot adapt to be accessible to all relevant agents in world politics. Once again the key to this argument is the notion of 'relevantly similar'. O'Neill's basic contention is that the notion of 'relevantly similar' at work in the particularist theory of Walzer and the liberal theory of Rawls is so restricted that it simply cannot generate principles of ethics that relate to the world as we know it. If proven, this argument would show that cosmopolitanism is the only viable theory in world politics.

The failings of non-cosmopolitan theory: Walzerian relativism

O'Neill's critique of particularist ethics is perhaps more easily explained and dealt with than her attack on contemporary universalism. Her occasional references to the 'myopia' of communitarianism and her brief but savage criticism of reliance upon virtue in place of justice leaves the reader in no doubt at all as to her general position. O'Neill outlines, and goes on to support, two criticisms of particularist reasoning that question its philosophical and political integrity.

> The most evident difficulty … in the writing of historicizing particularists is that by itself an appeal to local practices and traditions (however venerable, however passionately maintained) cannot but endorse evil practices and traditions, indeed vices. A further glaring deficiency is that particularists do not offer an account of justice that is adequate to the contemporary world. Modern societies have and need powerful and complex political and economic systems, whose influence cannot be confined within state or other boundaries, and whose construction and regulation must answer to standards that have more than local or traditional backing.[49]

These two criticisms are well-known condemnations of communitarianism and other forms of particularism. Put simply the charges are:

1 That particularist approaches to political theory are unduly relativistic, and
2 That such an approach is simply not relevant to a world in which international politics is as important, if not more so, than domestic politics.

However the present work aims to show that a constructivist, developmental communitarianism can answer, or evade both charges.[50]

These two criticisms, that particularist ethics are both conservative and lacking in any non-arbitrary vantage points and are therefore total misrepresentations of the modern world, stem from O'Neill's examination of an argument, associated with Walzer's *Interpretation and Social Criticism*, that

> [c]ontemporary friends of the virtues frequently attempt to meet such charges of arbitrariness by pointing out that social traditions and personal orientations always include tenets and practices for debating and criticizing, for reflecting on and revising, their own standards, practices and judgments.[51]

O'Neill rejects that a conception of 'internal critique' can take the place of universalist, objective criteria for two important reasons. O'Neill's first reason is that a developmental communitarianism lacks objectivity. The very fact that ethical development must begin as internal critique 'may in part account for the difficulty of discerning, challenging, let alone overcoming, well entrenched practices, such as class discrimination and deference, racism, sexism and statism'.[52] If we take statism as the most relevant example of the failings of 'internal critique' it is clear that it is a charge much associated with Walzer.[53] But simply to charge developmental communitarianism with being unable to transcend its starting point is to miss several pertinent points. Not only does Walzer address precisely those problems that O'Neill argues must be addressed but are unavailable to the communitarians (human rights and transnational justice) but he includes in his work two components that directly address O'Neill's claims. Walzer's work can, and must, be read as progressive developments of an attempt to address questions concerning the relation between the political embodiment of justice and wider, global problems (war etc.). His conclusions challenge those of O'Neill arguing that it is not (at present) possible or necessary to abstract beyond the political community to attain the sort of cosmopolitan objectivity O'Neill seeks. The way in which O'Neill presents the empirical claim of connectedness that licenses an abstract conception of justice is challenged in Walzer's work, not by making essentialist claims about the moral nature of the state in itself, but by focusing on the practical way in which politics is conducted at a domestic and global level. Walzer does not present an idealised account of community that adds certain predicates that are unattainable (indeed the abstracted concept of self-determination is simply that, argues Walzer, it is abstracted from its many reiterations: see chapter 6) but an account of international ethics that takes seriously the role of politics, an idea linked to the conception of presumptive legitimacy in *JUW*.[54] The second and related component of Walzer's challenge to O'Neill's depiction focuses on the notion of objectivity and motivation in ethics. For Walzer an abstracted account of ethics is not objective in the way O'Neill believes it to be. Walzer argues that:

> it is everyone's morality because it is no one's in particular; subjective interest and cultural expression have been avoided or cut away. And if we succeed in understanding this morality, we should be able to construct a complete objective and unexpressive code – a kind of moral Esperanto.
>
> But this hope is misbegotten, for minimalism is neither objective or unexpressive. It is reiteratively particularist and locally significant, intimately bound up with the maximal moralities created here, here and here, in specific times and places.[55]

This is quite obviously an aspect of the developmental communitarian challenge to the ethical supremacy of cosmopolitanism that O'Neill, and others, should at least confront. The claim is that O'Neill omits vital parts of a theory of agency and that Walzer's work can connect with the problems of international justice while retaining a realistic account of political agency. O'Neill's criticism rests on her cosmopolitan belief that vindicating principles which *could* be accessible to all relevant agents is a valid ethical and political exercise. The communitarian mindset typically rejects such claims, preferring to concentrate on what *is* currently accessible to all relevant agents given the fact of political and cultural pluralism. Walzer, for example, compares the 'eagle at dawn' and the 'owl at daybreak' in this respect yet strongly denies that a communitarian explanation of current events is irrelevant to current political problems. If this criticism is to be effective O'Neill *must* grapple with questions of motivation and what principles we are actually willing to enact as international policy to show the relevance of her cosmopolitanism to the politics of international relations. This does not, of course, prove that O'Neill is wrong. But her position here is by no means intuitively or obviously superior to that of Walzer. If Walzer's inability to consider seriously the pressing questions of international ethics is a central prop to her overall case, and I believe it is, then it needs to be shored up.

The second reason that O'Neill rejects the relevance of a politics based on internal critique, and one which is closely linked to the success or failure of the central argument of this book, is that the frontiers of ethical commensurability are also the junctures at which ethical questions are at their most urgent. A communitarianism that had no way of dealing with inter-cultural or inter-statal politics, that professed a kind of context-dependent ethical realism would indeed have no answer to the charge that 'internal criticism is unlikely to resolve problems of international justice, or of gender and justice, where the very boundaries and categories of justice are at issue'.[56] Yet Walzer's account of a reiteratively developed moral minimum that arises precisely to deal with the changing frontiers of political (and therefore moral) activity can obviously not fall prey to this aspect of O'Neill's criticism. Walzer's constructivist account of international ethics and internal critique seeks only to limit the development of principles of international justice with an appropriate account of interconnectedness. Nevertheless this is a criticism that has been at the forefront of O'Neill's anti-communitarianism in much of her writing. O'Neill's initial criticism of all communitarian and particularist work is typical of many reactions to work that openly criticises those 'friends of justice' that O'Neill also examines. The fact that thinkers such as Walzer, Rawls and Frost have attempted a communitarian constructivism that directly attempts to point out the deficiencies of such a critique seems to have been overlooked. Essentially O'Neill's project and that of the developmental communitarians is the same, the attempt to find a theory of international relations that is accessible to all actors in the relevant domain yet able to lay bare the shortcomings of those actors (both human and institutional) in some objective way. However, for O'Neill the communitarian attempt to vindicate political and ethical boundaries from within

> cannot take seriously – indeed may not be able to acknowledge – either the predicaments of those who have been excluded, or the alternatives for those who have been included. A ruthless relativism may suppress these concerns, at costs so high and implausible that I shall leave them unexplored.[57]

The simple fact, argues O'Neill, is that communitarianism has been overtaken by contemporary circumstances of justice, the political realities of today: 'The sphere of justice became that of the state, later also of that wider range of political and economic systems, even that of the system of states. Contemporary debate is increasingly about global justice.'[58] While a stereotyped communitarianism, or a non-developmental communitarianism, may fall prey to O'Neill's conclusions, it is important that developmental communitarianism is not seen to be tarred by the same brush. O'Neill's claim that for communitarians 'international justice is illusory, because it assumes that everyone shares categories and principles, whereas, as Michael Walzer put it, the largest sphere of justice is the political community'[59] will be shown to be an inadequate assessment of Walzer's position in chapter 6 and thereafter to have left unexplored a large element of liberal-communitarian thought.

The failings of non-cosmopolitan theory: Rawlsian idealism

If O'Neill's critique of particularism is incomplete (at least in respect to the work of Walzer) she must surely be on firmer ground when dealing with idealisation. Perhaps so, but in choosing Rawls as an example O'Neill has chosen badly. Rawls' constructivist and developmental communitarianism relies upon accessible, end-oriented and norm-oriented principles of practical reason. Only if, as O'Neill and others believe, Rawls rests his theory of international justice on ideas generalised from liberal theory could he be seen to fall into the idealising liberal category. I do not believe that this is the case. Here and in chapter 7, reading Rawls' work as constructivist yet non-cosmopolitan shows both the strength of the developmental communitarian position and weakens O'Neill's case still further.

O'Neill's critique of contemporary universalist thinking is also a two-pronged attack on the failings of contemporary political theory. Universalists are criticised for failing to provide accessible, abstract (non-idealised) conceptions of justice both from a philosophical and a political point of view. Philosophically some universalists are accused of covert reliance upon discredited or dubious metaphysical assumptions to ground their grand perfectionisms. Politically they are accused of ethical shallowness in assuming an 'inadequate, abstract (sometimes: "atomistic" or "deontological") view of the human agent, whose social relations and "situatedness" (also: "embeddedness", "specificity", "concrete reality") are not just overlooked but denied'.[60]

The principal charge that underpins both these criticisms is that universalists often provide not an overly *abstract* account of agency (a fully vindicable strategy) but an *idealised* account of agency. In doing so they provide an account of agency that is not accessible to all relevant agents and is thus not truly universal.[61] Rawls is repeatedly shown to be guilty of what, for O'Neill, is a common failing.

> Rawls' approach throughout this period has been criticized for relying on claims that when looked at more closely not merely abstract from established truths about human beings and human situations, but introduce various ideals and idealized conceptions of the human person as starting points for his construction of justice.[62]

Many of the criticisms that O'Neill lays against the work of Rawls are sophisticated versions of some of those points examined in chapter 3. Essentially the claim is that Rawls, in attempting to accommodate communitarianism has smuggled non-defensible, metaphysical and pseudo-empirical claims in to sustain his theory.

The distinction between abstraction and idealisation, it will be recalled, is very simple: 'Idealization requires abstraction but they are not the same thing. ... when we idealize we add a predicate to a theory, and the theory applies only where that predicate is satisfied.'[63] 'Mere abstraction', on the other hand, which simply omits certain predicates from a theory, does not face the same problem. The accusation of idealisation levelled at Rawls charges him with a double failing. The philosophical self-deception of an idealised account of agency, 'a preference-oriented conception of action governed by a rather idealised conception of self-interest'[64] even when vindicated by the 'considered moral judgment of society' is simply not good enough. Again the problem is twofold. Firstly the conception of agency is not universal (after all to claim a Kantian origin for all relevant conceptions of agency would be to stretch the limits of credulity). Secondly Rawls' response to the communitarian critics of his account of agency derives an account of agency from the 'public political culture' of a liberal society and therefore fails to take account of the appropriate 'scope' of justice. What, argues O'Neill, 'justifies Rawls' assumption that justice for society 'conceived for the time being as a closed system isolated from other societies' can serve as the paradigm for all justice?'[65]

O'Neill's account of Rawls' universalist writing on justice cites his later work as 'almost communitarian' constructivism. His constructivism is rejected because it is said to rely on idealisations and he does not make the transition to communitarianism because, O'Neill argues, he attempts to universalise the model of liberal justice developed in *PL*. There are however a number of weaknesses in O'Neill's critique of Rawls. If it is possible to show that this is a misreading of Rawls, that he does in fact succeed in vindicating a liberal account of justice in terms of its normative force in liberal political culture *and* that he does not simply apply this to international relations theory but develops a different and more relevant constructivist account of international relations theory, then O'Neill's critique is in trouble. Chapter 7 will show that O'Neill's account of Rawls' international relations theory is inadequate and quite wrong.

O'Neill's use of Rawls' idea of the closed society to show the fundamental flaws in his approach to justice is at the centre of her two main criticisms of Rawls. The central idea is that Rawls' conception of political justification or 'the reasonable' is constructed (in the first instance) in a liberal society where agents interact as fellow citizens in a liberal democratic regime and that this model of political interaction is then imposed on international society. Obviously if this were the case then O'Neill would be correct in her allegation that Rawls imposes an idealised and liberal account of political justice upon international relations. For O'Neill

> [m]uch of the effort of Rawls' complex construction of justice is needed in order to retrieve his intuitive idea of justice as fairness which is jeopardised by his – perhaps idealised – assumption that human reason is governed by self interest, whose adjustment behind a veil of ignorance can be justified in reference to the actual norms embodied in the 'considered moral judgements' of a liberal democratic society.[66]

However, if Rawls' use of the idea of a closed society has any bearing on his discussion of international justice at all (rather than being an irritating red herring) it is working to prevent precisely those failings, which O'Neill believes it expedites. While a detailed explanation of my argument here will can be found in chapter 7 it is perhaps enlightening to briefly lay out an alternative reading of Rawls' theory.

The main clue that leads to the conclusion that Rawls' use of the idea of a closed society does not lead him to impose liberal values on the international sphere is to be found in his use of the idea of the 'reasonable' and what he variously terms reasonable/doctrinal/political or full autonomy (see chapter 3). Throughout 'LOP' Rawls questions the assumption that a constructivist argument should provide a universal account of justice from the outset.[67] Yet this is precisely the charge that O'Neill brings against him. Her confusion stems from a misunderstanding of the role of the reasonable which, Rawls tells us, shows both how and why persons (and Peoples) enter into the political procedure that constructs principles of justice.[68] The idea of the reasonable is said to link a conception of practical reason with 'appropriate conceptions of society and the person'[69] and assumes both an analytical and a motivational form. Rawls' task, as he views it, is to provide a theory of justice that fosters reasonable pluralism and thus his search is for doctrinal or political autonomy, a conception of autonomy distinct from rational autonomy and the more Kantian version of autonomy which seeks to regulate all of life.[70] This goal is emphasised when Rawls argues that '[j]ustice as Fairness is not reasonable in the first place unless in a suitable way it can win support by addressing each citizen's reason as explained within its own framework'.[71] Rawls' reasons for conducting his construction of principles of justice in the way that he does militate against O'Neill's criticisms. Therefore when Rawls argues in *PL* that his constructivism seeks only to produce principles of justice for a well-ordered liberal society it is simply because that limited project is all that it is appropriate for liberal fellow citizens to aspire to when they are considering domestic political issues. In the case of *PL* Rawls argues that citizens of a liberal democracy are motivated to find a solution to questions concerning how a plurality of persons can live together justly as fellow citizens, questions found in the public political culture of a liberal democratic society. The strong forms of public justifiability, stability and toleration are constructed from ideas basic to that society. Interaction between persons is limited to fellow citizens by the idea of a closed society because the issues those persons are addressing are limited to questions concerning the basic structure of their society. *International* justice, on the other hand, is different and this is what O'Neill fails to take into account. In 'LOP' the analytical form of the reasonable is still the same as it was in *PL* – a conception of practical reason allied to appropriate conceptions of society and the person. The concrete or motivational form is different because the background conditions of international (as opposed to liberal democratic) society are different. A shared history of international law replaces public political culture, a conception of persons as citizens of a plurality of political powers replaces a conception of persons as free and equal citizens of a liberal society, and the search for stability and consensus is slowed down as the move from *modus vivendi* to even *constitutional consensus* is less evident. Rawls is most definitely not applying liberal cultural assumptions to international relations (see chapter 7). For Rawls an appropriate account of practical reason allied to a norm-governed framework provides both 'the form that practical reason requires for its application ... (and) the context within which practical questions and problems arise'.[72] If the idea of closed society does anything in Rawls' work it filters out potential idealisation.

The second difficulty with O'Neill's critique of Rawls relates to the cosmopolitan/communitarian distinction, or the dichotomy between justice and virtue, more generally. O'Neill's critique of Rawls' position is that his account of agency cannot deal with the scope of ethical consideration necessary for a theory appropriate to the modern age. In other words not all agents and agencies involved in questions of justice can meet the conditions of action that Rawls proposes and given that the circumstances of justice are more-or-less cosmopolitan, Rawls' reliance upon a non-accessible account of agency prohibits his theory from being seen as realistic. Furthermore, the attempt to overcome the crisis in liberal foundationalism by grounding principles in public political culture is itself a major ethical mistake. Rawls, it seems, is at once criticised for being too abstract and for not being abstract enough. The failure of his deontological liberalism to ground ethics in a (non-liberal) account of virtue and his reliance upon the *Sittlichkeit* of a liberal tradition to ground a universalist conception of *Moralität* both threaten the accessibility of his approach to political theory.[73] Having dealt with the charge of idealisation, thus implicitly moving Rawls to the particularist camp in O'Neill's analysis, we may turn to O'Neill's critique of normative theory once more. For O'Neill the Rawlsian derivation of a 'norm-governed practical reason' is illegitimate:

> appeals to the actual norms of a society or tradition, or to the actual sensibilities, attachments or commitments of individuals will seem at worst incomprehensible to those who do not grasp those norms an commitments and at best merely conditionally reasoned to those who grasp but do not share them.[74]

The reasons that O'Neill offers for this condemnation of Rawls' ideas are (1) that they are not accessible to all and (2) that there is no reason for believing that such norms are themselves vindicable. Both these reasons boast cosmopolitan origins. O'Neill's insistence that norm-oriented practical reasoning is ill suited to modern circumstances of justice rests on an inadequate account of the developmental aspect of communitarianism as exhibited by Walzer and Rawls and a cosmopolitan conviction that for practical reasoning to be followable by all it must go beyond politics in some way. They claim that while

> particularist reasoning can allow for the revisability of norms or commitments … it cannot allow for the thought that one stretch of practical reasoning may have multiple and differing audiences. Particularist reasoning is intrinsically 'insiders' reasoning. … Vindication of action is taken not to work across whatever borders there may be between 'insiders' and 'outsiders': it is reasoning for those who have internalised a given way of thought and its norms or traditions, its sensibilities, attachments or commitments.[75]

This clearly misrepresents the international dimension of the developmental communitarianism of Walzer, Rawls and Frost. It also fails to show that one stretch of universal and abstract act-centred reason must be cosmopolitan. All three of the thinkers presented as developmental communitarians in the following chapters show a relation between a communitarian politics and inclusive principles of international justice (see below). O'Neill's claim that practical reasoning must '*at least aim to be followable by others for whom it is to count as reasoning*'[76] does not in itself license the claim that practical reasoning must be universal in all its forms.[77] O'Neill must offer a fuller critique of developmental communitarianism if her 'doubly modal' account of practical reason is to license an automatic cosmopolitanism. The second criticism that O'Neill levels at norm-oriented conceptions of reason, that particularities are not necessarily vindicated by political experience, also rests on a commitment to cosmopolitanism. The following quotation is typical of many attacks on particularist politics.

> Particularists, who so often claim to take more sober account of the realities of human life, frequently fail to do so. Even when they do not introduce their own idealizations, they may support a meagre, even parochial vision of the real range of possibilities and capacities for societies or lives, whose aspirations they fix and blinker by current norms, commitments and sensibilities and of whose capacities and need to reason with differing others they take inadequate account.[78]

Not only is this an inadequate account of the developmental aspect of some forms of communitarianism but it begs the question that developmental communitarianism attempts to answer. If we are to develop an account of political and moral agency more appropriate to the modern world where do we start but with an accurate account of the present embodiments and sources of justice? O'Neill's repeated denial of the communitarian interest in international justice (supposedly obscured by their focus on 'insiders' virtue) itself obscures an important insight into the development of international relations and fails to make the case for a necessarily cosmopolitan starting point for inquiries into international relations theory.

Conclusions

Both constructivism and cosmopolitanism are among the most favoured liberal approaches to international relations theory. O'Neill in comprehensively uniting the two concepts portrays the inner logic of cosmopolitanism. Her argument, when stripped to the bare essentials, is that the logic of ethical judgment requires that we universalise principles of international justice across the range of relevant others and that this will produce a cosmopolitan international political theory. My criticisms of her theory (criticisms that I believe necessitate a close examination of constructivist communitarianism) suggest that there is nothing in the logic of ethical theory that requires that we ignore the existent plurality of political and ethical value-systems; the 'relevance' of other agents may or may not be attenuated by non-cosmopolitan concepts. Indeed the case made by the developmental communitarians for limiting the intrusion of universal principles into the political existence of a plurality of communities may seem stronger. The case for acting upon cosmopolitan principles of ethics that deny the relevance of a significant amount of the historically developed principles of domestic and international justice must be stronger than O'Neill offers. It is certain that a greater level of transnational action is necessary. It is equally certain that some historically developed political tools are inadequate for the present day. However without a solid argument that tells us that (for example) poverty or famine are world problems and that all vaguely connected parties have serious obligations to help (an argument that requires institutional change and personal sacrifice) the cosmopolitan case, no matter how intuitively appealing, is unlikely to succeed. Not simply because international agency is historically hard-hearted but because the dramatic changes in the name of an ethical international relations theory that O'Neill commands will require massive trade-offs both in terms of economic distribution and, more importantly, political autonomy. No argument has been successfully put forward that tells us that political autonomy is irrelevant in relation to the obligations accrued by the facts of international relations. It still stands as a powerful and counter-intuitive argument to the claim that a cosmopolitan account of agency generates true principles of justice, a claim that denies the ethical standing of many moral and political practices. The developmental communitarianism examined in the final chapters of this study argues that while there is an increased responsibility in international affairs we have no justification for requiring agents to surrender their historically developed autonomy. A different justificatory strategy, one that can take account of pluralism in world politics while recognising that the circumstances of justice and injustice have developed is required.

Notes and references

1 O'Neill, *TJV*, p. 3.
2 Ibid.
3 O'Neill, *Faces of Hunger: An Essay on Poverty, Justice and Development*, London, Allen and Unwin, 1986. O'Neill *Constructions of Reason: Explorations of Kant's Practical Philosophy*, Cambridge, Cambridge University Press, 1989. O'Neill, *Towards Justice and Virtue: A Constructivist Account of Practical Reasoning*, Cambridge, Cambridge University Press, 1996.
4 O'Neill, *CR*, p. x, *TJV*, p. 3.
5 O'Neill, *CR*, p. x.
6 See particularly O'Neill, 'Ethical Reasoning and Ideological Pluralism', *Ethics*, 98, 1988, pp. 705–722. 'Justice and Boundaries', in C. Brown (ed.), *Political Restructuring in Europe. Ethical Perspectives*, London, Routledge, 1994. 'Transnational Justice', in D. Held (ed.), *Political theory Today*, Polity Press, 1991, pp. 276–304.
7 O'Neill, *TJV*, pp. 63–64.
8 O'Neill, 'Abstraction, Idealization and Ideology in Ethics', in J. Evans (ed.), *Moral Philosophy and Contemporary Problems*, Supplement to Philosophy: 22, Cambridge University Press, 1987, p. 56.
9 O'Neill, *TJV*, p. 51.
10 O'Neill, *TJV*, p. 51.
11 O'Neill, *TJV*, p. 53.
12 O'Neill, *TJV*, p. 66.
13 O'Neill, *TJV*, p. 74.
14 This distinction in forms of universality will be shown to be a crucial feature in O'Neill's claims to have constructed an inviting cosmopolitanism.
15 O'Neill, *TJV*, p. 77.

16 Given that O'Neill believes she has rejected the starting point of most contemporary (and not a few historical) theories of justice and virtue it is hard to doubt the force of her formal account of practical reason.
17 O'Neill, *TJV*, p. 89.
18 O'Neill, *TJV*, pp. 89–90.
19 O'Neill, *TJV*, p. 91.
20 O'Neill, *TJV*, p. 97.
21 O'Neill, *TJV*, p. 101.
22 O'Neill, *TJV*, p. 112.
23 O'Neill, *TJV*, p. 113. Cf. the political consequences of these assumptions in 'Justice and Boundaries', passim.
24 O'Neill, *TJV*, p. 63.
25 O'Neill, *TJV*, pp. 114–115.
26 O'Neill, *TJV*, pp. 125–126.
27 O'Neill, *TJV*, p. 125, note 1.
28 O'Neill, *TJV*, p. 123. See also O'Neill, 'Justice and Boundaries', passim.
29 O'Neill, *TJV*, p. 167. On O'Neill's rejection of the idea of a world state see, for example O'Neill, *TJV*, p. 167 or 'Justice and Boundaries', p. 84.
30 O'Neill, 'Justice and Boundaries', p. 86.
31 O'Neill, *TJV*, p. 152.
32 O'Neill, *TJV*, p. 193.
33 O'Neill, *FH*, p. 32.
34 I will go on to argue that this pattern of argument changes significantly so that instead of this logical proof O'Neill offers the plausible suggestion that because all other theories are so far away from being relevantly accessible it would make sense to adopt cosmopolitan reasoning.
35 O'Neill, *TJV*, pp. 172–173.
36 O'Neill, *FH*, pp. 37–38.
37 O'Neill, 'Justice and Boundaries', p. 84.
38 O'Neill, 'Justice and Boundaries', p. 85.
39 J.L. Mackie, *Ethics: Inventing Right and Wrong*, Penguin Books, 1977.
40 Mackie, *Ethics*, p. 78.
41 Mackie, *Ethics*, p. 83.
42 Mackie, *Ethics*, pp. 97–98.
43 While the phrase 'plainly false' is a little strong the substitution of the phrase 'highly contestable' would serve my purposes here.
44 Ibid.
45 O'Neill, *TJV*, p. 117.
46 O'Neill, *FH*, p. 144.
47 O'Neill, *TJV*, p. 156. See also 'Ethical Reasoning', p. 714 and *FH*, p. 144.
48 Mackie, *Ethics*, p. 239.
49 O'Neill, *TJV*, p. 19.
50 While O'Neill predominantly cites MacIntyre in connection with particularist shortcomings she does use Walzer as an example of both failings.
51 O'Neill, *TJV*, pp. 21–22.
52 O'Neill, *TJV*, p. 22.
53 See, for one example, Luban, 'The Romance of the Nation State', *Philosophy and Public Affairs*, Vol. 9, No. 4, 1980.
54 See chapter 5. See also the discussion of O'Neill's distinction between abstraction and idealisation (above).
55 Walzer, *Thick and Thin*, p. 7.
56 O'Neill, *TJV*, p. 22.
57 'Justice and Boundaries', p. 70.
58 O'Neill, *TJV*, p. 27.

59 'Transnational Justice', p. 281. The limited codicil to this passage, 'Walzer does not wholly dismiss international justice, for he allows that the admission of individual aliens to membership of the community and conflicts between states raise issues of justice.' is both woefully inadequate as attempt to offer a realistic interpretation of Walzer's contribution to international relations theory *and* fails to alter O'Neill's evaluation of communitarianism's contribution to the debates and can therefore be discounted.
60 O'Neill, *TJV*, p. 18.
61 The distinction between abstraction and idealisation can be found in most of O'Neill's writing. See, for concise introductions, 'Ethical Reasoning and Ideological Pluralism', *Ethics*, Vol. 98, July 1988, pp. 705–722. or 'Abstraction, Idealization and Ideology' in J.D.G. Evans (ed.), *Moral Philosophy and Contemporary Problems*, Cambridge University Press, 1988, pp. 55–69.
62 O'Neill, *TJV*, p. 45.
63 'Ethical Reasoning', p. 712.
64 O'Neill, *TJV*, p. 47.
65 'Justice and Boundaries', p. 70.
66 O'Neill, *TJV*, p. 47.
67 Cf. 'LOP', p. 50.
68 Rawls, *PL*, p. 94.
69 Rawls, *PL*, p. 90.
70 Rawls, *PL*, p. 99.
71 Rawls, *PL*, p. 143
72 Rawls, *PL*, p. 110
73 See 'Ethical Reasoning and Ideological Pluralism', p. 713.
74 O'Neill, *TJV*, p. 51.
75 O'Neill, *TJV*, p. 55.
76 O'Neill, *TJV*, p. 51.
77 Cf. O'Neill, *TJV*, p. 53, para. 3, also Rawls on the relation between constitutive and doctrinal autonomy (below).
78 O'Neill, *TJV*, p. 63.

5 Secular Hegelianism

Mervyn Frost and the limits of developmental communitarianism

The Hegelian alternative to Kantian ethics is, in the history of political thought, one example of the philosophical divisions within the cosmopolitan/communitarian debate. The tensions between a philosophy based on *Moralität* and a philosophy that stresses the importance of the embodiment of ethics in political life, of *Sittlichkeit*, were raised to prominence by O'Neill's refusal to credit either Rawls or the particularists with being able to respond adequately to ethical problems in international relations. Yet Frost believes that his 'secular Hegelian' (or constructivist Hegelian) approach to international ethics can provide a theory of human rights almost as extensive as that derived from a cosmopolitan liberal theory, from within the normative framework of contemporary international relations. An explicit endorsement of the idea of *Sittlichkeit* associated with neo-Hegelianism is found in Frost's approach to what he terms the 'settled norms' of international society, the substance of which I discussed in chapter 1. To recap: Frost recognises that the traditional justifications of key ethical and political ideas in the history of international relations are no longer viewed as sound but argues that the 'norms' through which international relations are conducted are still considered 'settled'. This does not show comprehensive agreement on the content or importance of issues such as sovereignty and human rights but a general agreement that some idea of (for example) human rights is important to international politics. The full list of eighteen norms that represent international consensus upon key ideas such as sovereignty, international law, modernisation and domestic issues is given in chapter 1 and the argument that these norms are important to international relations is relatively uncontentious. For Frost the cosmopolitan argument that norms of human rights (or obligations) must take precedence over, or oppose in some way, the norms of sovereignty does not appear to make sense of the clear international commitment to upholding principles of sovereignty. The cosmopolitan position, that Frost terms variously the 'natural law/community-of-humankind approach' or the 'objection that issues arising in the modern state domain of discourse can only be settled from a wider moral point of view',[1] makes two claims. The first that Frost, citing Donelan, rejects outright is that there is a 'primordial community of humankind'. The problems associated with making claims of this kind have already been explored. A foundational approach fails to make its case because its basic premises are left unproven or seen to be false. An empirical claim of this sort runs into vast difficulties in interpreting available data as a move to globalisation rather than interdependence as was seen in chapter 1. Even a constructivist cosmopolitanism has difficulty with the notion of 'relevantly similar' that would be required to shore up such a claim. These criticisms of the cosmopolitan approach are also made, albeit differently, by Frost.[2] The second charge levelled by cosmopolitans is similar to the second argument O'Neill relied upon to make her case; that working within the state-centric domain of discourse confines one to maintaining the *status quo*. Frost's rejection of this charge relies, for its proof, upon the whole of his constitutive theory but can be summarised as his claim that

> [a]sserting the primacy of the modern state domain of discourse for my purposes does *not* commit me to holding that people will always live in states as we know them or that life in states, as we know them, is the only proper life for human beings, or that the way states are organized at present is the best way of organizing them. I simply contend that any discussion about what ought to be done in world politics (be the proposed action a small one or a large one such as, for example, the wholesale reorganisation of the global political system) must be conducted in the language of the modern state system. No other suitable language is available.[3]

Frost's basic argument is straightforward and undemanding even in the face of the debates surrounding interdependence and globalisation. For Frost,

> all normative issues in world politics today refer, either directly or indirectly, to the state, inter-state relations and the role of individuals as citizens of states. If this is correct then it is possible to encapsulate all the several normative questions into one central question: 'what in general is a good reason for action by or with regard to states?'.[4]

Nevertheless it is also clear (and Frost acknowledges it as such) that human rights play an important role in world politics. Frost's task is to produce a theory that can account for human rights and all other aspects of the 'institution' of international relations from outside the cosmopolitan camp. The method that Frost adopts is an example of developmental communitarianism, the approach to international relations theory that can, I believe, really attack the principal theoretical problems facing international relations.

While identifying what he terms 'the modern state domain of discourse' (see chapter 1) as the established context for problem solving in international relations, Frost firmly believes that he can provide the basis for solving hard cases in international ethics.[5] Normative issues, he argues, only arise in the context of shared understandings. To even begin to understand the problems of international relations assumes a shared context of ideas within which claims concerning an abuse of human rights or the right to self-determination can be judged as justifiable or not justifiable. Given the failings of so many of the traditional attempts to justify sovereignty or rights and the incomplete case even a constructivist cosmopolitanism offers for ignoring the current norms of international interaction, where else can we start?

> What we are dealing with in the first place in international relations are actions in the arena of world politics. ... The analysis must always start with reference to individuals, bureaucracies, states, multinational corporations or international organizations *doing things*. ... In order to understand what is being done (or what has been done) the investigator must ... understand the language of the actors, and, in order to do this, she must understand as a whole the social practice within which the action takes place. This in turn requires that she learn what would count as a mistake within that practice. Doing this will require of her that she understand the value systems of those active in the practice.[6]

From this beginning Frost believes that he has the basis of a substantial and practical approach to international ethics. Against 'conventional wisdom' that contends, as Frost puts it, that '[s]ince the underlying consensus which is necessary for the rational settlement of international disputes is lacking, there are only two possible ways of resolving such issues: either the parties may strike a bargain or they might resort to force'[7] he argues that there is a way of overcoming the impasse found in contentious normative issues. Against the 'thinner' but similarly norm-governed claims of Walzer's 'moral minimalism' or Rawls' initial 'modus vivendi' or 'constitutional consensus' Frost argues that '[m]y aim in doing this is to indicate that what is being put forward is not a "thin" raft of consensus, but is a set of commitments which is altogether more substantial'.[8]

Frost makes much 'thicker' claims against the 'here and now' than either Rawls or Walzer believe possible. By this I mean that Frost believes that his constructivist and norm-oriented theory can generate a more-or-less cosmopolitan theory from what are essentially communitarian premises. If this were shown to be the case then any exposition of the more limited conclusions drawn by Walzer and Rawls would be unnecessary. I do not, however, believe that all of Frost's conclusions are warranted. His method does indeed escape the problems of foundationalism and constructivist cosmopolitanism but this chapter will show that the price of this success is a more restricted (but still genuinely developmental) international relations theory. Frost's project takes a legitimate route but over-reaches itself when cashing out the political implications of its developmental communitarianism.

Frost's contribution to the philosophy of international relations takes the form of a constitutive theory of individuality that provides the background justification against which hard cases in international relations, that emerge within a framework of settled norms, can be tested. This background justification also forms a framework through which these settled norms can be understood. Yet despite Frost's *Towards a Normative Theory of International Relations*[9] and the subsequent reworking of his ideas in *Ethics and International Relations: A Constitutive*

Theory, Hegelian theories of international relations have not received the attention they deserve. In part this is due to the widespread acceptance of incomplete arguments in favour of cosmopolitanism and against communitarianism. Both foundational and constructivist arguments of this kind have been shown to be unconvincing. If a genuine constructivist communitarianism can be shown to address the relevant problems of international relations, as Frost's position can, then the claims of constitutive theory must command attention. To claim not only to identify the problem issues and the settled norms in international relations but also to claim to have formulated a shared background justification for the international 'institution' that can iron out discrepancies between the two surely merits attention. This chapter begins to redress the balance. The first difficulty that besets such an enterprise is that there is very little secondary literature to enhance the discussion of the Hegelian approaches to international relations that are found principally in the work of Frost but also in articles by C. Brown and J. Charvet.[10] However a close analysis of Frost's method and the claims he makes against it can prove to be a very fruitful introduction to the viability of the developmental communitarian alternative to Kantian ethics in international relations theory, of a reworked notion of *Sittlichkeit* rather than the more favoured *Moralität*. It is important to note at the outset that the notion of *Sittlichkeit*, sometimes translated as 'customary morality' is justified in many ways in Hegel's writings but the ultimate justification, one that is rarely invoked by even the most fervent Hegelian, relies on the notion of the Absolute Idea or Spirit (*Geist*) that forms the spring of Hegel's Absolute Idealism. Hegel's belief in the continuous process of history as striving to realise the idea of world-spirit is not, of course, shared by many contemporary Hegelian philosophers and it is vital that any attempt to construct a more secular Hegelianism (an exercise that Frost believes he is engaged in) is understood to stand or fall without the justification of the world's court of judgment.[11] Frost believes that his examination of what he terms the 'institution' of international society that is captured in the 'modern state domain of discourse' brings to light an altogether more secular image of Hegelianism: 'What is being argued is that individuals and states must have *some* moral position, for having such a position is partially constitutive of what being a person or being a state is.'[12]

Having *some* moral position, Frost argues, unites actors in international relations within a shared practice. In identifying the importance of community to individuality and of particularity to statehood, Frost believes that he has identified the basic importance of *all* communities, a recognition that unites all the state actors in international society within a shared practice. Without leaping ahead of the exposition of Frost's argument it would seem obvious that if his contention is justified then he has identified the basis for a swift move from particular to universal that could ground a substantial ethical theory. While this is a move that would, if defensible, be welcomed by developmental communitarianism, it is important to examine thoroughly the 'thickness' of the 'intra-practice' justification of settled norms in international relations that Frost offers. How sustainable is the idea of the modern state domain of discourse as a shared institution that requires a commitment to both sovereignty and human rights? How, to put it more contentiously, can we argue that one background justification for the status quo is better than any other? An exploration of these questions that follows closely Frost's line of reasoning and that pays attention to the issues surrounding a 'demythologised' Hegelian justification and to the cosmopolitan/communitarian debate can only prove beneficial.

The modern state domain of discourse: shared problems, shared solutions

Frost argues that we do not need grand metaphysical theories or complex contract doctrines to ground a justifiable yet genuinely developmental account of international ethics. Frost, like all theorists seeking to offer relevant ideas to international relations theory, has to recognise the force of the methodological critique of traditional justifications of international relations. But, as was the case with O'Neill, Frost notes that the force of anti-foundationalism is only felt by foundationalist theories and thus only rules out illegitimate premises. The consequences of this relatively straightforward recognition Frost terms 'the *constructivist* implication of the sceptical/relativist thesis'.[13] Frost does not claim any special ontological status for the modern state domain of discourse but equally he rejects the idea that non-cognitivism leads inexorably to amoralism, relativism or apathy.[14] For Frost

> What may be correctly drawn from the sceptical/relativist thesis is the conclusion that where there is an inter-practice dispute there is no guarantee that a right answer will, in the fullness of time, be found. ... If agreement is to be achieved it will have to be created (made) between the disputants. ... Saying that moralities have to be built does not imply that the building of a morality is not a worthwhile activity ... non-cognitivism establishes certain ways in which normative arguments are different from arguments about facts. It does not establish that normative argument is not worthwhile.[15]

Human flourishing, Frost argues, depends upon the creation of normative order and agreement upon the threats to human flourishing can provide (and has provided) the basis for an intra-practice debate on how to construct international ethics.

Frost begins his construction of an international ethics by listing thirteen of the central questions currently facing international relations. The list includes questions as intuitively engaging as:

1 Questions relating to the causes and conduct of war. When may states justifiably go to war? Once at war what are the normative constraints on the belligerents? What are the rights and duties of those states not directly involved in the war *vis-à-vis* other states?

5 When is intervention by one state in the domestic affairs of another state justified? What means may justifiably be employed in such interventions?

9 When may a state divide itself into several smaller states? (When is secession justified?)

10 Questions relating to the international use and distribution of the resources of the world. Who ought to get what, when, how? Ought a distribution to be achieved by the operation of a capitalist free market in which multinationals are allowed to operate? or should the distribution be governed by a worldwide democratic body of some kind?

12 What kind of international organisations ought to be established? What authority should they have *vis-à-vis* states?, and

13 What human rights are there and how ought they to be protected? Ought states to protect them? If a state fails to protect such rights ought other states to intervene? Should there be international institutions to protect these rights? If so what are states and individuals justified in doing in order to bring about the establishment of such alternative institutions?[16]

Frost offers no special arguments that place these concerns above others or that would give them ahistorical moral connotations. The claim is simply that many people agree that these are the pressing questions that beset international relations today. It is simply a matter of fact that we live in a world divided into particularistic entities called states and the list Frost provides simply outlines some of the problems generated by that fact. Yet for Frost 'agreement on the statement of the main issues is of fundamental significance, for by implication it indicates a common basis from which argument towards a solution of these key problems might proceed'.[17] It is this fundamental assertion that forms the basis of Frost's particular brand of developmental communitarianism, for it is here that a move from inter-practice dispute to intra-practice debate takes place. For Frost agreement on the fundamental issues of international ethical debate presupposes the existence of a domain of discourse, in this case the 'modern state domain of discourse', a contextually determined yet shared sphere of reference that can ground normative thinking. Herein lies the crux of Frost's argument. Agreement on the issues presupposes not only the existence of a domain of discourse but rough agreement on the norms within that domain of discourse. Norms that (whether we know it or not) can be (and are) premised on a philosophical 'background justification' that we could have recourse to in time of dispute. It is the link between positing the existence of a shared 'here and now' and saying that therefore we could all agree upon a constructed background justification that informs the content and ethical significance of the current norms of international society that needs to be explored as this leap is a very significant one.

Frost argues that agreement on the central issues at stake in international relations presupposes a shared understanding that international ethics are to be constructed in relation to the modern state domain of discourse, that is in relation to the state, inter-state relations and the role of individuals as citizens of states.[18] Such a shared understanding does not lead directly to the resolution of problems in international relations. We do not share a fully comprehensive understanding of the right way to act in any given circumstance. What we do share is the basic understanding of the institution that we mutually inhabit. This, Frost argues, following Dworkin's method for solving hard cases in law,[19] is enough to make a right decision even where there is no settled rule of international law or objective and established rule in international ethics. Using the example of chess rather than law, Frost, following Dworkin, shows the procedure a referee would have to go through to settle a dispute between two players where there were no previous rules, conventions or precedent concerning the particular dispute. Such a settlement would, both thinkers argue, be the *right* settlement if the following procedure were followed.

1 The requirement that the decision-maker start by inquiring into the *background-justification* for the *institution* as a whole.
2 In seeking an answer to 1 he must start with *'what everyone knows'* as the point or purpose of the institution. This inquiry will reveal certain guiding concepts capable of diverse conceptions. Thus, we all saw that all chess players would agree that chess is an intellectual game, but there is scope for diverse conceptions of just what this implies.
3 He must seek out that conception of the institution's point or character which best accords with the settled rules of the institution.
4 In the event of his being left (after completing step 3) with two or more conceptions which seem to fit the institutions settled practice equally well, he must decide which gives the deepest and most satisfying account of the concept. This may involve him in more fundamental philosophical questions about the nature of the basic commitments of the participants in the practice. But these are only of interest to him in so far as they reveal the character of the institution to which the participants have consented.[20]

In this procedure the decision maker is not free to make *any* decision but is constrained by the shared set of standards that allow us to determine the right answer to hard cases.

For Frost (and indeed for Dworkin) 'it is possible to settle hard cases (concerning law, chess and international relations), but not without getting involved in "deep" discussions about the basic justifications for the institutions within which these issues arise'.[21] In accepting (albeit temporarily – see below) that this method is fully applicable to international relations, it is important to note that Frost is not arguing that the status quo is all important to international relations. Any justification of the institution of the modern state domain of discourse will have to be *constructed* using a procedure that would overcome 'a lack of fit' between both the status quo and a coherent background justification and between some agents in international relations and the current situation with its background justification (the problem that Frost terms, following Hegel, alienation). If these procedures work in tandem we reach, Frost argues, 'reflective equilibrium' and avoid uncritical acceptance of the current situation. There is, Frost admits in reply to the criticisms of Gellner, some truth to the charge that his method is conceptually conservative, however:

> [t]he element of truth is that the procedure of the argument outlined above is conservative in that it starts from, and is tested against, the settled norms of the particular domain of discourse within which it takes place. What is false is the contention that the method involves *uncritical* reindorsement of the practice concerned ... there is a critical dimension to this process. In seeking an equilibrium parts of the settled corpus come to be challenged and thus over time the practice changes and develops.[22]

This argument and those that support it offer a fascinating insight into the developmental aspect of Frost's communitarianism. Given that Frost argues that agents in the international sphere are initiates in a shared practice, any dispute that arises will be about hard cases within that practice. The central idea here is that in constructing the background justification which will aid us in settling hard cases in international relations, we employ the procedure of 'reflective equilibrium', a procedure that encourages piecemeal change to the existing ethical and political situation. For Frost 'the technique of reflective equilibrium is designed to overcome an incompatibility (a lack of fit) between the body of settled rules and the background theory'.[23] It also allows for a developing understanding of the importance of existing or 'settled' social and intersocietal norms and the institution of new ones.

> In response to new situations new usages will emerge. These may be tested via the method of reflective equilibrium (the method of intrapractice critique) and thus, gradually, the ordinary language will change and grow.[24]

For Rawls this process would, over time, lead the actors in the international sphere to realise independently that toleration of reasonable pluralism is the chief virtue in international ethics. This realisation (in the most optimistic of possible interpretations of 'LOP') would lead to the move from the *modus vivendi* of international law to a fully overlapping consensus on the value of toleration. In Walzer's less confident brand of developmental communitarianism this process would lead (at the very least) to a shared understanding (and more optimistically a shared articulation) of the moral minimum. However for Frost it leads to much more.

The political and philosophical beginning of Frost's moral constructivism and therefore the only starting point for an analysis of Frost's theory is the modern state domain of discourse and the settled norms that are shared within this practice. The settled norms that Frost lists under the sub-headings '*the sovereignty (S) norms, international law (L) norms, modernisation (M) norms and domestic (D) norms*' are, he argues implied by the questions we commonly ask of international relations. Here, following the steps of Frost's argument that cohere with his presentation of

Dworkin's argument offers a fascinating insight into Frost's position. The first step in Frost's procedure for looking into the background justification for the modern state domain of discourse is to start with what everybody knows. This search reveals certain guiding *concepts* that are themselves capable of diverse conceptions. Essentially this process leads to the creation of the list of settled norms. It is important to remember that this seemingly comprehensive list of norms is (or could be) made up of some strikingly different conceptions of what each of the norms calls for. It is also quite clear (it will be recalled from chapter 1) that Frost shows there appears to be (or is commonly thought to be) a certain 'tension' between those goods that concern sovereignty and those that concern the rights of individual persons.[25] This pressure is itself a product of the development of international politics and leads to the central question of the cosmopolitan/communitarian debate and of international relations theory more generally. Frost shows that 'it may be argued that the primary question for a normative theory of international relations is *whether* the system of sovereign states is a justifiable way of organising the government of the world'. The problem with taking the cosmopolitan line of reasoning and questioning the settled status and primacy of S1 and S2 (the norms regarding the preservation of the society of states and sovereignty itself as good) is, Frost argues, that

> [t]here is good reason to believe that this would not be possible. One such reason is that a background theory, which requires of us that we reject this item, requires that we reject several other bits of the settled core, which are related to item 1. Of all the items on the list only five could possibly be thought of as totally independent of item 1. In such a case we are being asked to reject too many settled beliefs and are not left with a basis for argument at all.[26]

Cosmopolitanism is rejected on Frost's account because the way it privileges the concept of human rights over sovereignty does not cohere with the general understanding of what is important to international relations. While Frost's more recent work does begin to challenge the definitive role of sovereignty,[27] this process is not the product of what Frost scathingly refers to as 'mid-air reasoning' but of a historically bound dialogue between actors in the international arena. The process of development is theoretically and practically indispensable. While some current conceptions of D2 (norms of human rights) insist on the absurdity of the norms of sovereignty, they are not widely shared or theoretically justifiable conceptions of human rights and cannot serve to change the current domain of discourse. It can be said without too much scope for dispute that such conceptions do not cohere with a conception of the institution's character or point that best accords with the settled rules of the institution. Therefore they do not meet the standards set by point 3 of Frost's justificatory procedure (and thus rely on inaccessible reasoning). Nevertheless it is practically indisputable that much of the contemporary debate in international ethics focuses on human rights and that pouring scorn on 'mid-air reasoning' is not in itself a satisfactory way of overcoming the problem and the force of Frost's constitutive theory of individuality is brought to bear on precisely this tension. Essentially Frost's position recognises the importance of human rights issues in contemporary international relations theory but wants such claims to be adequately grounded in the shared discourse of international ethics. Having examined and rejected the claims of contract theory and order and rights based justifications[28] Frost proceeds to step 4 of his procedure.

The constitutive theory of individuality

Frost argues that:

> constitutive theory … does not seek to show that the sovereign state is a *device* which protects certain pre-existing rights. … Rather it contends that a person is constituted as a rights holder of a certain sort within the context of a specific social relationship. … I want to argue that neither is prior, but that rights and institutions presuppose and imply each other.[29]

For Frost the concept of human rights that plays a part in our shared practice developed in relation to those conventions and therefore any realistic conception of human rights must be shown to derive from the shared institution of international relations. In setting up his theory in opposition to contract theory Frost is engaging fully with one very basic (and sometimes stylised) aspect of the cosmopolitan/communitarian debate. While both Brown and Charvet make this connection explicitly Frost does not and so it is necessary once again to show the significance of Frost's position to the focus of my argument. The rejection of the contractarian and rights-based positions (basically cosmopolitan positions) is essentially a rejection of what Brown calls 'liberal individualism'[30] and what Charvet calls the 'Kantian fallacy'.[31] These conceptions of individuality do make sense in relation to a certain western European notion of human rights but not in relation to wider understandings of rights or other parts of international relations and therefore must be rejected. It is vital to remember, however, that as Brown notes '[t]his does not deny the notion of individuality. … What it *does* deny is the universalism of liberal accounts of individuality. Human beings live in different kinds of groups and these different types of groups create different kinds of individuals.'[32]

For Frost all states have agreed to abide by a concept of human rights, which necessarily incorporates various (but presumably not all) conceptions of individuality. His task, in engaging upon the fourth (and final) component of his justificatory procedure, is 'to make explicit the moral dimension that is already implicit in the simultaneous acceptance of the state and sovereignty norms (norms S1 and S2 on our list …) on the one hand, and the rights-related norms on the other hand'.[33]

Again (as Frost reiterates in a footnote) this procedure is not intended merely to justify the status quo. The fact is that:

> [t]he actors … may be acting according to a partial or incorrect understanding of the moral dimension implicit in their social arrangements. … Where a more satisfactory understanding of the moral dimensions implicit in the existing arrangements is produced, this will serve as a criticism of the previous understandings and will also guide their actions in new ways.[34]

The general thrust of the exposition of Frost's position in this chapter must now orientate itself to the concrete question of whether or not the conception of individuality that Frost constructs to explain the claims we make when referring to human rights or sovereignty is flexible enough to be justifiable. Does Frost's secular Hegelianism admit a concept of individuality that can really be said to be the focus of a substantially shared practice? Not only must Frost show that 'being a rights holder of a certain sort involves the other components of the practice within which the right is situated',[35] thus overcoming the presumed tension between these two key aspects of our existence, but he must show that this background justification is of practical merit.

That the current domain of discourse does utilise concepts of individuality is beyond dispute. Frost's task is to discover and articulate the reason that individuality became a shared value and the consequences an understanding of this entails. Frost's insight is that we have not developed the concept of individual right to challenge the authority of the state but that our current range of international political interactions and institutions entails the concept of individual right. The system we mutually participate in relies, at all levels, on the fact that we respect individuals as rights holders. The argument that 'individuality only becomes a value where it is the case that two or more people do, through their reciprocal recognition of one another, give concrete practical expression to valuing one another'[36] suggests that the rights we claim as individuals are the counterparts of the freedoms we claim in our existence within states. For Frost 'the point is that we would not be the individuals we are, were we not members of a specific set of social arrangements which are based upon specified sets of norms'.[37] We can no more deny that human rights are a part of our political world than we can deny that states and the system of states are a part of our political setting. In filling out the detail of this argument Frost goes on to give a relatively unchanged account of Hegelian individuality that is formed through the institutions of the family, civil society and the state (Frost also focuses on the society of states) once again arguing that 'constitutive theory … draws heavily on Hegel's political philosophy, but it is what may be termed a secular interpretation of his theory. Constitutive theory does not require of us that we understand or accept Hegel's metaphysical system.'[38]

However, while we may not have to accept Hegelian metaphysics it is absolutely vital that we understand them because a critical aspect of Hegel's political theory, its justificatory element, is tied up totally with the historical development of the notion of individuality. If Frost wants to discriminate between good and bad actors in international relations on the grounds that they do or do not honour his constructed concept of individuality, he must be able to show us why that concept of individuality is good. Before scrutinising Frost's secular Hegelianism let us state the problem more forcefully. Frost argues that 'individual freedom is not constituted by just any kind of state. ... In the *fully developed* state the citizens perceive a coincidence between what the state requires of them and what they require in order to be free.'[39]

Furthermore individual freedom is hampered if one's state is not recognised as autonomous and if the state is not what Frost calls the *fully developed* state then it cannot truly be recognised as autonomous. Frost's method is both descriptive and constructive. It seeks to explain how the current domain of discourse arose and in doing so to justify certain understandings of the current shared norms. It will be my contention that Frost does not fully explore the second aspect of his theory. It must be kept in mind that:

> despite the connotations of the word *Sittlichkeit*, Hegel's conception of modern ethical life makes strikingly little provision for cultural diversity between states. Hegel's *Philosophy of Right* must be read as a powerful contribution to the argument ... that the institutions of modern society must be held accountable before the bar of reason.[40]

Frost must also lay out the court before which his conception of ethical life, *the fully developed state*, must answer. My purpose here is not to dismiss Frost's enterprise, which I believe is a very fruitful one, but to charge it with recognising the consequences of its own secular Hegelianism.[41]

For Frost, constitutive theory begins by asserting that the person only attains individuality in 'a relationship of mutual valuation'. He continues, following closely Hegel's line of argument, that:

> [i]t is only in the state that individuality can be fully realized. Both (Hegel and Charvet) support this contention by examining how our individuality is partially constituted by subordinate wholes, like the family and civil society, and by showing how the shortcomings of the subordinate institutions are overcome by subsequent and higher institutions. This dialectical process culminates in the state.[42]

Frost, however, goes on to complete Hegel's insight and then to attempt to supersede it. Here simply laying out Frost's position makes his basic argument more accessible and so I will return to the detail of his proof in the following sections. For Frost our sense of what it is to be a free individual is tied up with our sense of what it is to be a free citizen. Our everyday claims concerning human rights or self-determination only make sense in relation to these specific modes of existence. Thus, argues Frost, for our individuality and freedom to be fully recognised we require both a fully developed state and recognition of that state by the international community. By a fully developed state Frost means one 'in which the people recognize each other as citizens in terms of the law which they in turn recognize as being constituted by them and constitutive of them as citizens'.[43] The basic idea here is that the concept of sovereignty and what we now see as the correlative notions of freedom and individuality makes no sense in relation to autocratic states. This is quite a claim. It follows from the claim that our specific idea of individuality is a consequence of the interaction of the social practices of family, civil society and the state. If, Frost reasons, we were the product of autocratic states, and were happy to be so, we would not even have the vocabulary to insist on rights. As agents with relatively fixed ideas about how one should treat children within the family or what freedoms one could expect in civil society (property ownership etc.) and a recognition that such 'rights' are objectified in the state, we have developed a clear idea of what it is to be a free individual and thus what rights such an individual should be accorded. From this position it is clear that the notion of rights we are dealing with requires the type of state Frost describes and cannot connect with totalitarian or patriarchal societies. Even those agents who do live in autocratic states have a surrogate history of the kind Frost's theory requires. Quite simply it is the history of the United Nations system of international politics that has promulgated the values of democracy and rights and created the global vocabulary of world politics. Thus individual rights entail democratic rights and democratic rights entail sovereign rights.[44] Hegel's full explanation, which Frost adopts, is more elegant (and far more lengthy) but the point is, I hope, clear. Constructivist Hegelianism attempts to show that there is no conflict between human rights and the idea of sovereignty because the social practice we are engaged in necessarily includes both. Human rights are associational or political rights of a special sort. Without them the state has no legitimacy and without the state the type of rights we claim make no sense. Frost's demythologised claim is that the type of individual freedom we demand reflects all the social institutions that are our history, our present, and all that we can construct in our immediate future. Accepting this argument overcomes the problem of the derivation of human rights and solves the problem of the apparent tension between rights and sovereignty and, Frost argues, carries with it a critical edge that is every bit as sharp as that of the cosmopolitan theory.

The political conclusions of constitutive theory

Continuing to employ secular Hegelian concepts Frost then moves explicitly into the international sphere and attempts to show how his reading of international ethics manifests itself in our international relations: 'The point here is that within the autonomous state all individuals are constituted as free citizens, but for their citizenship to be fully actualised their state needs to be recognised by other states as autonomous.'[45]

Again, following Hegel, Frost argues that in order to be recognised as autonomous the state must meet certain specific requirements. Here Frost excludes families, hordes, clans, multitudes, robber bands, liberation movements, tyrannies, oligarchies, patriarchies and any authoritarian or totalitarian state.[46]

In Hegelian terms they are excluded because they are not 'actual', they do not display the concept of individuality, which is in fact, Frost, argues, at the deepest root of the shared norms of international society. Frost realises that his claim is open to the objection that the background theory is too stringent arguing that if we were to apply this standard to our political world, few states indeed would qualify for recognition. While this does not concern Frost, Brown's reading of this aspect of Frost's work indicates that perhaps it should. Brown notes that while the disagreement concerning the value of state autonomy between cosmopolitans such as Beitz and communitarians such as Frost is fundamental to the cosmopolitan/communitarian debate:

> the logic of his [Frost's] position is that the vast majority of claims made by states to have their sovereignty respected are every bit as spurious as Beitz would say all such claims are. The disagreement between these two conceptions of the world is total at the level of theory, marginal at the level of practice.[47]

Frost attempts to resolve this problem by adopting Jackson's use of the image of 'quasi-states' and it is an image which must be carefully noted because it amounts to a defence of the shared nature of the underlying premises of the modern state domain of discourse. It is vital to remember that the shared nature of these underlying premises is the only justification for using this background justification in resolving tensions in international relations. Frost divides the world into developed states and quasi-states, the former being what he calls 'initiates' and the latter being 'novices'. Frost's argument is that the act of recognising a state's sovereignty is not 'a one off gate keeping act' (that is, it is not the case that a state is only considered sovereign and thus allowed entry into the community of states if it fulfils the conditions of Frost's constitutive theory) but that instead 'it must be understood with reference to a person or group of people learning how to participate in a given practice'.[48] In essence Frost portrays the development of international relations as the education by developed states of (willing) quasi-states that involves an initial recognition of the quasi-state's sovereignty (albeit at a lower level) until the novice becomes fully initiated in the rules of international relations. Returning to the example of an initiate chess player educating a novice chess player, Frost writes, casting himself in the role of initiate: '[m]y concern is prompted by the fact that what I ultimately want is for you to become a fully competent player. That you want this too, is indicated by the fact that you actively seek to play with me.'[49]

Nevertheless Frost emphasises that we are not to let this conclusion carry us away in a frenzy of constitutional change, we cannot simply ask 'in what type of state (or global system) can individuality flourish?' and expect our answer to prescribe the form of the next constitution (or series of constitutions) that we are to construct. To do so, Frost tells us, is to miss a fundamental point about constitutive theory.

> A constitution cannot simply be imposed on a people. It is a set of rules in terms of which they constitute each other. The people have to see the constitution as the proper way of doing things. They have to be educated into accepting it. They have to be convinced that it is necessary to their being who they are.[50]

Recognising the importance of human rights must lead to a world of free and self-determining democratic states.

There is still one more step in Frost's argument. In *Ethics* Frost had only reached the conclusions that I have laid out thus far. When writing about the possibility of a radically changed global order Frosts argues that: 'A world state would be justified if it came about through the voluntary actions of all states. … In short, any new order must grow out of the autonomous action of *states*.'[51]

However in work in progress and in a recent journal paper he has pushed his theory further down the time-line to the suggestion that all individuals now constitute each other as rights holders within global civil society.[52] A brief examination of this really emphasises the extent to which Frost believes his constitutive theory of rights can augment a non-cosmopolitan approach. Civil society, on Frost's account, 'is the realm of first generation rights'.[53] Our understanding of the importance of individuality and autonomy has reached the historical stage where rights can exist independently of a state and this, Frost maintains, may be the natural conclusion to the constitutive process. The critical edge is more apparent here. It is impossible, argues Frost, to conceive of a notion of free citizenship within a state in circumstances where the so-called citizens do not enjoy first generation rights. Here rights have made the transition and become the governing norms within our social practice. Here then Frost appears to have overcome the problem of the tension between rights and sovereignty and the claim that any such move will weaken the theory of rights too much. However some of the claims that Frost makes on the back of his 'secular' Hegelianism go too far.

The limits of secular Hegelianism

Brown, whose examination of 'demythologised' Hegelianism utilises the ideas of Frost and Charvet, highlights the central problem once in the abstract and later in relation to current international political practice.

> It should be noted that it is at this point that the attempt to provide a secular interpretation of Hegel's politics runs into difficulties. From the non-metaphysical perspective adopted here, this interpretation of the state can only

> be an 'interpretation' – a more or less plausible account of the salient features of modern states; it cannot be the only possible interpretation.[54]

More importantly it cannot be said to be the only interpretation of the state conducive to individuality and freedom. Brown notes that the central problem lies in the relationship between description and justification in Frost's theory.

> The first principle of prescriptive international relations, as promulgated by such bodies as the United Nations, is state sovereignty, and this notion is coupled with a refusal to distinguish between different kinds of states. From the UN viewpoint, a state is a state is a state – and any attempt to distinguish between those states that have earned the right to autonomy and those that have not is totally unacceptable. The problem from Frost's viewpoint is that it is essential to make this distinction, because if it is not made, the principles he enunciates become simply rationalisations for the status quo – and this is certainly not his intention. There is a dislocation between the starting point of his argument and its conclusion.[55]

Essentially the problem is that in dropping the justificatory element of Hegel's philosophy there arises a problem that is not overcome by applying Dworkin's casuistical legal theory to international relations theory.

Frost's self-imposed task, while Hegelian in character, is not the same as Hegel's project. It *must* rely on a different justification. Hegel's metaphysics and his philosophy of history combine to provide the background justification for the here and now. In this way Hegel really has the grounds to argue that specific concepts of freedom and individuality are constitutive of political actuality and that to be out of step with one's world is to be on the 'threshold of immorality'.[56] The idea that the 'theme' of history is that of the relationship between the individual, freedom and politics and that the substantive purpose of political philosophy is to overcome the problem of alienation, ideas utilised by Frost,[57] cannot seek the Hegelian justification that these values exemplify the spirit of an age and one vital moment in the struggle towards the Absolute *Geist*. The background justification that Frost constructs must receive its vindication from something other than world history or spirit. This is not an impossible task, indeed the general position held in developmental communitarianism is that grounding the universal aspect of *Sittlichkeit* in a different manner is an important part of international ethics. Without the absolute justification of Hegel's metaphysics we must, at the very least, be prepared to admit that not all problems in international relations stem from dealings with alienated or underdeveloped uninitiates (uninitiated, that is, to what are really the shared understandings of international ethics). We cannot infer the consent of the parties to the present structure of international ethics or the just nature of this ethical structure from the fact that everyone participates in international relations. At the very heart of Frost's enterprise is the tension between explanation and justification.[58] Frost, of course, does give up Hegelian justification in favour or Dworkin's method but I am not sure that this is acceptable. Here my dispute is not with Dworkin's argument as it pertains to law but with the purchase that his method could have on international relations. Frost makes a case for transposing casuistical legal reasoning from law to international relations and his claim must rest on his illustration of the character of the modern state domain of discourse as an institution comparable to that of a constitutionally supported law.

There are some basic points concerning the transposition of Dworkin's legal framework into the sphere of international ethics that must be borne in mind. Firstly, in order to determine the just nature of such a procedure we need to know that the starting point for our constructed morality (i.e. 'what everyone knows' about the institution) is itself just, or at least not radically unjust or partial, a matter that Dworkin, writing about a democratically supported legal system, is able to consider settled.[59] Another way of putting this is in the form of a question. Can there really be said to be shared (or even compatible) views concerning the purpose of international society or even the validity of the current 'norms' of international relations? Second: in what sense can it be said that the current participants have 'consented' to take part in the 'institution' Frost describes? One cannot secede from international society as one might choose to play draughts rather than chess. A state certainly cannot secede from the current norms of international relations without incurring penalties and given Frost's rejection of consent and contract theories in ethics it is a little odd that he does not question the relevance of this aspect of his thesis.[60] The main difficulty here is that in transplanting Dworkin's idea of casuistical problem solving from law to international relations Frost keeps rather a lot of inaccessible (to use O'Neill's phrase) justificatory material.

Dworkin tells us that '[i]n chess the general ground of institutional rights must be the tacit consent or understanding of the parties'.[61] These institutional rights are simply those rights that can be claimed only in relation to the relevant institutional framework. The idea is that in consenting to the rules of chess they also consent to play, as it were, in the spirit of the game, according to its general principles. Frost explicitly picks up on this point (even going so far as to complete the quotation above)[62] arguing, with Dworkin, that the known rules (of chess, law and the settled norms of the modern state domain of discourse) can be situated within a coherent background justification which represents the spirit of chess, law and international relations respectively (see below). Frost must therefore be claiming that actors in international relations share a substantial consensus on the meaning of the norms of the modern state domain of discourse, a consensus as substantial as that between players in a game of chess or voters in a democratic state.[63] The first point to keep in mind would therefore centre on the notion of consent in international relations. It is not too far fetched to imagine a state arguing that the current international situation and the norms that govern it are the product of a history in which they have either played no part, or in which they were exploited and given no chance to shape, or in which their most fundamental beliefs have had to be subverted and subordinated to western liberal beliefs for the sake of continued existence or economic sustenance. Even if those (theoretical) states had signed the treaty of Westphalia (regarding sovereign right) or of Vienna (regarding diplomatic relations) or the various United Nations declarations or had simply taken part in the day-to-day affairs of international relations, a good advocate could probably make the case that they were coerced into doing so. The key point here is that it is possible to claim that they are not alienated from current practice in the Hegelian sense (as Frost claims)[64] but that the modern state domain of discourse is alien to them.[65]

The second point to keep in mind relates to the 'substantiveness' of the consensus on the rules of the modern state domain of discourse. Given that the 'here and now' is not sacrosanct and we do not have a unified historical process that necessarily leads us to concur on the meaning of issues such as 'human rights', the process of 'political theory' that both Dworkin and Frost see as essential to the creation of background justifications is going to be more difficult. Frost's Hegelian position leads him to argue that the process he describes (essentially the process of solving ethical disputes in international relations) is a process of 'seeking to overcome the *alienation* a person might feel with regard to certain aspects of a practice (essential to her full flourishing within that practice) as hostile or detrimental to her well-being'.[66] The project eventually becomes centred upon a notion of the flourishing of individual freedom. Again, in Hegel this was justified in terms of the development of reason and *Geist* but in Frost it is simply a part of the 'here and now' and possibly a part of the 'here and now' that has many determinate conceptions, not all of which sit easily with each other. Dworkin foresees that the element of political theory that must take place in his procedure is indeed political and I think that it is an aspect of his thesis that *must* be borne in mind when applying his method to international ethics. Dworkin notes that his method of adjudication, what he calls his 'rights thesis' has two aspects. 'Its descriptive aspect explains the present structure of the institution of adjudication. Its normative aspect offers a political justification for that structure.'[67] If in international ethics the political aspect of decision making is partial (the alternative being a claim of political homogeneity, a patently absurd claim for the 'here and now') then the political justification for decisions must be watched closely for conceptual lacunae or the kind of claims that may be justified in a fully Hegelian international relations theory but not in a demythologised one. My point focuses on Dworkin's claim that the background justification itself and the decision maker's use of that justification must be just. It is well worth allowing Dworkin to make his point at some length. Using the example of Hercules (a fictitious lawyer of superhuman ability who is to make the decision in question) Dworkin argues that

> many of Hercules' decisions about legal rights depend upon judgements of political theory that may be made differently by different judges or by the public at large. … It does not matter to this objection that the decision is one of principle rather than policy. It matters only that the decision is one of political conviction about which reasonable men disagree. If Hercules decides cases on the basis of such judgements, then he decides on the basis

> of his own convictions and preferences, which seems unfair, contrary to democracy, and offensive to the rule of law. ... *However* ... That charge is ambiguous, because there are two ways in which an official might rely upon his own opinions in making such a decision. One of these in a judge, is offensive, but the other is inevitable.[68]

Given that Frost is not claiming that there is a Hercules to make judgments in international relations, we must be aware that the thought experiment he offers us is certainly subject to the charge of partiality. After all, reasonable people disagree considerably about international ethics. In what sense can a charge of partiality be avoided? For Dworkin the answer is simple and relies on the humility of the judges to recognise that they could well be wrong but more importantly upon the 'principle of democracy in political theory'.[69] Hercules must either make a decision based on his understanding of the existing constitution or, if many people disagree with that interpretation of the constitution, he must defer to the democratic process. In a legal system within a constitutionally regulated democracy this is a sound argument. In the international sphere, where certain 'thick' interpretations (what Frost and Dworkin call conceptions) of settled norms are likely to be incompatible with the organising principles of some sovereign states, we have a more difficult problem. There is no constitution that guarantees a democratic process and one (sovereign) judge's opinion may be non-negotiable. Either Frost must admit to holding a thinner consensus on the settled norms (a consensus so thin that all existent states can be a part of it) and his theory must provide a justification compatible with all world views, or Frost must justify the subordination of certain types of world view.

In adopting Dworkin's method and abandoning Hegelian metaphysics Frost wants to use the developmental aspect of the Hegelian dialectic without adopting the teleological aspect (or more accurately the notion of the self-actualisation of freedom). The difficulty with this is that the question of the origins of the value of individuality is left partially unanswered. Either Frost is arguing that the concept of individuality that he employs is simply a distillation of the values inherent in the here and now (which given the discriminatory work the concept must do is hard to presume) or he has to justify the focus of his thesis. There is however a way through this impasse but it questions the 'thickness' of Frost's vision of a shared domain of discourse and limits the work that his justificatory procedure can do.

A developmental communitarian restatement of constitutive theory

Following through on Frost's constitutive theory not only highlights these difficulties but also begins to indicate the way we must go if we wish to accept that a developmental communitarianism has the potential to further an understanding of international ethics. In the Hegelian version of the ethical state the tensions inherent in the concept of individuality are resolved in a higher unity. The lack of individuality in the family is resolved in civil society whose contradictions are in turn resolved in ethical life and we attain

> the consciousness that my interest, both substantive and particular, is contained and preserved in another's [i.e. the state's] interest and end, i.e. in the other's relation to me as an individual. In this way this very other is immediately not another in my eyes, and in being conscious of this fact, I am free.[70]

In Frost's terms, it is in the state that individual citizens recognise what they require for individual freedom. For Frost this conclusion carries with it a critical edge, not every state can be said to be suitable to the constitution of the kind of individuality that Frost seeks.

While this may indeed be an accurate portrayal of the current development of international relations it singularly fails to justify that developmental process. If Frost wants to argue that states that constitute individuality in the manner that he has outlined are in fact better (more just) than states that do not he must show more than the fact that those states that are considered developed in the here and now believe that they develop individuality (which they value highly) in this way and that they are educating others in their methods.[71] Such a description might merely portray a contingent power relation. There are two options open to Frost that might make his claims easier to agree with. The first would dilute the description of individuality that Frost puts forward and make the concept of individuality available to many more conceptions of individuality and citizenship or membership. This would have the effect of edging Frost further towards the pluralist perspective that he criticises but it would make the task of justification on the basis of the shared nature of the modern state domain of discourse much easier. The criterion for being recognised as an autonomous state would have to be lowered and the claims concerning the relationship between novice and initiate dropped or modified. Alternatively Frost could maintain the emphasis on the ethical nature of individuality as described in constitutive theory but recognise that it is a conception of individuality shared by 'developed states' only and that this must be taken into account when examining the modern state domain of discourse and any hard cases therein. These two alternatives are the core strategies of the two other examples of developmental communitarianism offered in this thesis. Examining these claims highlights the limits both of secular Hegelianism and of developmental communitarianism. These limits are, from a constructivist point of view, to be cherished rather than mourned.

An antifoundational, secular or demythologised Hegelianism that seeks its justification from a communitarian position rather than from a metaphysical history but nevertheless wished to incorporate some aspects of Hegel's political theory would have more reason than most to agree with Hegel that 'a general league of nations for perpetual peace would be the domination of one nation, or would merely be one people; its universality would be obliterated'.[72] It is perhaps indicative of Frost's misunderstanding of the consequences of secularising Hegel that he argues that the possibility of a world-state is not lost. Frost believes that the 'thick' intra-practice understanding of the constitutive theory of individuality presents us with a basic outline of what a just state would look like. I have argued that this 'thick' aspect of his theory is left unjustified. Frost's 'thick' interpretation of international relations leads him to argue that '[a] world "state" would be justified if it came about through the voluntary action of all sovereign states'.[73] However this is to misunderstand the communitarian consequences of secularising Hegel. For Hegel a state will cease to exist if it has no opposition either because it is afraid to fight for the freedom of its citizens or because it has attained its goals.[74] Because every articulation of a conception of freedom is necessarily subject to redefinition in the light of new understandings of the concept of freedom it is essential to the development of freedom that as many articulations of freedom as possible coexist. Here, the concept of freedom still does some discriminatory work but the various forms this critical edge can take are likely to fall short of Frost's novice/initiate relationship. This is because the state's right to stand in the international sphere as an individual or as a recognised articulation of freedom is tied up not with the conception of freedom held by initiate states but with the relationship between citizen and their state.[75] There follows from the fact that we have stripped Hegel's particular understanding of the form the concept of freedom can take from our justification (by denying claim to metaphysics or history) a starting point in international affairs that insists that as long as the state exhibits signs of a healthy relationship between citizen and state it must be recognised as sovereign.[76] What counts as a healthy relationship in this formulation of the starting point is still to be decided.[77] Following on from this and returning to Hegel's account of international relations it follows that contentious relations between states are healthy in the sense that it allows various conceptions of freedom to clash and thereby generate new (and, says the optimism of an Hegelian philosophy, better)[78] understandings of freedom. It is this developmental process that Hegel had in mind in his discussion of warfare. For Hegel the individual nature of the state is an embodiment of an ethical relation between citizen (or individual) and state, a relationship that cannot be transcended except internally in the development of that relationship. It is therefore logically necessary that a state defends its right to exist as a recognised sovereign power to its fullest capability. This is, as Brown rightly notes, 'resolutely communitarian'[79] but it does not sanctify permanent warfare. To argue that it does is to confuse something contingent with something ethical. The conflict between conceptions of freedom is necessary to the development of the concept of freedom, war is merely contingent upon this process. The current articulations of that concept are (provided they adequately model a healthy relationship between citizen and state) perfectly valid and one of the shared norms following from this watered down understanding of a Hegelian model of international relations would obviously be non-intervention in the case of a suitable relationship between state and subject.[80] Thus Hegel argues that 'one state should not meddle in the domestic affairs of another'[81] and this is simply a follow-on from the idea that freedom and individuality cannot be developed via coercion. These values can be developed via various forms of interaction but defence of sovereign integrity in the light of the concept of freedom or the 'ought' of international law is paramount. This does not have to take the form of armed combat and indeed the ends of war in a system where the language of freedom is used as a justification of sovereignty are such that 'war accordingly entails the determination of international law that it should preserve the possibility of peace'.[82] Here then is a putative theory of *Ius in Bello* and *Ius ad Bellum* and as Avineri notes: 'despite Hegel's insistence that international law always remains on the level of an "ought", his theory of sovereignty as based on reciprocal recognition brings forth a system of limited, yet effective, *comitas gentium*'.[83]

While this *comitas gentium* will (at least under present conditions) fall short of the global ethical order foreseen by Frost and other Hegelian scholars such as Vincent and Mitias,[84] it is perfectly possible to imagine a situation in which the necessity of war (which is based on contingency unlike the necessity for the dialectical conflict between conceptions of freedom) is no longer perceived as a necessity. T.H. Green's idealism picks up on precisely this point arguing that,

> [i]t is nothing then in the necessary organisation of the state, but rather some defect of that organisation in relation to its proper function of maintaining and reconciling rights, of giving scope to capacities, that leads to a conflict of apparent interests between one state and another. The wrong, therefore, which results to human society from conflicts between states cannot be condoned on the ground that it is a necessary incident of the existence of states.[85]

The central difference between Hegel's description of the international realm and Green's retort is formed in the historical contexts in which these two thinkers wrote and not in a difference of philosophical opinion. It displays the development of history examined in the light of the concept of freedom or the constitutive theory of individuality and charted by developmental communitarianism. The process is, however, limited by much more than historical contingency. It is limited by the communitarian underpinning of a Hegelian theory of international ethics. Such a theory may be happy to tell us, as Hegel does, that,

> [t]he European nations form a family with respect to the universal principle of their legislation, customs and culture, so that their conduct in terms of international law is modified accordingly in a situation that is otherwise dominated by the mutual infliction of evils.[86]

Indeed such a theory would (theoretically) be happy to take such a union further but not to the point of a world-state. This is simply because the concept of freedom that is at the heart of this description of international ethics is simply more indeterminate than the one Frost articulates. It is indeterminate because it is agnostic concerning the *Truth* claims made of certain conceptions of freedom and more concerned to focus on the concept of freedom.[87] The central difference is in the degree to which the concept of freedom can be said to be shared both in a secular Hegelianism and a developmental communitarianism.

Conclusions

The place of secular Hegelianism within developmental communitarianism has not been refuted, merely refined in relation to the consequences of the secularisation of Hegel. Of prime importance here is the method that Frost adopts and its ability to overcome the tensions between two key aspects of international relations. The basic idea that the human rights we claim stem from our participation in the 'modern state domain of discourse' is both theoretically more secure than the cosmopolitan construction of human rights and, in making sense of our practice, exposes human and political rights abuses as totally unjustifiable. While I have argued that Frost draws more aggressive conclusions than a constructivist Hegelianism can allow I do believe that a developmental communitarianism that stayed within the appropriate limits would be theoretically secure and still able to attack the problems of international relations theory. In order to spell out fully the significance of this reading of Frost's position it is useful to examine briefly the relationship between Frost and the other thinkers that I have labelled developmental and communitarian.

The association of Walzer's philosophy to Frost's constitutive theory is perhaps the easiest to deal with. In the next chapter the reiterative construction of a moral minimum (Walzer's brand of developmental communitarianism) shows that while the construction of the ethical standpoint in the work of Walzer and Frost is similar the outcome is significantly different. Essentially this is because the process of reiterative universalism that enables Walzer to see the construction of a moral minimum focuses on a very 'thin' band of shared concepts. In contrast to Frost's position the notions of justice that are shared cross-culturally (and so justify international action) are virtually non-deterministic because they are transient and not 'thick' enough to live by. On the question of the 'health' of the relationship between citizen and state, for example, Walzer can only allow intervention on the grounds of what he calls 'a radical lack of fit' between citizens and state because to go as far as Frost would be to privilege specific forms of social arrangement. Frost, for example, argues that in order to bring 'novice' states to a full understanding of international justice the 'developed' or 'initiate' states must practice 'forms of non-interference followed by interference'.[88] Frost must be very sure that the developed states correctly typify the concept of freedom. In order to justify a system of international ethics that rests on shared concepts Walzer believes that the eventual construction of international norms will have to be 'thin' enough so that it can really be said that they are shared. It is not a question of making everyone's conception of (for example) human rights consonant with the dominant western/liberal conception of human rights but of acting only on those principles that are in fact shared.[89]

Basically Walzer's international casuistry is limited by his recognition that there is no constitution against which we may test our principles. It does not, however, follow that if we accept the force of Walzer's communitarian position as a critique of Frost's communitarian position that we must necessarily share his conclusions concerning international relations. The position adopted by Rawls, which will be examined in the final chapter, overwhelmingly challenges this conclusion and without getting too far ahead of my argument it is useful to briefly compare an Hegelian interpretation of Rawls with Frost's theory.

Schwarzenbach's paper 'Rawls, Hegel and Communitarianism' can be seen as one of the many and often diverse responses to Rawls' philosophy after *Theory of Justice*. She argues that '[s]hould it emerge that Rawls in fact sides with the communitarian Hegel on numerous counts, the ground of contemporary debate should shift significantly'.[90] This supports my contention that Rawls should in fact be considered a developmental communitarian and that such an interpretation should lead to the reliberalisation of communitarian international relations theory. Here it is worth examining the relative strength of the claims that Rawls makes once it is recognised that 'Rawls's theory may appropriately be labelled "Hegelian" … once we have granted, that is, the possible separation of political theory from a full blown metaphysics'.[91]

In viewing Rawls as a secular Hegelian (or at the very least as a communitarian whose position is compatible with secular Hegelianism) it is necessary to recognise that while both thinkers can be said to share much, ultimately Rawls is a constructivist in ethics whereas Hegel is a moral realist.[92] Both Frost and Walzer also fit the category of constructivists. This means that while Rawls and Frost can share ideas such as reflective equilibrium (aka, argues Schwarzenbach, the political employment of the Hegelian dialectic) that adds the developmental aspect to communitarian political theory, it is important to remember that what determines the value of the principles of individuality etc. in the modern state in the work of Rawls and Frost is not 'the univocal theory of the "cunning of reason": (Hegel's) metaphysical philosophy of history' and that therefore 'while jettisoning all talk of world spirit, of the inexorable march of reason, or of the end of history, Rawls's theory nonetheless retains certain similar but far weaker assumptions'.[93] Without getting beyond an examination of Rawls' position it is vital (to an examination of the place of secular Hegelianism in developmental communitarianism) to briefly assess the relative strength or weakness of Rawls' claims in relation to those of both Hegel and Frost.

Firstly it is interesting to note that the development of the idea of freedom in Hegel's work that receives its justification from the philosophy of history and is articulated in the progress of spirit in the state is seen in Rawls' 'Aristotelian principle'. This principle argues, writes Schwarzenbach,

> that there is such a thing as moral progress in history (since the days of slavery), that a study of man discloses a strong desire for freedom and the

> exercise of his highest powers … and that our social and political institutions indeed reveal a minimal rationality and coherence.[94]

However in the work of Rawls this set of ideas takes its justification from the 'public political culture' of 'political liberalism' and while Rawls is not denying the possible universality of these ideas,

> a conception of political justice in his view (one appropriate for a modern, pluralistic democracy [or indeed an international system]) cannot rest on the truth or falsity of such strong theses and must even be compatible with a number of different positions concerning them.[95]

For Rawls' Hegelianism (argues Schwarzenbach) and for secular Hegelianism more generally this is the price of abandoning Hegel's metaphysical foundationalism. If we accept that the process of reflective equilibrium utilised in the work of Frost and Rawls has similar characteristics to Hegel's use of the dialectic in the development of political life we can draw some interesting comparisons. Recalling Frost's use of the idea of reflective equilibrium we find that,

> in seeking to construct a coherent background theory to justify the whole body of settled rules, the judge finds that it challenges (calls into question) some bits of the settled corpus of law. … Thus it is probable that in any piece of legal reasoning the judge will end up with some bits and pieces of the settled law which do not fit the proposed justificatory background theory. In this way bits of the settled law will become suspect and may well with time fall into disuse. This back and forth procedure is the procedure of reflective equilibrium.[96]

Similarly Rawls sees his task as attempting to formulate 'a deeper underlying basis of agreement' taking a historically specific situation as his starting point. This coincides with Hegel's view of the task of philosophy as coming to terms with one's 'own time apprehended in thoughts'.[97] For Hegel the overcoming of alienation is (put simplistically) coming to terms with a way of life sanctioned by historical process. Thus Hegel's claim that the 'Germanic Realm' (which is most of western and parts of eastern Europe) is destined to reconcile objective truth and freedom in the then current historical moment[98] is justified. However if we take the secularised versions of the Hegelian dialectic offered by frost and Rawls it becomes clear that Frost does not have the justification to claim that 'developed' states currently articulate objective spirit. In recognising this it is necessary that Frost adopt a position similar to that of Rawls who attributes a 'mitigated function' to this process.[99] In turning now to a close reading of the international ethical theory of Walzer and Rawls and the justifications of their positions found in their political theory the limits of developmental communitarianism exhibited in a critique of Frost's work can be seen to be at work.

Notes and references

1 M. Frost, *Ethics and International Relations: A Constitutive Theory*, Cambridge, Cambridge University Press, 1996, p. 84 and p. 88.
2 Frost, *Ethics*, pp. 84–88.
3 Frost, *Ethics*, p. 90.
4 Frost, *Ethics*, p. 79.
5 The tensions between the act of explanation and the act of justification will form a central part of this chapter.
6 Frost, *Ethics*, p. 34.
7 Frost, *Ethics*, p. 92, cf. note 31.
8 Frost, *Ethics*, p. 106.
9 M. Frost, *Towards a Normative Theory of International Relations*, Cambridge University Press, 1986.
10 Brown discusses the Hegelian approach to international relations in most of his work but the fullest discussions are to be found in *International Relations Theory: New Normative Approaches*, New York, London, Harvester Wheatsheaf, 1992, pp. 60–71, where he introduces Hegelian theories of international ethics as a general position and 'The Ethics of Political Restructuring in Europe: The Perspective of Constitutive Theory' where Brown makes a case for the constitutive theory of individuality. J. Charvet's *A Critique of Freedom and Equality*, Cambridge University Press, 1981 is a staple modern Hegelian text and much relied upon by Frost and Charvet's 'Contractarianism and International Political Theory', in D. Boucher and P. Kelly (eds), *The Social Contract From Hobbes to Rawls*, Routledge, 1994, chapter 10 offers an interesting and slightly different slant on Hegelian international relations theory.
11 World history is, of course, the court of judgment I refer to here. Cf. Hegel, *Elements of the Philosophy of Right*, §340 and also addition to §339.
12 Frost, *Ethics*, p. 47.
13 Frost, *Ethics*, p. 51.
14 For the detailed arguments see Frost, *Ethics*, ch.2.
15 Frost, *Ethics*, pp. 50–51.
16 For the full list see Frost, *Ethics*, pp. 76–77.
17 Frost, *Ethics*, p. 77.
18 Frost, *Ethics*, p. 79.
19 R. Dworkin, *Taking Rights Seriously*, Duckworth, 1981.
20 Frost, *Ethics*, p. 97.
21 Frost, *Ethics*, p. 98.
22 Frost, *Ethics*, p. 101.
23 Frost, *Ethics*, p. 99.
24 Frost, *Ethics*, p. 102.
25 Frost, *Ethics*, p. 137.
26 Frost, *Ethics*, note 7, p. 112, text pp. 229–230.
27 See 'Mervyn Frost Replies to Peter Sutch's 'Human Rights as Settled Norms: Mervyn Frost and the Limits of Human Rights Theory', *Review of International Studies*, Vol. 26, 2000, pp. 477–483.
28 Frost's rejection of contract theory incorporates a rejection of Walzer's position.
29 Frost, *Ethics*, pp. 138–139.
30 Brown, 'The Ethics of Political Restructuring', p. 167.
31 Charvet, 'Contractarianism and International Political Theory', p. 176.
32 Brown, 'The Ethics of Political Restructuring', p. 168.
33 Frost, *Ethics*, p. 141.
34 Frost, *Ethics*, note 7 to p. 141, text p. 233.
35 Frost, *Ethics*, p. 140.
36 Frost, *Ethics*, p. 141.
37 Frost, *Ethics*, p. 142.

38 Frost, *Ethics*, p. 143.
39 Frost, *Ethics*, p. 150.
40 Allen Wood, 'Hegel's Ethics', in F.C. Beiser (ed.), *The Cambridge Companion to Hegel*, Cambridge University Press, 1993, p. 229.
41 As Brown notes 'a completely demythologised Hegel is impossible. However it is still possible to hold that a secularised Hegelian account of International relations is the best available to us without accepting the full system.' Essentially this is done by recognising that Hegelian theory is 'theory' and not 'knowledge'. See *International Relations Theory*, pp. 70–71.
42 Frost, *Ethics*, p. 142.
43 Frost, *Ethics*, p. 152.
44 How justifiable a surrogate world history is thus becomes an important question. Hegel could ignore such questions as he could argue that despite (violent) contingency history exhibits a rational development. Frost has no such leeway.
45 Frost, *Ethics*, p. 151.
46 See Frost, *Ethics*, pp. 152–153.
47 Brown, *International Relations Theory*, p. 121.
48 Frost, *Ethics*, p. 154.
49 Frost, *Ethics*, p. 155.
50 Frost, *Ethics*, p. 150.
51 Frost, *Ethics*, pp. 158–159.
52 I do not intend to offer a critical exegesis to this section but just to lay out the direction that Frost's work is taking in order to emphasise the extent to which Frost believes his theory can go. I have received permission from the author to include unpublished work.
53 Frost, 'Reply to Peter Sutch', p. 478.
54 Brown, *International Relations Theory*, p. 64.
55 Brown, *International Relations Theory*, p. 121.
56 The phrase is Bradley's, see Brown, *International Relations Theory*, p. 62.
57 E.g. Frost, *Ethics*, pp. 140–141.
58 Neither Frost or Hegel are, however, committed to an unquestioning acceptance of the status quo.
59 This question is particularly pertinent because Frost claims that some participants may have misunderstood international relations and are therefore 'alienated' from its true point and that this licenses or requires their 'education'.
60 'I conclude that it is not possible to achieve the reconciliation between rights and sovereignty via the defense of contract (explicit or tacit) for most people have never made a contract and the theory of tacit consent is fraught with difficulties.' Frost, *Ethics*, p. 128 and p. 130 and Frost's discussion of Walzer.
61 Dworkin, *Taking Rights Seriously*, Duckworth, 1977 (7th impression 1994), p. 104.
62 Frost, *Ethics*, p. 96.
63 Either this or their understanding of the international system is flawed and they are alienated in the Hegelian sense.
64 Frost, *Ethics*, p. 140.
65 I am not here, or in the following exploration of this objection to Frost's position, suggesting a retreat to the 'conflict of ideologies' approach to international relations, there is no claim that actors in the international sphere are in any way 'hermetically sealed off' from one another. All I am questioning is the robust nature of the value system that Frost argues is inherent in his articulation of the modern state domain of discourse (see below).
66 Frost, *Ethics*, p. 140.
67 Dworkin, *Taking Rights Seriously*, p. 123. Frost argues that 'there is no way in which social scientists may legitimately avoid becoming involved in normative theory' and in doing so places the explanation/justification distinction at the top of the agenda. In

employing this distinction as the crux of an exposition of Frost's work I am merely fleshing out the consequences of his project and not importing isolated problems from Dworkin's work.

68 Dworkin, *Taking Rights Seriously*, p. 123.
69 Dworkin, *Taking Rights Seriously*, p. 125.
70 Hegel's discussion of Patriotism in *The Philosophy of Right*, §268 cited Frost, *Ethics*, p. 149.
71 It is interesting to note that like Hegel, Frost's account of what he terms initiate states or developed states is limited to constitutional democracies.
72 Hegel, *Jena Realphilosophie*, cited Avineri, *Hegel's Theory of the Modern State*, Cambridge University Press, 1972, p. 202.
73 Frost, *Ethics*, p. 157.
74 Here the state is enacting certain (but definitely not all) characteristics of an individual engaged in the master/slave relationship. Cf. Hegel, *Elements of the Philosophy of Right*, §324 and *The Philosophy of History*, p. 74.
75 Because the state as the summit of ethical life (but nevertheless itself subordinate to the concept of freedom) has consciousness in and for itself (*Philosophy of Right* §322) the relationship it has with other states cannot follow the form of the master/slave relationship and resolve itself in a higher form of ethical life.
76 Whereas, for example, Hegel's view concerning constitutional politics arise from an understanding of what it means to be free in this day and age.
77 One effect that this might have on Frost's depiction of international society is to force the recognition that there are not only developed states and quasi-states (chess players and wannabe chess players) but also what Rawls calls rogue states, states who know the rules but reject them. How would Frost class their legitimacy?
78 This faith in the developmental process is articulated (for example) by Brown, 'The Ethics of Political Restructuring', p. 179.
79 Brown, 'The Ethics of Political Restructuring', p. 173.
80 Intervention in the case of human rights violations (i.e. when the relationship between citizens and state is violated) would still be justifiable only more work would have to be done to explain what constitutes a healthy or not so healthy relationship. It is unlikely that Frost's criterion would be extensive enough.
81 Hegel, *Elements of the Philosophy of Right*, §331
82 Hegel, *Elements of the Philosophy of Right*, §338.
83 Avineri, *Hegel's Theory of the Modern State*, p. 204. This theory of the end of a Hegelian theory of international relations is similar to that of H. ten Bruggencate who argues that over time war gradually becomes restrained as each state through its own will relates to other states without the violent struggle for recognition as its initial thought. see 'Hegel's Views on War', *Philosophical Quarterly*, 1, 1950, pp. 58–60.
84 See Frost, *Ethics*, p. 157. A. Vincent, 'The Hegelian State and International Politics', *Review of International Studies*, Vol. 9, 1983, pp. 191–205. M. Mitias, 'Hegel on International Law', *Clio*, Vol. 9, No. 2, 1980, pp. 269–281.
85 T.H. Green, *Lectures on the Principle of Political Obligation*, Lecture K, p. 173. cited Brown, *International Relations Theory*, p. 68.
86 Hegel, *Elements of the Philosophy of Right*, §339 addition. See also Rawls' use of the idea of an overlapping consensus in international relations below.
87 The conclusions to Charvet, 'Contractarianism and International Political Theory', recognises the importance of states in international relations on the basis of what Charvet calls the assurance and indeterminacy arguments and shows how much 'thinner' than Frost's an Hegelian vision of international society must be.
88 Frost, *Ethics*, p. 154.
89 One cannot assume the alienation of others from the concept of human rights simply because they do not share one's conception of what it is to be a human individual.

90 S. Schwarzenbach, 'Rawls, Hegel, and Communitarianism', *Political Theory*, Vol. 19, No. 4, November 1991, p. 540.
91 Schwarzenbach, 'Rawls, Hegel, and Communitarianism', p. 542.
92 Schwarzenbach, 'Rawls, Hegel, and Communitarianism', p. 543.
93 Schwarzenbach, 'Rawls, Hegel, and Communitarianism', p. 547.
94 Schwarzenbach, 'Rawls, Hegel, and Communitarianism', p. 547.
95 Schwarzenbach, 'Rawls, Hegel, and Communitarianism', p. 549, square brackets mine.
96 Frost, *Ethics*, p. 100.
97 See Schwarzenbach, 'Rawls, Hegel, and Communitarianism', p. 543.
98 Hegel, *Elements of the Philosophy of Right*, §358.
99 See Schwarzenbach, 'Rawls, Hegel, and Communitarianism', p. 545.

6 Michael Walzer

Moral creativity and the minimalist universalism of reiteration

Frost's approach to international relations theory appears to offer a secure method for constructing principles of international ethics. However questions remain over whether the conclusions he draws from his theory are fully faithful to that method. The work of Walzer, on the other hand, is rarely charged with unfounded optimism. Indeed Thompson's critique of the tension between moral reasoning and political practice in Walzer's work and O'Neill's insistence on the unproductive relativism of Walzer's particularism have formed the principal introduction to his place in the political theory of international relations. It was also suggested in chapters 3 and 5 that the methods adopted by Frost and Walzer could be viewed as similar and the purpose of this present chapter is to build upon these suggestions to further explore the outline of the developmental communitarian method and to examine the theory of international relations that can be supported by this approach.

The principal task of this chapter is to flesh out Walzer's demand that under conditions of ethical uncertainty we must rely upon political sensitivity when constructing principles of moral judgment and political action. To this end this chapter is divided into four basic parts. The first section examines the link between developmental communitarianism and universal ethics that can be drawn from Walzer's writings. This essentially expository project forms the backbone of this chapter as it examines my claim that we are best served in viewing Walzer's ethical theory as both developmental and communitarian. The second section examines the basic link between Walzer's 'reiterative' or 'thin' universalism and international relations theory and offers a reinterpretation (in the light of this more recent evidence) of his construction of the 'Legalist Paradigm', his reworking of the concept of *Ius ad Bellum*. The following sections examine the difficulties that arise in attempting to transplant Walzer's (basically sound) ethical theory into the turbulent sphere of international relations (chiefly discussed in terms of aggression and warfare). The third section examines Walzer's insistence on the primacy of the principle of self-determination and his rigid attachment of the doctrine of non-intervention to that principle in his arguments concerning the question of when going to war may or may not be justifiable. The fourth section then examines the problem of the status of ethical principles once such action has been declared legitimate. My reasons for focusing upon these two applied aspects of Walzer's theory are straightforward. In the first instance Walzer demonstrates the real consequences of accepting the fact of pluralism and the requirement that principles of political action be fully justifiable and offers a full response to his cosmopolitan critics. In the second instance Walzer outlines the full (or rather not so full) ethical conclusions that he believes we are obliged to accept. In approaching Walzer's work in this manner I combine a much needed re-examination of the ethical premises of his argument, an account of the application of his thesis and an illustration of the less-than-optimistic conclusions that Walzer believes we must be committed to.

Given that the cosmopolitan premises of international ethics and Frost's conclusions remain largely contestable it is important to show that Walzer's developmental communitarianism relies only upon what O'Neill called 'accessible' predicates while accounting for the observable developments in international ethics. These two possibilities were, it will be recalled, ruled out by O'Neill in her critique of Walzer's method in chapter 4. If Walzer can be shown to construct a viable project, not relying upon idealised or inaccessible premises, and to account for the changing and developing norms of international relations that Frost shows are part of the 'modern state domain of discourse', then his claims to have successfully constructed an international ethics will have been given a solid base. Walzer's reiterative development of a moral minimum, his norm-oriented/communitarian method attempts to account for the development of international relations. His conclusions may not be what the cosmopolitans (or indeed Walzer himself) might wish, but in constructing a philosophically viable ethical theory a preferred outcome cannot form part of the theory.[1]

Developmental communitarianism and universalism

Beginning with Walzer's ethical theory presents two opportunities. Firstly, in the context of this chapter, it supplies at the outset the information that many of Walzer's critics were lacking when they approached his rendering of just war theory in *JUW*. A clear example of this can be found in Beitz's review of this work.[2] Beitz, writing about the lack of metatheoretical analysis in Walzer's early work, makes the following observation.

> 'This is a book of practical morality' Walzer writes, and throughout he abstains from inquiring into 'profound questions of moral philosophy'. This practical focus helps to redress a much-remarked imbalance in contemporary moral philosophy, but, as we shall see, at some cost. It makes a difference to the justification of some of Walzer's conclusions how more profound, and apparently more abstract, philosophical issues are settled; to ignore these issues is to leave the conclusions in doubt.[3]

The critical conclusions of Beitz, indeed of most commentators, owe much to this insight. Central to much of the criticism levelled at Walzer are doubts concerning the basis of claims concerning the moral standing of states and his postulation of universal rights to life and liberty. If he can be seen to construct such claims fairly then these criticisms can be bypassed. Secondly, in the wider context of my general argument, using Walzer's construction of his ethical theory as a way into his work offers the opportunity to continue an analysis of the problem of moral universalism and its political expression. One of my central claims is that the developmental communitarian project offers an important way to overcome theoretical and practical problems in international relations theory and it is therefore vital that Walzer be shown to reach the standards required by this tradition of thought.

There can be little doubt that Walzer should be portrayed as a communitarian. In 'The Communitarian Critique of Liberalism' (and in many other works) he does reject the association but it is a limited rejection, a rejection only of communitarianism's 'current American versions' and he goes on to 'offer a version of my own – less powerful, perhaps than the ones with which I shall begin, but more available for incorporation within liberal (or social democratic) politics'.[4] Walzer's goal, and to some extent the goal of this book, is to transcend this divide or, at the very least, to 'redescribe it in less conventional terms'[5] to make the liberal aspect of developmental communitarianism more accessible.

> Advocates of liberal enlightenment confront advocates of communal tradition; those who aspire to global reach confront those who yearn for local intensity. We all know one another's lines. ... I want to argue from within what I, and many others, have taken to be the opposing camp; I want to take my stand among the universalists and suggest that there is another universalism, a non-standard variety, which encompasses and perhaps even helps to explain the appeal of moral particularism.[6]

This explicit account of the aims of his moral theory is echoed by Walzer in *Thick and Thin*. The ideas in the Tanner lectures and in *Thick and Thin* develop the moral theory implicit in his political theory (both international and domestic) making these two texts absolutely indispensable to an understanding of Walzer's viewpoint. Given that Walzer's just war theory predates the elaboration of his moral theory it may seem methodologically dubious to use his later work as an interpretive tool both in the exegesis of his international relations theory and against his critics. However this chapter progresses on the assumption that these later texts are indeed an elaboration, an extension of ideas inherent in *JUW*, particularly of the idea of universal rights to life and liberty that gave his earlier critics so much ammunition. Any seemingly anachronistic criticism of Walzer's earlier commentators is simply intended to shed some light on a muddied issue. In *JUW*, and in subsequent work[7] Walzer argued that there was one universal, 'thin' morality that was elaborated in various ways in the many 'thick' cultures of the world. However in *Thick and Thin* and 'Nation and Universe' Walzer shows both how this understanding has the equation totally inverted and explains what a communitarian universalism would look like.

> 'There is a thin man inside every fat man,' George Orwell once wrote, just as ... 'there's a statue inside every block of stone.' Similarly, there are the makings of a thin and universalist morality inside every thick and particularist morality – but the story of these two is not at all like the statue and the stone. They are differently formed and differently related, as we shall see.[8]

The language employed by Walzer in the elaboration of his moral philosophy is not uniform. In *Thick and Thin* he describes the two forms of morality as 'minimalist' and 'maximalist', in 'Nation and Universe' he contrasts 'covering-law universalism' with 'reiterative universalism'. But the differences in language are not intended to divorce one set of ideas from the other. Not only is there much that unites these two texts philosophically but the idea of reiteration is also found in *Thick and Thin*. Considering the standard view of moral minimalism Walzer argues that,

> it is everyone's morality because it is no one's in particular; subjective interest and cultural expression have been avoided or cut away. And if we succeed in understanding this morality, we should be able to construct a complete objective and unexpressive code – a kind of moral Esperanto. But this hope is misbegotten, for minimalism is neither objective or unexpressive. It is reiteratively particularist and locally significant, intimately bound up with the maximal moralities created here, here and here, in specific times and places.[9]

The idea of reiteration is extremely important in Walzer's moral theory as it is the vehicle by which we move (albeit temporarily) from particularism to universalism and therefore from a rigid communitarianism to a developmental communitarianism. The two forms of universalism are initially distinguished in terms of Jewish religious history. Covering-law universalism stems from the idea that there is one God and therefore one justice and only one possible salvation, the Jews, knowing this, are therefore instrumental to a universalist end and those other nations who do not accept guidance from the enlightened are simply missing the point of existence.[10] The second form of universalism fits much less comfortably with its place in a monotheistic religion (something Walzer acknowledges) but provides an appropriate contrast. Again the example is taken from Jewish history, more specifically from the prophet Amos, and focuses on the idea that there 'is not one exodus ... one moment of liberation. ... Liberation is a particular experience, repeated for each oppressed people'.[11] The central idea here is that the exodus of the Jews from Egypt is different from the exodus of the Syrians from Kir, or of the Philistines from Caphtor and that all these separate, liberating experiences are equally valuable.[12] The value that is found in all these segregated experiences is somehow intensified as all come to realise the importance of the process of liberation itself as it is reiterated over time and in many different ways. The central difference between the two types of universalism is neatly summed up by Miller who writes that

> 'covering-law universalism' ... affirms the rightness of a particular way of life, and sees one nation as the bearer of that way of life ... 'reiterative-universalism' ... recognises that, subject to certain minimal constraints imposed on all, there are a number of radically different and valuable forms of life which flourish in different places.[13]

Our main focus here is on the content of those 'minimal constraints' and upon their construction. If it can be shown that a communitarian position can lead to the construction of some universal moral code then the cosmopolitan/communitarian debate and constructivist international relations theory would seem to have gained an extra dimension.

The notion of a moral minimum plays a vital role in Walzer's developmental communitarianism. He argues that '[t]he minimal demands we make on one another are, when denied, repeated with passionate insistence. In moral discourse, thinness and intensity go together, whereas with thickness comes qualification, compromise, complexity and disagreement.'[14]

The moral minimum is often expressed in the language of rights or in terms of a covering law such as 'oppression is always wrong'. For example, in Walzer's just war theory he premises any prohibitions on the execution of a war on the rights of individuals, more specifically on their rights to life and liberty.[15] That this can be considered communitarian may seem to be puzzling, the language of rights and individuality is part of the liberal culture that emerged out of the enlightenment. It is, as Walzer notes, a part of the language of our own moral maximalism.[16] Yet this position is not as inconsistent with Walzer's position as it might at first seem because

> [r]eiterative universalism can always be given a covering-law form. ... But these are covering laws of a special sort: first, they are learned from experience, through a historical engagement with otherness ... second, because they are learned in this way they impose upon us a respect for particularity.[17]

The way in which we arrive at the formulation of the universal law is distinctly communitarian. We abstract from the particular to the universal through repeated experience. The 'critical enterprise', as Walzer terms it, of explaining how our moral lives progress from thick to thin may well sound liberal, indeed at the very heart of Walzer's philosophical project is the idea that there is no non-expressivist language, no impartial discourse that does not originate within a maximalist morality, but this is not a necessary feature of that enterprise. Describing this minimalist morality in terms of rights is merely contingent, so Walzer would argue, upon the context of whoever is articulating the description and in any case the language we may use to describe the moral process is assumed to be translatable.[18]

> minimalism when it is expressed as Minimal Morality will be forced into the idiom and orientation of one of the maximal moralities. ... Still we can pick out from among our values and commitments those that make it possible for us to march vicariously with the people in Prague. ... Perhaps the end product of this effort will be a set of standards to which all societies can be held – negative injunctions, most likely, rules against murder, deceit, torture, oppression, and tyranny.[19]

This all sounds very optimistic but Walzer's initial position is not so up beat. He argues that the very thing that allows us to form these minimalist positions necessarily prevents them from developing into maximalist ones. It is here, rather than in the reiterative process of moral constructivism, that Walzer differs with O'Neill who, it will be recalled, claims that his particularism prevents him from accounting for the real connectedness of agents in world politics. O'Neill achieves her abstraction to a transcendental conception of agency by arguing that only a universal recognition of the value of all agents reflects the actual assumptions we make when acting. Walzer, on the other hand, does not believe that all agents make such thick or sustained assumptions; his conclusions are casuistical rather than transcendental. In essence he argues that we do make such assumptions but only in the context of international political crises and that we do not go on to incorporate these assumptions into the moral hierarchy of our everyday lives. There is no reason why this process could not eventually encourage us to do so but, Walzer maintains, it has not happened yet and thus the structure of our present ethical construction must rely upon other premises. The question that remains is simply 'what premises'?

Richard Bellamy explores precisely this question, taking account of Walzer's recent work, in relation to social justice and democracy. The question he poses models the next generation of criticisms that take over from the questions concerning the absence of an ethical theory to question the substance of Walzer's argument. Bellamy writes,

> [q]uite how the 'collective' and uncoerced reflection necessary to generate such moves towards democracy (*one could easily substitute international justice here*) could get going in the absence of certain general preconditions remains something of a mystery.[20]

The question concerns the dynamic of the developmental communitarian method. Following Raz, and taking a similar line to O'Neill, Bellamy argues that the method of intra-practice critique that Walzer employs is either conceptually incoherent; that 'it implies the paradox that the prevailing morality' (which Walzer is obliged to accept as contextually true) 'contains both true and false propositions'; or it is extremely weak consisting 'of pointing out false deductions from accepted premises, uncovering duplicity and the like'.[21] Bellamy continues, arguing that,

> [t]he only ways Walzer can consistently hold to an interpretative morality … is for him to adopt some form of progressive immanent teleology. … Or he has to argue that existing 'thick' moral systems involve far more 'thin' universal elements than he usually wants to admit, but that these are shockingly poorly observed by many of those who claim to profess them.[22]

He concludes that the first of these positions is hopelessly optimistic and the second empirically dubious and ethically vacuous. The first of these strategies is unavailable to Walzer's brand of developmental communitarianism. The second option, which Walzer does, in part at least, defend does appear to form the basis of Walzer's constructivism. Walzer's argument builds out of the experiences we have shared in international politics and can be thought of as an expression of normative development similar to that of Frost's account of the modern state domain of discourse. His conclusions are more reticent than those Frost offers because Walzer remains within the boundaries of constructivist theory. His conviction that we must stay within the justifiable bounds of political theory (and hence his plea that we allow the process of moral development to continue while 'hanging in there') largely accounts for the limited and somewhat pessimistic conclusions he reaches. Bearing Bellamy's point in mind it is important to examine how Walzer believes his position would cash out in international politics in order to see just how 'thin' he believes a developmental communitarianism would have to be.

International politics and reiterative universalism

For Walzer,

> justice seems to be universal in character for the same reason that autonomy and attachment are reiterative – out of recognition of and respect for the human agents who create the moral world and who come, by virtue of that creativity, to have lives and countries of their own.[23]

Here it seems that the foundational assumption concerning human nature in *Spheres of Justice* (*SJ*), that we are all 'culture producing creatures', is still at the base of Walzer's moral philosophy and that his (quasi) communitarianism is in fact supported by a universalist ethic. However, if we take seriously the idea that Walzer remains faithful to the process of reiteration it is clear that we cannot leap from a thin or minimal understanding of the value of autonomy or social freedom to a fully fledged concept of agency as the thin, reiterated concept is non-deterministic. If we take autonomy as an example we find that from Walzer's perspective

> [i]f we value autonomy, we will want individual men and women to have their own lives. But if all lives are radically covered by a single set of covering laws, the idea of 'own-ness' has no scope. … There is no single

> mode of 'having' a life of one's own. ... In any account of autonomy then, there has to be room not only for different self-determinations but also for different types of self possession.[24]

Walzer's construction of principles of international justice rests on a cashing out of the reiterated conception of the value of autonomy that leads to the acknowledged value of self-determination and a particular view of the consequences of not allowing human creativity to flourish. For Walzer:

> It is certainly possible to build an account of justice on the foundation of agency. Start with equal respect for agents (and every man and woman equally an agent), and there is probably no clear stopping point short of a fully elaborated description of a just society. ... Why should we value human agency if we are unwilling to give it any room for manoeuvre and invention.[25]

International justice is not a universalist ethic in the traditional sense. It is a product of a recognition of a multiplicity of claims to justice as a series of family resemblances, a distillation of what it means to have a claim to justice. It is a consensus on a minimalist position that is not sufficient to guide our lives but that recognises each family resemblance for what it is, a glimpse of oneself in a totally separate 'other'. International justice is the product of a developmental communitarianism.

> We stand where we are and learn from our encounters with other people. What we learn is that we have no special standing; the claims that we make they make too. ... But it is a moral act to recognise otherness this way. If reiteration is, as I believe, a true story, then it carries in its telling the sorts of moral limits that are usually said only to come from covering-law universalism.[26]

In this sense international justice, like the articulation of its foundation as supporting culture production, is the product of a consensus, a historically conditioned formulation of a moral minimum that achieves its universality in the here and now. It is forged in a more developed (and continually developing) understanding of the importance of community. Self-determination is its primary value but that value is itself arrived at reiteratively.

To take on Walzer's metaphor from *Thick and Thin* when we march in the name of 'justice' for the rights to life of citizens betrayed by an illegitimate government we are marching in recognition of a 'partial commonality' formed in response to a particular situation. Walzer stresses

> that what is recognised is just this (partial) commonality, not the full moral significance of the other cultures. Most people most of the time do not see the others, in context, as carriers of value; most people are not pluralists.[27]

For Walzer cultural pluralism is a part of liberal maximalism, 'a thickly developed liberal politics', a reiterative universalism relies on something much weaker, on 'overlapping expectations' about the behaviour of others.[28]

Thus far Walzer's construction can be usefully viewed as taking a similar direction to that of Frost. Like Frost, Walzer's views concerning the critical force of a normative approach lead him to insist that the argument for a norm-governed derivation of morality 'is not to suggest that we can do nothing more than describe the judgements and justifications that people put forward. We can analyse these moral claims, seek out their coherence, lay bare the principles they exemplify. ... The proper method of practical morality is casuistical in character.'[29] Casuistical moral reflection is designed to solve problems within a given practice. Walzer must therefore argue that international relations form such a practice and that its demonstrable rules (the product of a dynamic but not fully developed consensus) offer the basis of a critique of international political activity. The breakthrough comes if Walzer can show that the 'universal rights to life and liberty' he places at the heart of global justice are a product of a universally accessible account of international political practice (that is they do not rely upon any restricted form of moral/political reasoning) and that they can provide solutions to widely acknowledged problems in international relations. That the reiterated concepts at the heart of international relations are not central to any or all maximalist moralities does not matter, as these are the principles that are recognised as essential to the *international* sphere.

Essentially Walzer applies this norm-governed morality to international affairs by invoking the just war traditions of *Ius ad Bellum* (the legalist paradigm) and *Ius in Bello* (the war convention). The first step in his exposition of the norms of international relations relies upon 'clear evidence'. 'The clearest evidence for the stability of our rules over time is the lies our statesmen tell. They lie in order to justify themselves, and so they describe for us the lineaments of justice.'[30] His basic position is, of course, more complex than this. For Walzer the beginning of moral enquiry is to embark upon a study of moral discourse, in judgments of conduct and not the conduct itself. Moral reality, for Walzer is 'all those experiences of which moral language is descriptive or within which it is necessarily employed'.[31] For Walzer,

> neither the words nor the actions have any single authoritative source ... the 'judgment of history', as it is called ... [is] the judgment of men and women arguing until a rough consensus is reached. ... International law arises out of a radically decentralized legislative system, cumbrous, unresponsive, and without a parallel legal system to establish the specific details of the legal

> code. … the task of the moral theorist is to study the pattern as a whole, reaching for its deepest reasons.[32]

As a description of the basis of international ethical theory this leads us almost directly to one of the main difficulties with norm-oriented ethical theory in international relations, the problem of identifying the 'deepest reasons' of international consensus. As Walzer and others before him acknowledge, there is no true legal authority through which we can identify these principles. The dangers of non-constructivist reasoning derived from a single maximalist morality are clear. Thus the 'deepest reasons' Walzer seeks must be drawn out of international public political culture. Walzer argues that in the contemporary international system '[r]ights are only enforceable within political communities where they have been collectively recognised. … The globe is not, or is not yet, such an arena. Or rather the only global community is pluralist in character, a community of nations, not of humanity.'[33] Yet for Walzer (as for Frost) the concept of individuality is also central to the minimalist morality created in response to the problems of international relations. These values are not good in themselves. Walzer argues that 'the value of minimalism lies in the encounters it facilitates, of which it is also the product. But these encounters are not – not now, at least – sufficiently sustained to produce a thick morality.'[34] Nevertheless Walzer believes that they both do important work in international politics.

Walzer argues 'aggression is the name we give to the crime of war. We know it is a crime because of our knowledge of the peace it interrupts – not the mere absence of fighting, but a peace with rights, a condition that can exist only in the absence of aggression itself.'[35] The basic argument is this: individuals obtain rights by virtue of their membership of a state. The wrong an aggressor commits is to force people to risk their lives for these rights.[36] It is important that we remember that the use of the language of rights is not a necessary feature of Walzer's plan but it is equally important to note that in the absence of defensible covering-law universalisms the community protects the ways of life that people appear to freely endorse.[37] All states hold the rights of political sovereignty by virtue of their relationship with the citizens that form them and while it is the rights of individuals (specifically, Walzer argues, the rights to life and liberty) that are at the base of judgments we make about war and aggression, we do not assign moral responsibility to private individuals in the international sphere. We judge the collectivities they represent or the communities whose orders they are obliged to obey.[38] We do, however, have a reiteratively universal standpoint to judge them from, a perspective from which a global ethics is a possibility and from where the right of sovereign powers to go to war or to act in certain ways towards their citizens in the name of *raison d'état* is limited. Walzer begins his analysis of international relations with a 'thin' universalist conception of persons because

> these two rights (life and liberty) seem to account for the moral judgments that we most commonly make in time of war. They do real work. … Men

> and women do have rights beyond life and liberty, but these do not follow from our common humanity; they follow from shared conceptions of the social goods; they are local and particular in character.[39]

For Walzer the 'thin' moral sense (as he was later to call it in *Company of Critics*) can only act as a guide to political and social knowledge, in order to apply it in any meaningful way we must look to the plurality of actualisations of this sense, to the communities where this sense is worked out. This idea has a deep philosophical provenance, not just in the works of communitarian writers such as Hegel whose twofold argument for the idea of the state as the principal actor in international affairs (the irrationality of suggesting that private interests are represented and the idea that the state embodies the substantive freedom of its citizens)[40] closely parallels Walzer's argument, but also in the writings of Rousseau, and, for very different reasons, Hobbes. The idea that states are moral agents is by no means unproblematic and some of the criticisms that Walzer's version of this doctrine generates will be considered after his basic position has been explored.

Walzer, in attempting to explain the political process whereby agents build a communal life uses the metaphor of social contract. It is important to note that Walzer's 'contract' much like Rawls' 'original position' (as constructed in *PL* rather than *A Theory of Justice* (*TJ*)) does not place him in the tradition of social contract theory. For both thinkers the contract is used to simplify the exposition of a normative theory. Walzer begins with existent communities just as Rawls relies upon public political culture and the background conditions of society (see below). If Walzer were to rely upon a contract theory he could be accused of artificially vindicating the political community. Starting with existing communities (and assuming for the purposes of my exposition a condition of relative peace) Walzer argues that we have no grounds to assume that any existing community is not the result of human development under conditions of liberty. While

> the process of collectivisation is a complex one … it is best understood, nevertheless, as it has commonly been understood since the seventeenth century, in terms of social contract theory. Hence it is a moral process which justifies some claims to territory and sovereignty and invalidates others.[41]

Through his version of contract theory Walzer updates the just war thesis of *Ius ad Bellum* which takes the form of 'the legalist paradigm'. Using what he terms the 'domestic analogy' he argues that the rights of individuals are represented by (or passed on to) the state and his theory of justice, or the crime of aggression, is formed into six propositions and five revisions.

1 There exists an international society of independent states.
2 International society has a law that establishes the rights of its members – above all the right to territorial integrity and political sovereignty.

3 Any use of force or immanent threat of force by one state against the political sovereignty of another constitutes aggression and is a criminal act.
4 Aggression justifies two kinds of violent response: a war of self-defence and a war of law enforcement by any other member of international society.
5 Nothing but aggression can justify war.
6 Once the aggressor state has been repulsed it can also be punished.[42]

These rules and their revisions are taken to arise historically and reiteratively, a developmental theory similar to that of Rawls and Frost. While they are often criticised for defending the status quo it is more helpful to view these as examples of developmental communitarianism and to examine the role of social criticism in the construction of such a position.

The most elemental of these propositions are the first two. The first is grounded in the historically developed idea that agents are, in international politics, protected and represented only by their own governments and that the governments therefore stand in relation to each other as sovereign powers. This Walzer believes is simply historical fact. This leads to a second and vital idea that is taken to model the 'deepest reasons' of international relations theory that Walzer has been searching for. For Walzer 'although states are founded for the sake of life and liberty, they cannot be challenged in the name of life and liberty by any other states'. Hence the principle of non-intervention (proposition 2). These laws refer only to states but the fundamental rights they protect, argues Walzer, are the rights of men and women to build a life and risk this common life only when they freely choose.

There are a number of potential difficulties with this position, not least the idea that the communal or political lives of agents are 'freely chosen' that underwrites Walzer's principle of self-determination. In order to test the strength of some of the claims that Walzer makes it is useful to examine in more detail the arguments Walzer has to employ in order to defend his construction of the legalist paradigm, more specifically the principle of non-intervention.

The legalist paradigm; the moral basis of non-intervention

In order to introduce this vital issue it is worthwhile returning to the more abstract reasoning that lies at the base of Walzer's position and to focus briefly on the language employed in the first part of this chapter. For Walzer 'we are, if only by default, advocates of non-intervention. But not only by default, for reiterative universalism derives in part from a certain view of what it means to have a history of one's own. So non-intervention can claim a positive foundation.'[43] Indeed Walzer's principal case is that the universal values such as 'independence, inner direction, individualism, self-determination … freedom, autonomy' and the like, those values that cosmopolitan thinkers argue lead necessarily to 'thick', global conceptions of justice, have important particularist implications.[44] Writing specifically on non-intervention in *Thick and Thin* Walzer argues that:

> [n]or can every moral rule that we are able to describe in minimalist terms serve to justify the use of force. We are more likely to be called on to speak up for 'truth' than to fight for it. 'Justice' too is better defended with the moral support of outsiders than with their coercive intervention. We might even say that this preference is a feature of the moral minimum. Nonetheless, there are times when it is morally justified to send armed men and women across a border – and minimalism alone (ultra-minimalism?) defines the time and fixes its limits.[45]

The question of non-intervention and its more positive formulation (self-determination) plays a pivotal role in the construction of Walzer's just war theory yet it is the aspect of his theory most often highlighted as a target for cosmopolitan critics. For Walzer 'The state is presumptively, though by no means always in practice, the arena within which self-determination is worked out and from which, therefore, foreign armies must be excluded.'[46] This statism is compounded, argue Walzer's critics, by the fact that 'domestic tyrants are safe'. Because of Walzer's refusal to acknowledge covering-law universalisms the point of the legalist paradigm is primarily to create independent states rather than liberal or democratic ones.[47] Yet the history of international politics and international relations theory tells us that the state is often the arena in which great injustices are perpetrated. What then are the implications of Walzer's insistence that he cannot allow a challenge to a state in the name of life and liberty?

For Walzer, as I have attempted to show, the established government's claim to sovereignty is based upon a further claim to protect and represent the common life freely chosen by its citizens. In effect the state's legitimacy rests upon consent, a type of social contract where 'contract is a metaphor for a process of association and mutuality, the ongoing character of which the state claims to protect against external encroachment'.[48] While this assumes a degree of cultural homogeneity, Walzer's second amendment to the legalist paradigm allows for intervention where this is obviously not the case and a separate community is attempting to free itself.[49] Walzer continues (following Mill's 'Stern doctrine of self-help') that even if the *de facto* government is incapable or illegitimate the rule of non-intervention is still to be observed because there is a duty of self-determination. This view of the state, argue two of Walzer's critics, leads to patent injustice. This dispute is set amidst 'significant philosophical disputes about the nature of political life'.[50] Doppelt and Luban, Walzer's critics, are arguing from the perspective of globally applicable human rights, Walzer on the other hand is arguing in favour of enforceable, recognised individual rights formed through citizenship. Both Doppelt and Luban argue that Walzer's contract is rather Hobbesian and contains similar problems. For Doppelt,

> even if a group of individuals 'consent' to (that is collectively and voluntarily make) an independent community to which they are loyal, it does not necessarily follow that *any* government which protects this community 'in some degree' deserves the right of sovereignty or defence.[51]

Luban's critique, while similar, is more forceful and shows the conceptual gap between communitarian and cosmopolitan theorists. Initially Luban argues that one of the main problems in assigning rights to states is that the state as the supreme linguistic being (to adapt a Hobbesian concept) may simply adapt these moral rules to be nothing but convenient.[52] While the laws of war are radically incomplete and lack a neutral judge and so lack political authority, moral authority, argues Walzer, is merely the ability to evoke commonly held principles in a persuasive manner.[53] While this argument is closely linked to the second point (the pervasiveness of relativism in international relations which I will discuss below) it does seem that Walzer has to sacrifice some authority to his highest principle – pluralism. Abstract or universal moralism in the international sphere tends to define the internal aspect of states as well as making them regulate their external relations which, on Walzer's view, leads to more invasions of individual liberty than the diluted relativism of international affairs. Indeed Walzer, among others, makes a strong case for the argument that there is a connection between pluralism and individual liberty as the alternative is a universal state with no political alternatives.[54] This argument is developed with much more force in *Thick and Thin* and 'Nation and Universe' as Walzer comes to develop what Frost would call his 'background justification'. Moral minimalism does not entail self-determination as a foundational assumption but the conception of reiterative universalism generates an understanding of the value of self-determination. Self-determination is not a covering law but stems from what Walzer sees as the 'values and virtues of human creativity'.[55] With the additional information offered in these later texts, it is possible to read Walzer's seemingly foundationalist assertion that humans are culture producing creatures in a different light. To constrain cultural or human creativity via covering laws is to move away from procedural reiteration and towards forced imitation, towards the imposition of an alien maximalist morality.[56] It is to violate the rules of philosophical constructivism and to derive (and enforce) international ethics from inaccessible premises. For Walzer the constructed community and the constructed morality have real importance and it is perhaps better to let him answer his critics in his own words.

> There is a general principle that we can think of as the expression of moral minimalism in international politics. The principle is 'self-determination'. We will most readily understand it as a claim for democratic rights, and so it is in our time and place. But the principle has been reiterated in many different times and places, always in some local idiom and with a set of maximalist accompaniments. 'Self-determination' is abstracted from all of

> its reiterations ... what is at stake ... is the value of a historical or cultural or religious community and the political liberty of its members.[57]

Luban's second and more incisive point is that Walzer has actually failed to make a case for grounding moral agency in state sovereignty. For Luban,

> wars are not fought by states, but by men and women. There is therefore a conceptual lacuna in such a definition. It can be bridged only by explaining how a crime against a state is also a crime against its citizens, that is by relating men and women to their states in a morally cogent fashion. This I take it is what the concept of legitimacy is supposed to do. A legitimate state has a right against aggression because people have a right to their legitimate state.[58]

The crux of Luban's argument is that Walzer's contract is of the Lockean, horizontal variety, where individuals contract with each other rather than the Hobbesian, vertical variety where individuals contract with the state. Thus argues Luban, Walzer has succeeded only in grounding the rights of nations and not of states, of individuals and not (as he claims) of sovereign powers.

Walzer's initial response is that Luban and Doppelt would license more interventions on the basis of defending human rights than reason would allow. Their case, Walzer argues, is too permissive. More fundamental to Walzer's case however is his theory of community. Walzer's initial response to Luban is that the horizontal contract he envisages does not fail to ground the rights of states: 'Against foreigners, individuals have a right to a state of their own. Against state officials, they have a right to political and civil liberty. Without the first of these rights the second is meaningless: as individuals need a home so rights require a location.'[59]

The moral agency of a state for Walzer has two foundations. The first is its relationship with its citizens and this is an internal and domestic matter only. Like Rousseau, Walzer reconciles individual freedom with political community. Through his arguments in *Obligations* and 'The Moral Standing of States' ('MSS'), Walzer argues that, in a very real sense, individual liberties, goods and moralities are heightened through objectification in a political community where their meanings are constructed and shared. Indeed central to Walzer's argument in *SJ* is the idea that

> actual men and women ... claim justice, and resist tyranny, by insisting on the meaning of social goods among themselves. Justice is rooted in the distinct understandings of places, honors, jobs, things of all sorts, that constitute a shared way of life. To override those sorts of understandings is (always) to act unjustly.[60]

As Nardin points out, Walzer does not advance an irrefutable claim for the validity of his principles but it can accommodate the fact of pluralism. The exclusive context for real rights, Walzer argues, is real life.[61]

There is however a second stage in the development of this argument. For Walzer '[T]he international standing of governments derives only indirectly from their own citizens. The derivation is complex because it is mediated by foreigners and because foreigners are not confronted (as citizens are) by a naked government but by a state.'[62] The argument here is, in Walzer's work, simply stated but we must not confuse simplicity with philosophical shallowness. Walzer argues that for most of the time foreigners are in no position to deny the reality of the union between citizens and their state and that this means that we should respect the doctrine of non-intervention, basing our judgments on 'presumptive legitimacy' unless the rules of disregard are enforceable.[63] One question that arises here is in what sense are wars fought (as Luban contends) between men and women and not states? Certainly not in their private capacity but in their collective capacity, as citizens obligated to their state. Again this assertion is taken as an endorsement of the status quo by many cosmopolitan writers, including Beitz who takes a poor view of what he terms Walzer's 'communal integrity thesis' but this is primarily because he did not have access to Walzer's background theory.[64] On this interpretation of Walzer as a developmental communitarian a 'state' with certain claims to sovereignty and self-determination is what foreigners see in international relations, a 'nation' is, by virtue of the social contract (to use Walzer's metaphor) the arena within which autonomy is developed in the multitude of ways consistent with that concept (see above) and embodied in the maximalist morality of that society.

> The nation is by no means the most important of the collectivities within which moral ideas and ways of life have been elaborated. ... Even with reference to self-determination, the national entity, itself differently constituted and understood in different historical periods, could as easily be replaced by the clan or the tribe or the city-state or the community of faith.[65]

Thus the question 'what is so important about the nation-state?' relates to the legalist paradigm and principles of non-intervention as they are here and now (according to our present minimalist positions) and not to the moral standing of the nation in domestic mode. The freedom to fight or the freedom to rebel does not transfer easily to foreigners.[66] Thus, the Hobbesian argument Doppelt saw in Walzer's work, the idea that any stable state is legitimate, is in fact directed to a very different audience – to those outside the state not those within it.[67] An interesting way of examining the distinction between Luban's cosmopolitanism and Walzer's communitarianism is to look a little more closely at the debate over intervention. Walzer's 'rules of disregard' that indicate those times when the absence of fit between the government and the people is radically apparent is termed 'the politics of as if'.[68] On the basis of this model international politics is based upon what Walzer terms 'presumptive legitimacy' unless extreme forms of oppression indicate this absence of fit. The purpose of this model is, Walzer argues, to rule out intervention in cases of 'ordinary oppression'. While this phrase is not particularly pleasing, Walzer's point, provided the reader is at least committed to a modicum of plurality, is realistic.

> By democratic standards, most states throughout human history have been oppressive (and illegitimate), but those are not necessarily or usually the standards by which they are judged among their own people. On the other hand, we can always assume that murder, slavery, and mass expulsion are condemned, at least by their victims.[69]

This position, argues Luban, is just another symptom of Walzer's fixation with the 'Romance of the nation-state'. We are not, he argues, ignorant of the internal affairs of a state, there are 'experts, experienced travellers, expatriates, scholars, and spies'.[70] Radical abuses of what Luban calls 'socially basic human rights' can be disguised so that 'the government fits the people the way the sole of a boot fits a human face' and still Walzer would not sanction intervention and so, Luban argues, we should disregard his rules and act upon 'ordinary oppression'. R.J. Vincent, also a human rights theorist, is deeply critical of the 'rashness of Walzer's attachment of the principle of non-intervention to that of self-determination'.[71] He argues that Walzer accepts a conservative, Burkeian, notion of self-determination and 'virtual representation' that 'comes not from moral satisfaction with the society of states ... but from the fact that righteous intervention will be received as imperialism'. A reply to these criticisms, on behalf of Walzer, should make two points. The first, building on Vincent's criticisms, would note that the latter of those criticisms is, in fact a complement, the status quo is not considered the best form of international affairs and moral imperialism is indeed a major issue. The positions occupied by the cosmopolitans are indeed 'noble' but only in the sense in which Walzer uses the description in 'Nation and Universe'.

> Machiavelli suggests a class basis for such understandings: 'If we consider the objects of nobles and of the people, we must see that the first have a great desire to dominate, while the latter have only the wish not to be dominated'. ... Conceivably, there are 'noble' and 'plebian' nations, the first always a threat, the second always threatened.[72]

The second point would focus on the notion of 'presumptive legitimacy' and would note that while it is a vital concept here it has a very important flip-side. Understanding morality as reiteratively minimalist does lead to a notion of presumptive legitimacy but it also leads, occasionally, to presumptive intervention, that is, intervention based on a morality derived from a consensus and not simply one's own maximalist position.

> But minimalism makes for (some) presumptive occasions. ... We will use force, for example, to stop a person committing suicide, without knowing in advance who he is or where it comes from. Perhaps he has reasons ...

> confirmed by his maximal morality, endorsed by his moral community. *Even so 'life' is a reiterative value and defending it is an act of solidarity*. And if we give up the forcible defence out of respect for his reasons, we might still criticize the moral culture that provides those reasons.[73]

Presumptive legitimacy is a concept that derives directly from an understanding of the importance of self-determination. Presumptive intervention also stems from the notion of self-determination when this value is reflected upon in the light of international interaction.

There are many areas of difference between thinkers such as Doppelt and Luban, and Walzer, however the most important rests on a misunderstanding of the communitarian position. Both Luban and Doppelt argue that Walzer in defending his just war theory through an appeal to individual liberties *must* recognise that he has set a limit to pluralism. As Doppelt notes:

> The moral exceptions to the rights of national autonomy allowed by Walzer, in particular, intervention in cases of official murder, expulsion or enslavement are intelligible only if we assume that some human rights are more basic to international morality than Walzer's foundational rights.[74]

In this Walzer's critics are falling prey to a misunderstanding of one of the basic distinctions of Walzer's developmental communitarianism. Walzer argues that his reluctance to abandon his particularist position does not preclude 'serious or radical social criticism', indeed the most obvious form of criticism is the internal or 'immanent' critique: 'We often criticize friends and colleagues for not living up to a set of standards that we and they profess to honour. We measure them against their own pretended ideals; we charge them with hypocrisy or bad faith.'[75] While this form of social criticism is an internal venture, historically contextualised understandings of the moral minimum are also subject to criticism and elaboration and those states that profess this minimal code yet act differently are equally subject to the charge of hypocrisy and bad faith and the difficulties it will bring them in international interactions.

Walzer's ontology does not blind him to human suffering, what it does, however, is to make him wary of permissive principles that would justify wars in the cause of social justice or democracy, wars that would establish rights, rather than defend them. There must, argues Walzer, be more than the opposition of philosophers to raise an army.[76] Walzer's critics argue for a singular right, Walzer, on the other hand argues for pluralism based on presumptive legitimacy. There is an international minimum standard through which the relationship between citizens and their states may be judged based on the rights of individual liberty and aside from appeals to a 'common humanity'; it is unclear that abandoning the principle of non-intervention would further their cause. Through the process of reiteration and social criticism concepts such as individuality and rights become important to us, more important (given the circumstances in which they arise) than many aspects of our maximalist moralities. For example, the redistribution of economic gain in a society is important to us as welfare liberals but in the international context there may be more pressing issues, issues that we *can* form a consensus on, rather than the more disputed issue of economic right. In an earlier exposition of his moral theory Walzer argued that

> we might best think of them not as discovered or invented but rather as emergent prohibitions, the work of many years, of trial and error, of failed, partial and insecure understandings – rather as David Hume suggests with regard to the ban on theft (for the sake of the 'stability of possession') which 'arises gradually, and acquires force by slow progression and by our repeated experience of the inconvenience of violating it'.[77]

These rules are constructed (possibly unconsciously) from within our social context and while they may be framed as 'covering laws' they are historically conditioned and certainly not sufficient to mould a maximalist account of international ethics. The rights to life and liberty are, however, based on a commonly held perception (or a family of perceptions) of what it means to be a human being. Nations (domestically) and states (in the international sphere) are products of moral and political reasoning and producers of moral and political reason, the fount of our understandings of the moral reality of international politics. In an uncharacteristically optimistic moment Walzer outlines the full range and derivation of his international theory and it is worth quoting him at some length here.

> These two arguments – first for what might be called the moral usefulness of the (nation-) state and the solidarity it generates, and second for the possible legitimacy of the citizenship/ethnicity or citizenship/culture connection – do not commit those who accept them to resign themselves to the 'drastic inequalities' of international society. They only require that the fight against those inequalities begin within existing political communities and that it aim at the progressive expansion, but not the abolition, of existing solidarities. … They embody … the admission of refugees to full citizenship; increased foreign aid, economic unification, and cooperation across borders; multilateral political, and if necessary, military interventions for humanitarian purposes; extensions of sovereignty to stateless persons; experiments in regional devolution and transnational agency. And the motive for all this can only be the hope of ordinary people in their diverse national, religious, and political communities for their own survival and well being, and for that of their neighbours, under conditions of peace and justice.[78]

Walzer's method does not have the capacity to demand these reforms in world politics but he is suggesting that these actions are already considered a part of the necessary framework for international survival and well-being. His reiterative universalism is intended to describe the basic reasons that can be given for this recognition. Walzer's claim is that non-constructivist or covering-law theories do not have the theoretical grounds to demand any more and cannot account for the way in which international relations have developed to this point. To employ a covering-law explanation of world politics would be to deny the right to self-determination, deny the plurality of maximalist moralities, without justification.

Nevertheless it is clear from the history of world politics that optimism is not enough to prevent the dissolution of peaceable relations and the advent of irresolvable conflict. The concern many critics have with Walzer's theory is that the concern for communal autonomy will ultimately conflict with a concern for human rights and that in such a conflict Walzer is obliged to retreat to a more realist version of the morality of states argument. This objection is a sound one and is best explored not in relation to the legalist paradigm but in relation to the war convention, the rules of *Ius in Bello*, where we already assume that two political communities are engaged in armed conflict. To begin here is to really test the relative strength of the rights of sovereignty against the universal rights to life and liberty.

The war convention: the moral responsibility of states

As Brown argues,

> the 'war convention' is the modern code governing *jus in bello*. In one respect at least the notion of a war convention is less controversial than the legalist paradigm: whereas the latter involves the difficult task of determining guilt and innocence on the part of the states on the basis of general principles that are always difficult to apply, the war convention applies to all participants in a war – irrespective of the issue of just cause – and its content is embodied, albeit imperfectly in international treaties and conventions.[79]

However many ambiguities remain, how can we tell what restraints are moral? How can we tell whether a state will (or indeed should) make a moral rather than a prudential decision? When states are already countenancing the killing of human beings how can we tell at what stage their orders become unjust? The answers to questions of this sort are, of course, always essentially contestable; they rest on assumptions that are far from unambiguous. While Walzer does not escape these difficulties he does, by virtue of his acceptance of conventions that are (for the most part) already accepted, avoid most of the difficulties concerning the acceptance of rules by sovereign states. In this section, as in the last, I am primarily concerned with normative issues rather than the intricacies of practical ethics. The principal area I will explore is the question of the character and possibility of rules of warfare in a sphere often thought of in terms of 'the mutual infliction of evils'.[80] The international society described by Walzer is best thought of in Hegelian terms. 'The relationship between states is a relationship between independent units which make mutual stipulations but at the same time stand above these stipulations.'[81] This description focuses on two interrelated issues that normative discussions of the war convention must focus upon. The first issue focuses on the formation of a common morality and the second on the obligations of independent states to follow the rules of warfare and the issue of relativism. For Nardin, as for Walzer,

> the basic premise underlying the idea of just conduct in warfare is the same as that underlying the idea of international society itself. … Underlying the historical, cultural and circumstantial diversity of warfare is the core notion that military conduct, like all conduct, falls under the jurisdiction of moral and legal constraints as well as considerable agreement concerning the content of those restraints.[82]

The war convention refers to laws, principles and codes of conduct that have, through history, emerged to govern the act of war. The relativism that many cosmopolitan thinkers see in communitarian accounts of international relations has, Walzer argues, been radically over-exaggerated. For Walzer, the war convention rests on the equality of combatants and, more crucially, on a view of non-combatants, which holds that they are men and women with rights that cannot be used for any military purpose (even a legitimate one).[83] The normative question that this raises rests on what Walzer calls 'the sliding scale of utilitarianism' or the relationship between *Ius ad Bellum* and *Ius in Bello*, and on the issues, cultivated by Walzer's developmental communitarianism, concerning the possibility of constructing and enforcing these moral laws.

The war convention is concerned with the protection of individuals as opposed to states, a seemingly contradictory position given that the legalist paradigm claims to protect the rights of communities. However to assume this is to misunderstand both the relationship between *Ius in Bello* and *Ius ad Bellum*, and the foundational principles of Walzerian and much communitarian morality. As I attempted to show (above) Walzer in *JUW*, *SJ*, *Interpretation and Social Criticism* and more specifically in, *Thick and Thin* and 'Nation and Universe', posits 'a kind of minimum and universal moral code'.[84] In *SJ* this rests upon the fact that we are all equal by virtue of the fact that we are culture producing creatures,[85] in *JUW*, this is articulated as the rights to life and liberty. While social meaning is often not apparent and is subject to interpretation (one of the main reasons why there must be a radically apparent 'lack of fit' between citizens and the state to license intervention), the point Walzer makes is that paying attention to particularity (the area in which these rights are actualised or exercised) does not lead to a denial of the possibility of social criticism. Indeed if a society is not allowing the process of 'culture production' then we are justified in intervening.[86]

In terms of the constraints that Walzer's developmental communitarianism can place on the conduct of war it can be argued that his position checks both the particularist egoism of the nation-state and the 'forced imitation' threatened by the cosmopolitan positions. The charge that Walzer is in fact supporting the nationalist tendencies of the *status quo* in international relations is met head on as he argues 'I want to argue now that the theory of reiterative universalism provides the best account of nationalism in general and the most adequate constraint on its various immoralities.'[87] To make his point Walzer contrasts his position with the covering law universalists arguing that '[t]he advantage of the reiterative mode is that is recognizes the value of what it admonishes'.[88] The reiterative mode values self-determination and therefore, to a certain extent pluralism, but it must be a reasonable pluralism (to borrow a phrase from Rawls). Provided those nationalisms are legitimate in the eyes of their own people and provided the attitude they adopt towards other nations is one of mutual accommodation[89] then international society will be peaceful. What is required by the moral minimum is 'an international consensus that validates a variety of choices, supporting any political arrangement that satisfies the tribes at risk'.[90] The moral minimum therefore dictates that in time of war individuals, particularly non-combatants, still retain rights and, Walzer argues, a warring state that violates these rights is acting unjustly.

One problem that is generated by Walzer's community centred position is that a just war is one that is morally urgent to win as critical values are at stake[91] and so, run the arguments of realists such as Morgenthau and some universalist liberals, the more just our cause, the more right we have to violate certain commonly held rules. Not so argues Walzer. Walzer's main problem is that in many commentaries on international law the tensions between necessity and morality are resolved into an oversimplified opposition. He is wary of the 'sliding scale of utilitarianism' writing that,

> on this view, the rules have no standing in any war that is worth fighting. They are at most 'rules of thumb', general precepts of honour (or utility) to be observed only until observing them comes into conflict with the requirements of victory. But this is to misunderstand the war convention.[92]

Similarly he is aware that the absolutist stance, 'do justice even if the heavens fall', is not really a plausible doctrine. As Nardin notes, to defend an absolute morality as a guide to action in extreme situations appears to make one's position rendered untenable by its own rigidity.[93] Walzer's alternative position is what he terms 'the utilitarianism of extremity', do justice unless the heavens are (really) about to fall. The difficulties with a position of this kind are many. Firstly, as Nagel notes, absolutist ethics 'are often the only barrier before the abyss of utilitarian apologetics for large scale murder'.[94] The idea that a state at war, regardless of the justice of its cause, may when it perceives a threat to its continued existence do whatever is necessary to prevent its eradication does seem rather permissive. For Nardin, Walzer's insistence that it is sufficient to argue that the consequences of a violation of the rules of war are good for the state in whose interest the rules are broken is nothing but a variant of the doctrine of *raison d'état*.[95] In one sense Nardin is correct and Walzer is caught somewhere between the criticisms of realism, in another sense Nardin is wrong but Walzer falls fouls of the criticisms of utopianism, an idea summed up, I believe, by Walzer as he attempts to limit the realm of necessity.

> Utilitarian calculation can force us to violate the rules of war only when we are face to face not merely with defeat but with a defeat likely to bring disaster to a political community. But these calculations have no similar effects when what is at stake is only the speed or the scope of victory.[96]

Political leaders, argues Walzer, have to make utilitarian judgments, it is the ethic of responsibility. However in a desperate bid to avoid the pessimistic conclusions of the realists Walzer attempts to formulate a position through which such statesmen are not relieved of moral blame. The dishonouring of Arthur (bomber) Harris is a colourful example. Harris, although under orders, coordinated and carried out the terror bombing raids throughout the second world war, these bombings (though morally indefensible in themselves) are taken as an example of what Walzer calls the dirty hands problem. The failure of Churchill and the British people to honour Harris after the war was over is taken as a form of national atonement: 'the refusal to honour Harris at least went some small distance to re-establishing a commitment to the rules of war and the rights they protect. And that, I think, is the deepest meaning of all assignments of responsibility'.[97] I do not think that this example truly strikes the chord that Walzer was searching for. As Rengger notes 'if we are not to end adopting effectively realist assumptions, whatever we add by way of pious language, international society must be able to create at least some obligations that are binding on us whatever our self interest'.[98]

Walzer, when pressed on this issue seems to substitute moral *sensitivity* for moral responsibility. In *The Company of Critics* Walzer sets his position out further.

> Liberty, justice, democracy, domination, oppression, exploitation, cruelty, violence, terror, mass murder, totalitarian rule – this is the language of politics in the twentieth century, a time of large hopes, high risk, desperate efforts, fearful culminations. Who can doubt that this language is better employed by a person of moral sensitivity without a theory than by a morally obtuse person with the grandest possible theory? In any case, the sensitive critic, still tied to his fellows can 'hang in there', though he may be hurt while he is hanging in; moral sensitivity is the armour of survival.[99]

Walzer's principal task is social criticism, a laudable beginning, but I cannot help but hear the echoes of Rousseau's 'politics of despair'. In a short article on political method Walzer contrasts his position with realism, arguing that, for the realist, decision making comes down to maximising values beyond rational dispute such as that of national security and argues that the difference between his position and the realists is to be found in the fact that he assumes that there is a moral that is acknowledged even when we fail to live up to it.[100] This, however, is the most pessimistic reading of Walzer's project. The relationship between moral sensitivity and moral responsibility is more dialectical than this. Walzer's biggest problem, I believe, is not in the argument for the existence of the war convention (war after all is usually fought with an end in mind (either recognition or reparation of some kind) and therefore tends to be fought so as to preserve the possibility of peace) but in not working out fully claims to its efficacy within a communitarian position.

Walzer's imagery in *Thick and Thin* is similar to the idea of 'hanging in there'. While we may march vicariously for 'truth' and 'justice' alongside those in Prague we always return to our own parades. We do not move from a thin notion of international justice to a notion of cultural pluralism. We cannot infer a notion of complex equality from the understanding of procedural equality enshrined in the notion of mutual respect. Walzer argues that,

> we can give thin accounts of accommodation and adaptability, and sometimes it is politically useful to do that, arguing for a social or personal version of a minimalist liberalism. But such arguments will only take us so far; they can't reach to the reality of our private or our collective lives.[101]

However the principal advantages of a developmental communitarian account of the normative construction of principles of international justice is that agents do not have to be committed to a thick universalist and cosmopolitan ethic in order to conduct international affairs. One of the principal criticisms of Walzer's position, put forward by thinkers such as Doppelt and Beitz (above), is that the only way in which Walzer's international theory can be effective is if there is a more basic and universal position underlying his communitarianism. Yet even the most idealistic cosmopolitan must realise that an international agreement between states with opposing ideologies or religious doctrines upon principles that regulate the conflict between them is not the same as an agreement on 'thick' moral principles that ground full political cooperation. The distinction in Rawls' theory between *modus vivendi* and overlapping consensus is a more fully developed articulation of this contrast and the next chapter will lay out its full potential. The notion of 'development' that the cosmopolitans search for in Walzer's work is understated because Walzer believes it is impossible to argue that constant reminders of the usefulness of cooperation in international affairs would lead to the progressive homogenisation of international society. However the possibility of a more stable consensus on international law and morality is not necessarily ruled out by a developmental communitarian position.

If, as Walzer does, we wish to emphasise the moral role of the community in realising and representing individual rights we must, during times of crisis, recognise that *raison d'état* is going to transcend individual rights. However the concern of Walzer's critics (and it seems of Walzer himself) that his developmental communitarianism can guide action in times of 'ordinary oppression' or conflict but cannot promote peace in times of 'extreme oppression' or ultimate emergency rests on an unnecessary total identification of the principles of the legalist paradigm with the principles of the war convention. The developmental communitarianism that underpins the legalist paradigm is the norm-oriented and constructivist procedure that can identify the basic principles of international ethics. The norms of the war convention are built on top of this. They are adhered to because there is a consensus on their value. In *JUW*, Walzer argues that we have learned the value of the war convention. Yet if the international community were once again threatened by Nazism (Walzer's own example)[102] the principles underlying self-determination would surely outweigh the war convention. However, the majority of international conflict does not take this form and when self-determination is not threatened then the principles of the war convention preserve the minimum standard of cooperative relations. To be sure judging when an international conflict is 'ordinary' or 'extreme' will be difficult but it seems to be an important distinction. In later works Walzer, in similar style to Frost and Rawls, suggests that the political consensus has become much fuller but not to the point of altering the prime value of self-determination. The passage taken from Walzer's 'Response to Veit Bader' and cited above really indicates the extent of this transition but as Walzer does not fill in the process of development under conditions of ordinary international relations himself I propose to show how the work of Rawls develops the idea of a developmental communitarian consensus.

What Walzer offers us through his developmental communitarianism is a position from which to survey the carnage of international history and a language to discuss the issues arising from it with a view to finding a more productive position. He argues that 'if principles determine decisions, decisions in turn modify and refine principles: This is the way that both law and morality change over time. And in this process, it is not only authoritative decisions that count [but the judgments of all citizens]'.[103]

Here then we see the historical context for the formulation of shared meanings both within a concrete community and within a developing international society. Walzer is not offering a blueprint for immediate development but attempting to show the manner in which his casuistical theory can influence (perhaps should influence) the possibility of a future peace. The importance of casuistry lies in the fact that it is a reflective process for everyone. His method indicates how the 'deepest reasons' of a fair and just construction of principles of international ethics should be viewed. This theory is consistent with the tensions between the norms of sovereignty and the norms of human rights that emerge out of a slowly developing system of international interdependence and while Walzer believes this process to be at a delicate stage it seems more realistic to ask that we 'hang in there' rather than over-reach this just development by leaping to covering law or cosmopolitan conclusions. Perhaps Hoffmann, who calls Walzer's project 'a pious hope', is the more utopian in searching immediately for a 'praxis ante et contra bellum'.[104]

Conclusion: ethical uncertainty and political sensitivity

The claim that Walzer substitutes political sensitivity for ethical uncertainty does seem to capture the spirit of his enterprise. We must remain uncertain about the validity of covering-law universalism and thus guard against the construction and imposition of principles of ethics on inaccessible grounds. It is Walzer's emphasis on this point that makes his theory appear tenable where O'Neill's cosmopolitanism and Frost's secular Hegelianism show flaws. Walzer's moral minimum provides us with the ethical substance of the claim that political sensitivity is necessary and shows the basic product of a developmental communitarianism that remains within the framework of its constructivism. In doing so Walzer's theory overcomes the problems that were seen to remain in the theories of O'Neill and Frost. In opposition to O'Neill's cosmopolitanism Walzer continues the project outlined in Frost's constitutive theory. Walzer's entire approach to international relations theory begins from the position that it is not possible to construct an account of agency that is both accessible *and* still able to adhere to the three cardinal principles of cosmopolitanism outlined in chapters 2 and 4. While O'Neill did not explicitly adopt a liberal-individualist account of agency, indeed she referred to her account of agency as 'banal' and undemanding, it was shown that her cosmopolitan conclusions relied upon the assumption that the contemporary circumstances of justice required such a conception of agency. This position was not derived (as O'Neill claimed) from the structure of moral reasoning itself but from contentious claims concerning the extent of interconnectedness in world politics and the incomplete argument that only a cosmopolitan account of morality was workable under such circumstances. Frost's counterclaim, one that Walzer agrees with, is that there is not enough evidence to support such a claim and that in order to ensure that international justice is accessible to all relevant others we must start our construction elsewhere. For Walzer the emerging 'thin moral sense' that is supported by the evidence in international politics does not license O'Neill's abstraction to an individualist conception of agency and therefore her cosmopolitanism, that is in turn supported by this abstract account of agency, has to be rejected or modified to take account of a viable or accessible construction of the international community. Perhaps Walzer's strongest case against O'Neill's cosmopolitanism stems from the fact that he does construct a genuinely developmental account of international ethics from a communitarian position, something that O'Neill is convinced is impossible. For Walzer, as international society recognises the emergence of shared dilemmas in international politics it is possible to construct a more substantial theory of international justice. Deciding in advance what the most urgent problems are or what the most appropriate theory of justice is simply leads to charges of partiality. Frost, it will be recalled, also began from this position but argued that it is still possible to construct a valid account of individual agency. His method contained a similar methodological approach to constructivism as that of Walzer but it was shown that his claim that international relations could ground a liberal conception of individuality similar to the cosmopolitan account over-reached that method. The conclusions drawn by Frost and O'Neill both extended far beyond that licensed by constructivist liberal theory. Walzer in adopting a similar approach to Frost ensures that the predicates to his theory are tested against the criterion of accessibility or constructivist reasoning. The developmental communitarian method shared by these two thinkers ensures that their theory of international justice relies only upon sustainable evidence derived from an observable consensus of actors in international politics. No other starting point is possible. However, in taking seriously the restrictions on the construction of principles of international justice imposed by such a method, Walzer argues that it is at present impossible to construct a viable cosmopolitanism. His conclusions are a more accurate portrayal of the type of principles that can be supported by a secular liberalism. Because one cannot be sure that the political arrangements of liberalism can be justly universalised (indeed because there is a lot of evidence to the contrary) principles of international politics and ethics must defer to a fully vindicable understanding of the shared principles of the international community. When Frost's conclusions are stripped of their unvindicated predicates it must look more like Walzer's reconstructed version of just war theory. The norms that are emerging in international politics concerning human rights and a developing account of sovereignty do have positive implications and while such 'reiterative universals' may in time be reiterated and developed to become fully incorporated into international politics any attempt to force this development along cosmopolitan lines risks the charge of hijacking the process of development without cause. Until there is a universally shared, fully worked out, conception of human rights then international politics must operate upon principles accessible to all legitimate actors. This is the consequence of having to rely only on principles that can be generated by secular liberalism that many cosmopolitan theorists are reluctant to accept.

However, there is a little more scope for the development of international politics within the tradition of developmental communitarianism than Walzer allows. Walzer does not really complete the arguments necessary to show precisely what form political sensitivity does or could take or how far international institutions or norms can extend beyond boundaries under peaceful conditions. His concern with ethical problems in extreme circumstances rather leads him away from this point. His method conforms to the requirements of constructivism and accounts for the two principal norms that are characteristic of international politics, the norms of sovereignty and human rights. Nevertheless Walzer's reticence in elaborating the way in which the developmental communitarianism he employs accounts for the 'ordinary' international political consensus and his focus upon the failings of ethics under drastic circumstances does leave certain important aspects of the tradition unexplored. I do not believe that Walzer's temporary minimalism demonstrates the full reach of developmental communitarianism. In turning to examine the work of my final example of developmental and communitarian constructivism it will become clear that developmental communitarianism can offer a more complete account of international relations than Walzer envisages while remaining within the constructivist limits that Frost transcends.

Notes and references

1 Cf. O'Neill's critique of the universalisability of instrumental reasoning outlined in chapter 4.
2 C. Beitz, 'Bounded Morality: Justice and the State in World Politics', *International Organization*, Vol. 33, No. 3, Summer 1979, pp. 405–424.
3 Beitz, 'Bounded Morality', p. 410.
4 M. Walzer, 'The Communitarian Critique of Liberalism', *Political Theory*, Vol. 18, No. 1, February 1990, p. 7.
5 M. Walzer, 'Nation and Universe', *The Tanner Lectures on Human Values XI 1989*, G. Peterson (ed.), University of Utah Press, 1990, p. 509.
6 Walzer, 'Nation and Universe', p. 509.
7 E.g. Walzer, *Interpretation and Social Criticism*, Harvard University Press, 1987.
8 Walzer, *Thick and Thin: Moral Arguments at Home and Abroad*, Notre Dame, Indianapolis and London, University of Notre Dame Press, 1994, p. xi.
9 E.g. Walzer, *Thick and Thin*, p. 7.
10 Walzer, 'Nation and Universe', p. 510.
11 Walzer, 'Nation and Universe', p. 513.
12 Walzer is a little reluctant to allow the that the idea of equality follows from the idea of reiteration ('Nation and Universe', p. 514.). Nevertheless it would seem that if we express reiteratively universalist laws as covering laws a notion of equality must apply (see below).
13 Miller, *On Nationality*, Oxford, Clarendon Press, 1995, p. 10. The word 'nation' in this quotation could (probably should) be replaced with tradition as Walzer notes that the territorial element of community is contingent rather than necessary to the understanding of a tradition of ethics.
14 Walzer, *Thick and Thin*, p. 6.
15 E.g. Walzer, *JUW*, p. 54, see my discussion of *JUW*, below.
16 Walzer, *Thick and Thin*, p. 10.
17 Walzer, 'Nation and Universe', p. 515.
18 Walzer, *Thick and Thin*, p. 10.
19 Walzer, *Thick and Thin*, p. 10.
20 R. Bellamy, 'Justice in the Community: Walzer on Pluralism, Equality and Democracy', in D. Boucher and P. Kelly (eds), *Perspectives on Social Justice*, Routledge, 1998, p. 176.
21 Bellamy, 'Justice in the Community', p. 177.
22 Bellamy, 'Justice in the Community', p. 178.
23 Walzer, 'Nation and Universe', p. 522.
24 Walzer, 'Nation and Universe', pp. 519–520.
25 Walzer, 'Nation and Universe', pp. 522–523.
26 Walzer, 'Nation and Universe', p. 527.
27 Walzer, *Thick and Thin*, p. 17.
28 Ibid.
29 Walzer, *JUW*, pp. xxix–xxx.
30 Walzer, *JUW*, pp. 13–19
31 Walzer, *JUW*, p. 15
32 Walzer, *JUW*, pp. 44–45.
33 Walzer, 'The Moral Standing of States: A Response to Four Critics', in *Philosophy and Public Affairs*, Vol. 9, No. 18, 1980, p. 222 ('MSS').
34 Walzer, *Thick and Thin*, pp. 18–19.
35 Walzer, *JUW*, p. 51
36 Walzer, *JUW*, p. 58
37 See the discussion of self-determination in the third section for an examination of when we are free to intervene in the case of a 'lack of fit' between citizens and state'.

38 Cf. Walzer, *JUW*, p. 54
39 Walzer, *SJ*, p. xv.
40 On the first point see for example, Hegel, *Early Theological Writings*, trans. T.M. Knox, Chicago, 1948, pp. 164–165. On the second point see for example Hegel, *Elements of the Philosophy of Right*, Wood (ed.), trans. H.B. Nisbet, Cambridge University Press, 1991, §270 addition.
41 Walzer, *JUW*, p. 54
42 For the legalist paradigm see Walzer, *JUW*, pp. 61–62.
43 Walzer, 'Nation and Universe', p. 515.
44 Walzer, 'Nation and Universe', p. 518.
45 Walzer, *Thick and Thin*, p. 16.
46 Walzer, 'MSS', p. 210
47 Cf. G. Doppelt, 'Walzer's Theory of Morality in International Relations', *Philosophy and Public Affairs*, Vol. 8, No. 1, 1978, pp. 3–26 and D. Luban, 'Just War and Human Rights', in *Philosophy and Public Affairs*, Vols 8 and 9, 1980. See also Walzer, *JUW*, p. 94.
48 Walzer, *JUW*, p. 54
49 Walzer, *JUW*, p. 90.
50 Walzer, 'MSS', p. 4
51 Doppelt, 'Walzer's Theory of Morality', p. 16.
52 Luban, 'Just War and Human Rights', p. 160.
53 Walzer, *JUW*, p. 287.
54 Walzer, 'MSS' p228. Cf. T. Nardin, *Law, Morality and the Relations Between States*, Princeton, Princeton University Press, 1983, p. 237.
55 Walzer, 'Nation and Universe', p. 518.
56 See Walzer, 'Nation and Universe', pp. 519–520. See also the discussion of autonomy above.
57 Walzer, *Thick and Thin*, pp. 67–68.
58 Luban, 'Just War and Human Rights', p. 165.
59 Walzer, 'MSS', p. 288.
60 *SJ*, p. 314.
61 See also the discussion of autonomy above.
62 Walzer, 'MSS', p. 212.
63 Walzer, 'MSS', pp. 212–216. The rules of disregard (cf. Walzer, *JUW*, pp. 89–108) entail a radical lack of fit between community and government. The idea of presumptive legitimacy is developed in *Thick and Thin* (see below)
64 C. Beitz, 'Nonintervention and Communal Integrity', *Philosophy and Public Affairs*, Vol. 9, No. 4, 1980, p. 305.
65 Walzer, 'Nation and Universe', p. 536. NB: It could not, however, be replaced by 'world', the experience of otherness is vital.
66 Walzer, 'MSS', p. 214. Hegel offers a similar argument in his work on international convention and law.
67 Walzer, 'MSS', p. 215.
68 Walzer, 'MSS' pp. 212–218
69 Walzer, 'MSS', p. 218.
70 Luban, 'The Romance of the Nation-State', *Philosophy and Public Affairs*, Vol. 9, No. 4, 1980.
71 R.J. Vincent, *Human Rights and International Relations*, Cambridge University Press, 1986, p. 116.
72 Walzer, *Nation and Universe*, p. 537.
73 Walzer, *Thick and Thin*, p. 16. Emphasis added.
74 Doppelt, 'Statism without Foundations', *Philosophy and Public Affairs*, Vol. 9, No. 4, 1980.
75 Walzer, *Thick and Thin*, p. 42.

76 Walzer, 'MSS', p. 228.
77 Walzer, *Interpretation and Social Criticism*, pp. 24–25.
78 M. Walzer, 'Response to Veit Bader', *Political Theory*, Vol. 23, No. 2, 1995, p. 249. Here Walzer is responding to Bader's demand for large-scale economic redistribution and open borders.
79 Brown, *International Relations Theory*, p. 139.
80 Hegel, *Elements of The Philosophy of Right*, §339.
81 Hegel, *Elements of the Philosophy of Right*, §330 addition.
82 Nardin, *Law, Morality and the Relations Between States*, p. 228
83 Walzer, *JUW*, p. 137. The idea of equality presupposed here is a 'thin' conception of the equal right of states to self determination. There is no suggestion that each state must value the internal position of the other on an equal level to its own, see 'Nation and Universe', p. 514.
84 Walzer, *Interpretation and social criticism*, p. 24, cited S. Mulhall and A. Swift, *Liberals and Communitarians*, Oxford, Blackwell, 1992, p. 144.
85 *SJ*, p. 314.
86 Cf. Mulhall and Swift, *Liberals and Communitarians*, p. 145.
87 Walzer, 'Nation and Universe', p. 547.
88 Walzer, 'Nation and Universe', p. 554.
89 Cf. 'Nation and Universe', p. 554 and *Thick and Thin*, p. 80.
90 Walzer, *Thick and Thin*, p. 81.
91 Walzer, *JUW*, p. 110
92 Walzer, *JUW*, pp. 227–228.
93 Nardin, *Law, Morality and the Relations between States*, p. 295.
94 Nagel, *War and Massacre*, p. 56, cited Brown, *International Relations Theory*, p. 142.
95 Nardin, *Law, Morality and the Relations between States*, p. 302.
96 Walzer, *JUW*, p. 268.
97 Walzer, *JUW*, p. 325.
98 N. Rengger, 'A City which Sustains all Things: Communitarianism and International Society', *Millennium*, Vol. 21, No. 3, 1992, p. 365.
99 Walzer, *The Company of Critics: Social Criticism and Political Commitment in the Twentieth Century*, Peter Halibran, 1989, p. 229.
100 Walzer, 'Political Decision Making and Political Education', in Richter (ed.), *Political Theory and Political Education*, Princeton University Press, 1980.
101 Walzer, *Thick and Thin*, p. 101.
102 Walzer, *JUW*, p. 253.
103 Walzer, 'Political Decision Making', p. 170, brackets mine.
104 S. Hoffmann, *Duties Beyond Borders: On the Limits and Possibilities of Ethical International Relations*, Syracuse University Press, 1981, p. 82.

7 John Rawls, developmental communitarianism and international ethics

Rawls' place within the structure of the present argument has been prefaced throughout this work. Rather than offer another introductory passage here I wish to state boldly the role Rawls' theory plays in my construction of a developmental communitarian tradition and to pull together some of the most important arguments that I have already made in relation to Rawls' *political* liberalism.

The idea of a constructivist and developmental communitarian approach to questions of international political theory has been developed in opposition to cosmopolitanism (in its traditional and constructivist forms) and through an exegesis of the method of Frost and Walzer. The communitarian or norm-oriented approach taken by Walzer and Frost allows them to meet the requirements of constructivist theory, something, I have argued, that the cosmopolitan liberals cannot do. I have also argued that meeting the requirements of constructivist theory is an essential aspect of a claim to have legitimately produced or described principles of international ethics. While the method of Frost and Walzer was seen to be both legitimate and useful there are still problems with their characterisation of international justice. These problems stemmed, I have suggested, not from their methodological approach to the problem (a difficulty which affects all other theories which rely upon inadmissible or inaccessible premises) but with their cashing out of their approach. Frost's constitutive theory, developed as a background justification for the shared norms of international relations, does appear to offer an accessible account of the current developments in international politics but it cannot support some of the conclusions that Frost draws. Frost's conclusions appear to overreach the developmental communitarian method. Walzer's moral minimum, on the other hand, appears to understate the potential of developmental communitarianism. In focusing upon the functioning of principles of international morality under extreme conditions he leaves much of the potential of such an approach unexplored. The work of Rawls overcomes both of these difficulties. In this chapter I will further develop my claim that Rawls successfully constructs principles of international justice along developmental communitarian lines and show how such a construction facilitates the dual development of the two key concepts of international politics; the principle of equal respect for the self-determination of peoples (enshrined in a developing understanding of the principle of sovereignty) and the principles of human rights.

Essentially this chapter examines Rawls' extension of his political theory into the field of international ethics, a task that he assumed in the Amnesty Lecture 'The Law of Peoples' ('LOP'), briefly continued in a short article in *Dissent* entitled '50 years after Hiroshima' and extended in a recent book also entitled *The Law of Peoples.*[1] My exegesis of these essays is closely tied in to an examination of Rawls' more detailed exploration of his theory in *PL*. This approach is instructive in two primary ways. Firstly it offers a chance to examine one of the principal claims of Rawls' critics who maintain that in his construction of international ethics Rawls illegitimately takes ideas suited only to a political construction of principles of justice by and for members of a liberal society and simply transplants them on to international society. This claim will be shown to be absolutely false and its refutation shores up my assertion that Rawls must be viewed as outlining a developmental communitarian position. Many cosmopolitans claim that no liberal theory of international justice can derive from non-cosmopolitan reasoning. Indeed it was this claim that O'Neill was shown to rely upon in order to make her case that only cosmopolitan international theory is suited to the present circumstances of justice. In showing that Rawls' developmental communitarianism can produce principles of justice suited to the current situation in world politics and that it does so using truly accessible arguments – something cosmopolitanism fails to do – my case concerning the viability of this revised liberalism is strengthened. Once again, the term communitarian is used to stress the distinction between the constructivist method of Rawls and the tradition of liberal cosmopolitanism in international relations theory. This distinction is, I believe, vital as for too long debates concerning the extension of liberal ideas into international politics have focused on how the realities of the world can be moulded to cohere with a liberal point of view. For Rawls, liberalism in international politics is not a starting premise but a conclusion, the background justification of which must be drawn from potential consensus by the existent plurality of political communities. In seeking to recover Rawls' meaning from the claims of his critics I believe we should take very seriously indeed his claim to have constructed principles of international justice that necessarily fall short of the Kantian principles he associated his early work with.[2] Secondly, in linking an exposition of 'LOP' to the appropriate arguments of *PL* it is possible to flesh out Rawls' position on international political theory. In this chapter I achieve this by examining the consensual mechanism that plays such an important part in the construction of justice as fairness in *PL* and applying the idea of 'constitutional consensus' to 'LOP'. The more general claim that follows from reading Rawls' work in this manner is simply this: liberalism does have important implications for international politics but unless that liberalism is constructed along developmental communitarian lines it is in danger of being theoretically unjustifiable and of producing unjust and politically dangerous principles and policies.

Thus far in my argument the work of Rawls has been introduced in two ways.

In chapters 2 and 4 I introduced the idea that Rawls' liberalism cannot be read as part of the cosmopolitan tradition. While Schwarzenbach's 'Rawls, Hegel and Communitarianism'[3] makes a strong case suggesting that Rawls' work resembles what Brown or Frost call a 'secular' or 'demythologised' Hegelianism and Paden follows Barry's acknowledgement of Rawls' shifting perspective towards communitarianism[4] it is more usual to see Rawls' principal commentators refer to his work as a weak liberal-cosmopolitan. The examples I gave in chapter 2 centred on the work of Beitz and Pogge[5] and in chapter 4 on O'Neill's critical examination of Rawls' idealised theory.[6] Much of the small but emerging literature on Rawls' international relations theory argues that Rawls is not liberal enough to be counted as cosmopolitan. To take this route is, I will argue, simply to miss the point of Rawls' constructivism. The second way in which I introduced the role Rawls' theory plays in this argument was my suggestion in chapters 3, 5 and 6 that Rawls' approach to international relations theory is similar to those of Frost and Walzer. In this final stage of my argument all that is required to show that Rawls does indeed construct a theory along developmental communitarian lines and that such a construction can be usefully related to the ideas of Frost and Walzer is a full and systematic exegesis of his position.

John Rawls and the extension of political liberalism

The attempts of liberals to redefine their philosophical roots without the justification of Kantian or Hegelian metaphysics calls into focus questions concerning the scope of liberal ethics. If O'Neill's recent *Towards Justice and Virtue* represents the Kantian/cosmopolitan attempt to delimit the scope of liberalism in the modern age, Rawls' *Political Liberalism*, I argue, represents the liberal-communitarian position.[7] The attempted extension of liberal ideas of justice into the international realm should highlight the consequences of the secularisation of liberalism and Rawls, I believe, is more successful here. Yet despite the claim that Rawls' recognition of the political limits engendered by secular liberalism places him in the communitarian camp, I also claim that *'political'* liberalism can play a vital role in world politics. Rawls' theory is designed to show that the revised constructivist procedure that he developed in *PL* is, contrary to the view of O'Neill and many other liberal cosmopolitans, able to provide a genuinely accessible liberalism for modern world politics. As Rawls commenting on his own project argues:

> In the absence of this extension to the law of peoples, a liberal conception of political justice would appear to be historicist and to apply only to societies whose political institutions and culture are liberal. In making the case for justice as fairness, and for similar more general liberal conceptions it is essential to show that this is not so.[8]

When coming to Rawls' international theory (particularly for the first time) there is an important point to note here. Rawls is not attempting to construct a general theory of international justice (one that aims to be universal in the cosmopolitan sense). Rather, Rawls is attempting to show what liberals should be committed to in world politics and thereafter to show what needs to be done to make such principles universalisable in the sense that they could be the object of consensus for a more heterogeneous group of agents. The point is that liberals should acknowledge that the principles they adopt among themselves to regulate domestic politics would not be the same principles that they would adopt in international politics. Still less would they be the principles that one could reasonably expect the peoples of the world to adopt. There are two reasons for noting this here. Firstly, this fact speaks volumes about the method that Rawls adopts. We begin from what we know about liberal society and *then*, as Rawls puts it, 'extend the what are ordinarily thought of as the limits of practical possibility' (see below). Secondly, unless we grasp from the outset that Rawls is speaking to liberals, in an attempt to show what they must concede in international relations if they are to view themselves as just, it is very easy to misunderstand the text.

In order to facilitate a complete exposition of Rawls' international relations theory I wish to introduce and defend the three following claims.

1 That Rawls' law of peoples begins from developmental communitarian premises and that a recognition of this has important implications for any interpretation of his international relations theory.
2 That the developmental communitarianism articulated by Rawls has goals consistent with many liberal-internationalist aspirations and that these goals are only limited by the just limits of political interaction, and, most importantly,
3 That Rawls' account of the law of peoples makes use of a dynamic conception of political consensus capable, over time, of linking liberal and non-liberal accounts of human rights. This form of consensus is adapted from the idea of a *constitutional* consensus in *PL* and expedites a full understanding of 'LOP'.

To explain further: *PL* was written to address 'a serious problem' that Rawls found in *TJ* namely the

> unrealistic idea of a well ordered society as it appears in *Theory*. An essential feature of justice as fairness is that all its citizens endorse this conception on the basis of what I now call a comprehensive philosophical doctrine. … Now the serious problem is this. A modern democratic society is characterised not simply by a pluralism of comprehensive religious, philosophical and moral doctrines but by a pluralism of incompatible yet reasonable comprehensive doctrines.[9]

The dominating idea of *PL* is that justice as fairness is a 'political conception' of justice, that is a conception of justice that all citizens can affirm regardless of their reasonable moral, philosophical or religious beliefs: a conception of justice that is constructed out of political ideas that all parties can affirm and not founded upon inaccessible metaphysical claims. This is said to offer a vision of politics as freestanding[10] and a sensitive and interpretative understanding of this point informs the analysis of 'LOP' given in this chapter. In order to focus on the problems involved in not seeing Rawls as a communitarian thinker in this context, I will look briefly at the criticisms of Jones and Pogge who both specifically attack what Jones terms Rawls' 'parsimonious conception of human rights'[11] and at the work of Moellendorf who attempts a more cosmopolitan construction of the law of peoples.[12] At stake here, I shall argue, is a conflict concerning what it means to be liberal in the modern age. Rawls' developmental communitarianism, grounded in his political conception of justice and the changes this forces to his discussion of the ideas of stability and consensus, does have significant importance for the extension of his theory to the international sphere.[13] Secondly I want to show that despite this communitarian starting point Rawls, like Walzer and Frost, can extend a significant theory of justice into the international sphere, a claim met with substantial scepticism by those less sympathetic to the claims of communitarian liberalism.[14] Finally I want to suggest that there is a thick and thin (or liberal and minimal) account of Rawls' international relations theory. The 'thick' idea of the law of peoples is presented as formed out of a fully overlapping consensus on points of international justice arising out of an affirmation of the value of reasonable pluralism. The 'thin' idea of global justice is said to be based on a single component of this idea, a working consensus on traditional ideas of the equality of states. There are two points that follow from this interpretation. Firstly it is only the minimal conception of international justice that can be said to have legitimate purchase on international politics in the here and now. Cosmopolitan attempts to introduce aspects of the liberal consensus into international politics overstep the limits of constructivism. However the potential of the developmental communitarian position becomes clearer as it becomes apparent that Rawls can offer a conception of human rights and international law as a dynamic *constitutional* consensus that is capable, over time, of linking fairly both liberal and non-liberal accounts of world politics.

Rawls' communitarianism: the background conditions of international society

As I noted in chapter 4 in response to O'Neill's claims concerning the premises of Rawls' argument, there is, at the most basic level in Rawlsian constructivism, an important division between the Kantian and communitarian elements of his thought. For example, the regulative role of what Rawls calls Kant's theory of 'constitutive autonomy' (the comprehensively liberal attachment of value to a 'thick' conception of individual agency) is abandoned in favour of the political value of a shared public life.[15] In separating his constructivism from Kant's 'deeper' and comprehensive approach Rawls notes that 'the full significance of a constructivist political conception lies in its connection with the fact of reasonable pluralism'.[16] A recognition of the importance of this 'fact' means that the in-built universalism of constitutive autonomy is replaced by 'doctrinal', 'political' or 'reasonable' autonomy; a thin conception of practical reason that is allied to a normative framework that gives full weight to the autonomy of 'appropriate conceptions of society and the person'.[17] Here the stress should be on the word appropriate. The significance of this theoretical development has been largely overlooked primarily, I think, because its importance is obscured in Rawls' construction of principles of justice appropriate to a liberal democratic citizenry in *PL*. The principal idea here is that a constructivist theory may not include a notion of agency as a predicate to its thesis unless that notion of agency is found in the public political culture (or background conditions) of the political arena that is being examined. In *PL* Rawls focuses on the principles that fellow citizens within a liberal democracy would feel justified in proposing and abiding by. He thus feels vindicated in using a normatively derived notion of agency that conceives of individual persons as free and equal citizens (that is as being normal, cooperative members of society over a complete life) with a capacity for a sense of justice and a capacity for a conception of the good.[18] Persons are then described as 'reasonable and rational' and any difference between agents beyond this conception is described as reasonable pluralism. This, as can be seen, is a fairly full conception of agency and thus the move from constitutive autonomy to doctrinal autonomy (from a metaphysical liberalism to a political liberalism) does not appear to do much work. Because the phrase 'reasonable pluralism' rather than simple pluralism reappears in every extension of Rawls' theory beyond the closed society of *PL*, many commentators assume that Rawls is employing the same criterion of what it means to be reasonable. Analytically this may be the case but, as I pointed out in response to O'Neill's critique of Rawls, the substance of the idea of the reasonable has radically changed because the normative domain that the theory must draw on is radically different. The significance of this fact, this norm-oriented method of constructing an appropriate conception of agency, must not be overlooked. This move towards a particularist stance is indicative of Rawls' move towards a broadly communitarian position.[19] Rawls, in developing a philosophy of international relations based on his domestic political theory, acknowledges the force of the empirical claims of the cosmopolitan thinkers (that international society is moving away from a purely state orientated system)[20] and attempts to account for the practical and philosophical shifts that have placed (or are placing) the issue of human rights firmly on the political agenda. Essentially Rawls does this by arguing that even though (or perhaps because) international society is characterised by a plurality of reasonable yet incompatible social systems (what he terms the 'fact' of reasonable pluralism), human rights, or a version of that doctrine can, and should, be supported by any legitimate state. For Rawls the background conditions (in *PL* of a liberal society, in 'LOP' of international society) are central to the construction of any principles of justice. In Rawls' international relations theory it is the background conditions of world politics that limit the cosmopolitan practice of methodological abstraction and oblige us to focus on the claims of peoples and their governments rather than a liberal conception of the person.[21] The communitarian focus on international society (rather than a cosmopolitan focus on individual agency) leads thinkers such as O'Neill to argue that their work has no ethical or political potential. If, however, Rawls can be shown to derive an effective theory from such premises without illegitimately substituting liberal ideas developed by and for citizens of a liberal democracy (as was the case in *PL*) for those found in, and accessible to, international society, then the central claim of my argument is sustainable. The best place to begin an exposition of Rawls' international relations theory is therefore with his conception of the background conditions of that political arena.

In applying the limited 'political' principles of the new Rawls to international political theory it is important to note that Rawls' international relations theory rests not so much on a shared public political culture as a shared history of international law.[22] In the international arena the traditional principles of international law *plus* the 'dramatic shift' in international law since the second world war grounds the conception of the agent.[23] This 'dramatic shift' informs a wide ranging acknowledgement of some shared problems in contemporary world politics and the vital role of international law in solving such problems. Essentially then the political culture of the international sphere is weaker, specifying an agent (the people themselves as politically organised)[24] with the capacity to participate in a reasonable law of peoples, a capacity to rationally pursue its domestic good and that recognises certain historically developed constraints on its sovereignty (the most important here being a right to war only in self defence and a duty to protect a certain minimum version of human rights).[25] Rather than supporting an idea of international society as a fair system of cooperation for reciprocity or mutual advantage (the background conditions of liberal society that Jones, among others, believes apply[26]) I think this supports a conception of international society as a fair system of cooperation for peaceful coexistence.[27] This position seems more defensible than that which characterises international society as a fair system of cooperation for reciprocity.[28] It is important as it removes from the conception of international society that sense of homogeneity and social cohesion that provides the normative and motivational support needed for the difference principle (along with other egalitarian concerns) to be effective (something that Rawls argues cannot be expected in IR)[29] while retaining the notion that real international society is unlike the popular characterisation of the Hobbesian international state of nature.

This acknowledgement of the more fragile conditions of international as opposed to domestic society does not restrict Rawls' aspirations to international justice unduly. Indeed, Rawls argues that the fact of reasonable pluralism licenses the question 'where are the reasonable limits of toleration to be drawn'[30] on this understanding of international society. In itself this question raises many concerns about the foundational status of liberal values in Rawls' theory. Toleration is undoubtedly a value associated with metaphysical liberalism. Yet Rawls is careful to show that the idea of toleration in use here is a political idea rather than a value associated with liberal foundationalism. Perhaps the most significant of the ideas that informs Rawls' view of the international sphere and certainly the one that necessitates the transformation from *TJ* to *PL* is the fact of reasonable pluralism. For Rawls:

> The fact of reasonable pluralism is not an unfortunate condition of human life, as we might say of pluralism as such, allowing for doctrines that are not only irrational but mad and aggressive. In framing a political conception of justice so it can gain an overlapping consensus, we are not bending it to existing unreason, but to the fact of reasonable pluralism, itself the outcome of the free exercise of human reason under conditions of liberty.[31]

In this passage, and throughout his work, Rawls is not, as many critics suggest, advocating a conception of justice that simply applies the liberal principle of toleration.[32] Justice, it might be argued, can more easily be based on a liberal principle of toleration when it is worked out to apply to a liberal culture yet in extending his theory to non-liberal societies Rawls shows that notions of cultural diversity and sovereign freedom should be limited by a developing understanding of the benefit of political values that do not conflict with other religious or philosophical values. The central idea is that of political neutrality rather than a 'thick' conception of toleration. Some commentators pursuing this line of thought argue that this distinction is not secure. Pogge, for example, argues that at the second level of extension the idea of 'political' neutrality falters when it comes across states that do not value toleration as highly as a liberal democracy would.[33] However in this case Rawls begins by making a case for toleration based on a notion of the international equality of states that hold a common good sense of justice[34] and in doing so creates a minimal set of criteria capable of setting out the basics of a political conception of justice while retaining the possibility of future development. Essentially Rawls' case for a political conception of international justice is that any state capable of international cooperation or even of peaceful coexistence would be capable of affirming this conception of justice even if initially they did not do so for the right reasons.[35] Both Pogge and Jones criticise Rawls' use of the idea of toleration. They argue that Rawls, in 'tolerating too much',[36] threatens both the foundation of human rights and his own liberalism. Yet for Rawls this 'toleration' is simply the consequence of what it must mean to be liberal in the modern age. Rawls' vision of the 'here and now' and the 'political' grounding of liberalism means that ideas of what it is to enjoy political stability and of what we recognise as 'reasonable' must be weakened, that ways of life that are not specifically liberal must be given equal weighting in *international* politics. These recognitions, found predominantly in Rawls' use of the idea of 'constitutional consensus', do not curtail his liberalism, they are a bold statement of the necessary limits and the possibilities of politics in the 'here and now'.

The premises of Rawls' international relations theory thus derive from a norm-governed constructivism. The background conditions of international society are laid out to reveal a political society of peoples who recognise the benefits of international law in relation to the advancement of their own ends. Rawls then goes on to construct the tools we can legitimately use to describe the processes of international politics, to create the background justification through which we can critically assess the justice or injustice of certain international actions. That is, Rawls constructs the legitimate structure and content of the law of peoples to show how we arrived at our present understandings and what tools we have used and may legitimately continue to use to advance international politics. It is to this aspect of his theory that I turn now.

The extension to liberal societies

The first stage in Rawls' ideal theory is the attempt to construct a 'thick' law of peoples for a society of liberal states. Rawls' use of two constructions in 'LOP' has caused concern in some quarters primarily because it seems a little odd that we should need to have a social contract for liberal peoples followed by a social contract between all peoples. However Rawls' imagery here is meant to be illustrative of a normative theory rather than a social contract theory. The original position simply allows the reader to see legitimate reasoning in action. As Paden notes:

> by making two parallel arguments, he hopes to defuse what he anticipates will be a major criticism of his approach. Given that his method and the principles of international justice it generates will be generally similar to the liberal method and principles that he discussed in *A Theory of Justice*, Rawls is concerned to avoid the appearance of imposing liberal Western values on societies that may subscribe to a variety of non-liberal comprehensive doctrines.[37]

It is useful to follow Rawls in this endeavour and to begin with a brief look at his construction of the law of peoples for well-ordered liberal societies as it does precisely this job. For Rawls the idea implicit in the emerging political culture of international society is that societies capable of international cooperation *are already* contributing to, *and will continue to develop* a workable system of, human rights. The focus, like that of Walzer's moral minimum, is that international cooperation rests on domestic legitimacy.

The basic principles of the law of peoples that have evolved historically as a *modus vivendi* are unsurprisingly traditional. The seven-point law of peoples reads as follows:

1. Peoples (as organised by their governments) are free and independent, and their freedom and independence is to be respected by other peoples.
2. Peoples are equal and parties to their own agreements.
3. Peoples have the right of self defence but no right to war.
4. Peoples are to observe a duty of non-intervention.

5 Peoples are to observe treaties and undertakings.
6 Peoples are to observe certain specified restrictions on the conduct of war (assumed to be in self-defence).
7 Peoples are to honor human rights.[38]

This list is relatively uncontroversial; it describes the prevailing *status quo* much as Frost's list of settled norms or Walzer's legalist paradigm can be seen to do. The importance of the developmental communitarian approach lies in the way this list is arrived at and how our traditional understandings of these concepts alter as we come to accept the validity of the background justification that these thinkers construct for these norms. Many of Rawls' critics argue that the seven-point law of peoples is unduly conservative.[39] One particularly clear example of how a misunderstanding of Rawls' constructivist method leads to unsound criticisms of this kind is to be found in Moellendorf's addition to the law of peoples.

In his article on 'LOP' Moellendorf argues that Rawls' account of the law of peoples is *ad hoc* and that a true construction of the principles would include two further principles. These are

8 Peoples are to honor the principles of liberal democracy, and
9 Peoples are to honor principles of egalitarian distributive justice.[40]

Moellendorf's conclusions here rest on two major, inter-related misunderstandings of Rawls' position which can profitably be explored before I go on to offer a developmental communitarian reading of 'LOP'. The first misunderstanding stems from Moellendorf's failure to grasp that Rawls is offering a normative construction. Moellendorf argues that:

> Rawls's account appears internally *ad hoc* insofar as it permits piercing the shell of sovereignty in order to defend human rights, but not in order to defend liberal democracy or egalitarianism. He seems to have neglected Kant's advice not to advance a political morality that is tailored to the concerns of statesmen … the goal of political morality is not to establish principles that leaders are likely to accept, but ones which they ought to accept, that is ones to which citizens might hold them accountable.[41]

Here Moellendorf is assuming that human rights arise in opposition to sovereignty, a position that has been critically explored throughout my argument. He is also assuming that one can construct a universal conception of human rights that is intrinsically bound up with liberal egalitarianism, another position that has been critically examined throughout this book. Indeed Moellendorf goes on to suggest that unless the international original position models the interests of persons rather than peoples, Rawls has no grounds for including point 7 in his theory at all.[42] In this he singularly fails to note that Rawls' method (which models the appropriate limits of constructivist theory) requires a reinterpretation of the justification of the principles of sovereignty and human rights. In part this misunderstanding stems from the second of Moellendorf's interpretations of 'LOP'. Moellendorf appears to argue that the first image of the original position that Rawls outlines (international agreement between liberal states) has a legitimate priority over the second extension of Rawls' procedure. That liberals have grounds for rejecting the completed procedure simply because the traditional liberal conception of the relationship between citizen and state is not represented.[43] The argument that a specific world view has grounds for rejecting principles of international justice because its moral viewpoint is not fully represented is clearly unstable. Neither Rawls nor any other constructivist can privilege an inaccessible (and thus non-universalisable) moral position in their construction of international ethics.[44] To return to the language adopted in response to O'Neill's position in chapter 4, the only conception of the relevantly similar political agent available to constructivist theorists of international politics is an accessible one. The claim that we have the normative or theoretical grounds to abstract to a conception of international political agency that includes a 'liberal' conception of the relationship between citizen and state pushes, and breaks, the bounds of credibility. Therefore, as Paden notes,

> although Rawls does construct two different original positions to bring out these points (concerning the fairness of situating liberal and non-liberal equally) he argues that, in the end, nothing of substance depends on the fact that he uses two such constructions. Instead he holds that the principles selected in his two stage account would also be selected by an original position in which delegates from both kinds of well-ordered society would be present.[45]

All peoples must be able to agree upon the political principles they are supposed to share and the two-step construction of international justice can usefully be thought of as showing what a comprehensively liberal conception of human rights (the dominant historical tradition) must give up if it is to claim to be just in international politics. What would vindicate Moellendorf's contention (which he maintains is constructivist) that a liberal understanding of the relationship between citizen and state be universalised? The burden of the present argument has been (in part) to show that all three of the arguments offered by Moellendorf fail to meet the necessary requirements of constructivist political theory. Essentially Moellendorf's position stems from his belief that the requirement that all well-ordered societies respect human rights entails the 'proto-liberalisation' of all well-ordered societies.[46] Nothing could be further from Rawls' theory.

The key to Rawls' project in 'LOP' lies in a developmental communitarian understanding of point 7, that 'peoples are to honor human rights'.[47] The empirical claim that since the second world war human rights have been on the agenda of international relations theory is supplemented by a justification of their prominence as for Rawls the existence of cosmopolitan human rights discourse is unstable in the sense that it lacks the normative justification appropriate to the international sphere.[48] The idea of justification that Rawls applies to international relations theory is modelled on that found in *PL* IV and Rawls completes his sketch of the first original position for well-ordered liberal societies by arguing for two further conditions that lend normative and practical stability to his project. The first of these two conditions is that the international order should be stable in the right way, that it should be more than practical so that,

> given the existence of a political society of such peoples, its members will tend increasingly over time to accept its principles and judgements as they come to understand the ideas of justice expressed in the law among them.[49]

The second condition is that the law of peoples should ideally be the object of an overlapping consensus. That is, that the parties to the law of peoples should

> be able to say that the doctrine of the law of peoples for such societies, more than any other doctrine, ties together our considered political convictions and moral judgements at all levels of generality, from the most general to the more particular, into one coherent view.[50]

The conditions of stability and consensus represent the philosophical justification of the seven-point law of peoples that Rawls argues is consistent with both liberal and non-liberal perspectives. Yet elements of international law that are controversial in character (human rights for example) are likely to receive whatever justification they get from a variety of incompatible philosophical or doctrinal sources. It is here that Rawls' notion of a developing consensus plays its most important role.

Human rights, in the first extension of Rawls' theory of justice, represent a 'thick' conception of rights founded on specifically liberal ideas. They signify that each person is 'assigned a certain status, the status of members of some human society who possess rights as human persons'.[51] Yet human rights in the fully extended law of peoples represent a 'minimum standard of well-ordered political institutions for all peoples who belong, as members in good standing, to a just political society of peoples'.[52]

Rawls is acutely aware that much of international society does not hold a western individualist conception of the person and therefore assigns rights differently, and that this fact alters his discussion of stability and consensus. In extending his theory to non-liberal states Rawls has to create a conception of human and international right that can appeal both to liberal and what he terms hierarchical societies without relying too heavily on one tradition or becoming superficial in a universal form. If Rawls can be seen to complete this argument without abandoning his constructivist principles then my three central claims are sustainable.

The extension to hierarchical societies

Still working in ideal theory Rawls aims to extend his theory of international justice to non-liberal, but *well-ordered*, societies.[53] These well-ordered hierarchies have to satisfy three basic requirements.

1 They must be peaceful
2 Their system of law must a) impose moral duties and obligations on all persons within its territory and b) be guided by a common good sense of justice. These aspects will establish a state's legitimacy in the eyes of its own people.
3 They must respect basic human rights.

To continue a defence of my second claim. A society that supports the three requirements of well-orderedness will be what Rawls calls a consultation hierarchy and will give its people the rights to life, liberty and property in some way as well as a measure of formal equality.[54] These are necessary conditions of membership in good standing of a society of states. It models, Rawls maintains, the rational and reasonable nature of these societies without using a liberal conception of the person that may be unacceptable to these peoples.

The key question here is whether Rawls' principles are necessary to a state's legitimacy in the eyes of its own people or just for it to achieve membership in good standing of a society of states and, if we argue in terms of the last, how such a distinction is reached. Legitimate domestic arrangements can take many forms some of which may not appeal to our liberal conception of legitimacy. Recalling Walzer's plausible observation,

> by democratic standards, most states throughout human history have been oppressive and illegitimate, but those are not necessarily or even usually the standards by which they are judged by their own people.[55]

Rawls, in attempting to keep this in mind, has identified a three-tier system. In the first instance there are those societies, which in achieving the recognition that they not only accept the seven principles of the law of peoples but do so for the right reasons, attain membership in good standing of a society of states (an extra form of legitimacy). This legitimacy is gained via a recognition of a kind of transnational political and ethical affinity that breeds stability of the right kind. Secondly there are those states who may adopt the seven principles of the law of peoples as a developing *modus vivendi* and whose domestic organisation, while legitimate in the eyes of its own people, is not as accessible to the other members of international society and so does not promote this kind of stability. They nevertheless enjoy what Walzer calls presumptive legitimacy and thus freedom from military and economic intervention in belonging to this international order, although the reasonable society of peoples may urge reform (through example and enticement etc.). Thirdly there are those states (outlaw societies) which neither abide by the principles of the law of peoples nor by the basic principles of human rights and they achieve neither international recognition of their domestic legitimacy nor the additional benefit of membership of a society of states. The central idea is that the benefits of true stability only derive from a fair construction of principles of justice among consenting and dependable parties. The three requirements that indicate well-orderedness are the minimal indicators of such dependability that do not radically conflict with liberal conceptions of justice or common good conceptions of justice. The rights they engender, argues Rawls, are politically neutral in the sense that they are not specific to western liberal culture.[56] Yet for some liberal commentators Rawls' position dilutes the conception of *human* rights too much and here I can begin to defend my third claim.

A more assertive version of human rights theory, and one that is built out of a direct criticism of 'LOP', is found in Pogge's 'An Egalitarian Law of Peoples'. The argument that Pogge offers in this paper was explored briefly in relation to Rawls' rejection of cosmopolitanism in chapter 3 and here it is worth exploring the distinction between Pogge's cosmopolitanism and Rawls' developmental communitarianism at greater length. Pogge argues that Rawls' project 'holds little promise' because the fundamental conflict between a liberal's desire for the rights of persons to be protected by an international code and a non-liberal's desire for the rights of peoples to be represented in this law cannot be resolved via a politically neutral law of peoples.[57] Furthermore, when Rawls premises the acceptance (by liberals) of hierarchical societies into the international order on the basis of 'liberalism's own principle of toleration' he abandons his liberal values. This is simply because,

> [t]he hierarchicals, unencumbered by any principle of toleration, get their favoured law of peoples, while the liberals, 'to express liberalism's own principle of toleration,' surrender their egalitarian concerns and some important human rights. This fits the witty definition of a liberal as someone who will not take her own side in any disagreement.[58]

In seeing Rawls' project as an attempt at liberal universalism Pogge is unable to deal with Rawls' treatment of the fact that international society is not (or more, optimistically, not yet) liberal. It does, however, share some characteristics of a liberal society (as described in *PL*) in that it consists of a plurality of incompatible, yet valid, political systems. It does not, however, share a political culture but something much weaker (a shared history of international law). There is little doubt that Rawls believes political liberalism to be the best organising principle for such a system but wants to see the progressive liberalisation of international society achieved through the more stable procession of consensus between states. Essentially Pogge's criticisms of Rawls are informed by a misunderstanding of the limits of secular liberalism and a misguided view, that follows from this misunderstanding, of the relation between the background conditions of domestic and international justice. Recalling Pogge's argument from chapter 3,

Pogge argues that the following statements represent a liberal and non-liberal stand respectively.

1′ A liberal society must leave room for certain non-liberal communities and lifestyles.
2′ It would be illiberal to impose liberal institutions on a society that contains many persons who do not share our liberal values.[59]

These statements, said to represent the argument in the domestic case, show that Rawls would accept (1′) and reject (2′) because 'while our society can contain many different kinds of communities, associations, and conceptions of the good, some liberal in character and some not, it can be structured or organised in only one way.'[60] The essential point to note here is that in international politics Rawls would not reject (2′) because the political culture of the international sphere simply does not license the belief that a liberal global order is an appropriate political mechanism with which to administer international justice. Rawls' is not abandoning his liberal convictions, as Pogge would have it, but arguing (quite consistently) that there are no (non-comprehensive) grounds for believing that liberalism is just in this instance. Here Rawls' emphasis on a dynamic political consensus avoids the 'greater international conflict' in the area of human rights engendered by Pogge's 'more assertive liberalism' and other cosmopolitan theories of human rights. Fundamentally, Rawls avoids Pogge's criticisms by suggesting that, at a very basic level, any ethical attachment to principles of human rights must be constructed out of the minimal, but developing, shared political culture of the international system and this is something that Jones picks up on. For Jones it is not so much the particularist, reiterative construction of shared principles that is at the heart of Rawls' argument but the peculiarly 'objective' standard of well-orderedness that means a society will recognise these principles.[61] For Jones '[r]espect for rights is therefore built into the very foundations of his argument; it is not delivered by that argument'.[62] Yet if we look at Rawls' position from a communitarian point of view the notion that we can only begin to talk about basic rights when there is a vague consensus about the need for and purpose of such rights seems less difficult to sustain. Furthermore the concerns of Pogge and Jones that Rawls' starting point makes human rights at best a hostage to contingency and at worst a reaffirmation of a flawed *status quo* seem overly pessimistic.

A developing theory of human rights

Jones offers one of the best interpretations of 'LOP' currently available. He offers a full engagement with Rawls' project and is correct, I believe, in all but one (albeit major) respect. His reading of Rawls does not treat his work as developmental communitarianism and so misses the force of Rawls' argument. He argues that if Rawls is offering a purely political theory of human rights then that conception of rights cannot do any real work, or at least cannot do the work a human rights theory is supposed to do. In this respect Jones recognises that for Rawls all human rights denote are 'a set of standards that peoples (not persons) have good reason to adopt and to follow in their relations with one another' but goes on to argue that this defeats the point of human rights theory.

> This parsimonious conception of human rights departs significantly from the conventional conception. In moral and political philosophy, human rights have generally been conceived as rights possessed by human beings as such and as rights that must therefore be respected in all the various contexts and circumstances in which human beings find themselves.[63]

If Rawls' method dictates that he abandon this course then he is, as Jones points out, committed to condemning all 'comprehensive' theories of human rights in the strongest terms.[64] Yet if Rawls persists in his method, recognising that the more we add to the substance of a theory of human rights the more problematic it becomes, all Rawls presents us with is a new image of diversity and dissensus.[65] In order to overcome the limitations of his method, Jones continues, the critical burden of Rawls' human rights thesis is carried not by the political conception of justice but by the criterion of well-orderedness that Rawls insists that parties to the law of peoples meet. The idea of well-orderedness is, Jones argues, a moral, as well as a political conception. It plays a foundational role in Rawls' theory and should be thought of, we are told, as a fourth 'fundamental idea' underlying the law of peoples.

> Rawls therefore confronts a commonplace dilemma. He is understandably anxious to develop a conception of international justice that respects each society's own values. Indeed he claims to work from ideas that are the common currency of the international community. Yet if he accepts the legitimacy of every practice and institution that a culture might sanction or a people endorse, he risks tolerating too much. If, on the other hand, he limits the forms of society that are tolerable, he can be accused of imposing values upon peoples which conflict with their own self-understandings that goes against the very nature of his project.[66]

This is another version of the principal criticism of the developmental communitarian method that has been explored throughout this work. A lot, therefore, turns on Rawls' position. Here I wish to contest both the idea that Rawls' project relies upon the foundational conception of a well-ordered society and the suggestion that without such a foundation Rawls' human rights project has no vitality. By examining the consensual mechanism that Rawls employs in *PL* it is possible to see that the idea of an international society of well-ordered peoples can be thought of as the product of what Frost calls the norms of the modern state domain of discourse and that the work Rawls asks this concept to do in international affairs is a result of a legitimate construction of an appropriate background justification, a reiteratively derived and therefore accessible account of human rights in the 'here and now'.

The most telling questions that Jones raises are ones concerning motivation. He asks:

1 Why should well-ordered societies, taken severally, be committed to a common set of rights?
2 Why should those societies want to make individual rights a matter of international concern rather than limit their concerns to the rights of their own members.[67]

Rawls, on Jones' account, offers two possible answers to these questions. The first is primarily empirical and argues that as a matter of fact no population would find the non-recognition of the basic rights accorded to citizens of a well-ordered society acceptable.[68] There are two problems here. Firstly Jones shows that Rawls accepts that there are many societies that appear to have popular endorsement that do not meet the standard of well-orderedness and therefore popular endorsement is not enough to admit a state in to the political society of well-ordered peoples. Secondly Rawls, in a bid to show that by popular endorsement he does not require the presence of liberal democratic institutions, suggests that relevant judges of the regime's legitimacy are the officials and rulers of that regime rather than the population at large and this, Jones argues, 'makes internal endorsement even less satisfactory as a guarantor of human rights'.[69] The second argument that Rawls offers in defence of the criterion of well-orderedness, and the argument that does all of the work, is philosophical rather than political. This second argument stems from Rawls' own liberalism and not from his constructivism and culminates in the three requirements of well-orderedness set out above that cannot, Jones suggests, be the product of international consensus. To recap: the basic structure of Jones' well thought out criticism of Rawls is this: Many societies do not appear to fulfil the criterion of well-orderedness and we cannot therefore infer their consent to this standard. Thus Rawls relies unjustifiably upon a moral conception (a *non-constructivist* moral conception) of state legitimacy to effectively ground his human rights theory. I believe that both of these objections can be dealt with from within the boundaries of Rawls' argument.

In answer to the first of Jones' objections it seems useful to return to the construction of what Frost called the modern state domain of discourse and Walzer called the legalist paradigm. Both of these thinkers recognised that international society does not always (or even very often) live up to the ethical standards it sets itself. Nevertheless it is clear that there is a substantial agreement on what might be considered to be the basic elements of 'best practice' in international politics. Neither Frost's list of settled norms nor Walzer's six principles that are grounded in his conception of the moral minimum rely upon continual adherence to these norms but both theorists argue that there is a moral consensus strong enough to limit action premised on the ideas associated with the doctrine of *raison d'état* internationally or simple tyranny in the realm of domestic politics. Rawls' case in 'LOP' lends itself to a reading of this sort rather than to the interpretation Jones offers. The fact of injustice does not rule out the construction of justice. Indeed the construction of an accessible background justification, that is a justification that all parties can relate to, is designed to shore up and strengthen the conception of justice implicit in the 'best' or most beneficial practices in international politics. Simply imposing an inaccessible account of justice may provide the theorist with a series of arguments that have a highly critical edge but there is no reason to expect that agents in international politics will adopt that conception of justice. At best a dominant power may impose their view of justice but this will not meet the standard of stability that Rawls convincingly argues characterises justice. At worst such an imposition will deny the possibility of the development of a truly accessible and shared conception of justice. Leading on from this, and in answer to Jones' second point, in setting out the requirements of well-orderedness Rawls is not asking that we maintain a very thick account of political legitimacy. He suggests that a state that appears to be legitimate will (a) have a system of law rather than a system of coercively enforced commands, (b) will take seriously (or at least allow for some form of expression of the claims of its citizens, (c) will not persecute minorities, (d) will allow emigration and (e) will be peaceful in its relations with other states.[70] Rawls has to show that these requirements can be built out of an existing international consensus (a possibility that Jones denies). This task should be (indeed it is) less difficult and more powerful than constructing the idea of a constitutive theory of individuality from the settled norms of international politics or the reiterated values of life and liberty from repeated international encounters.

Here I wish to explore the idea of consensus that Rawls uses in his theory. Rawls suggests that we can usefully categorise the form of agreement reached by political agents into three types. These are *modus vivendi*, constitutional consensus and overlapping consensus. Rawls principally refers to the move from *modus vivendi* to overlapping consensus as the goal of politics but on my reading of Rawls the process of shifting our allegiance from principles of a *modus vivendi* to principles of justice is vital as the force of Rawls' conclusions relies upon the legitimacy of their developmental communitarian construction rather than their goal. The idea of *modus vivendi* has clear implications and a long pedigree and it is not necessary to offer a detailed discussion of what this form of political existence might entail. For Rawls,

> [i]t is easy to see how there might be a reasonably just *modus vivendi* between a plurality of conflicting comprehensive doctrines. We simply suppose that historical circumstances have so turned out that for the time being at least, the balance of forces keeps all sides supporting the current arrangements, which happen to be just to each of them. However, when two salvation religions clash, can there be any resolution of the conflict that goes beyond that? I have noted that sometimes a *modus vivendi* might develop into an overlapping consensus of reasonable doctrines ... the idea of an overlapping consensus is moral in its object and motivation, rendering the consensus

> stable over the distribution of doctrines. This gives stability for the right reasons and this distinguishes the idea of such a consensus from a *modus vivendi*.[71]

Stability for the right reasons is an essential aspect of the force of Rawls' position. A *modus vivendi* agreement is stable in the sense that it is not advantageous for a state, as party to that agreement, to violate its terms.[72] As soon as this is no longer the case (if, for example, the relative strength of one party increases so that it could enforce its will upon the other parties) the agreement may effectively end. Agreements based on overlapping consensus, on the other hand, will not end at this point. The agreement is based on moral grounds and has a moral object and will be affirmed regardless of the relative strength of the parties.[73] Here 'all are moved to adhere to their common law accepting it as just and beneficial for all'.[74] But how, Jones is perfectly right to ask, can Rawls get from *modus vivendi* to overlapping consensus and the benefits it brings without building in a moral foundation. In Rawls' depiction of international society it is more than likely that only liberal societies would achieve an overlapping consensus on the law of peoples because one aspect of the overlapping consensus rests upon a specifically liberal understanding of the *value* of reasonable pluralism. There is however some middle ground between *modus vivendi* between states (as described in *PL*)[75] and full overlapping consensus that seems to depict the 'just' relations between states in a more appropriate manner.

The form of consensus reached between liberal and hierarchical states is likely to be analogous to the idea of constitutional consensus in *PL* where,

> a constitution satisfying certain basic principles establishes … procedures for moderating political rivalry within society. … While there is agreement on certain basic political rights and liberties … there is disagreement … as to the more exact content and boundaries of these rights.[76]

Constitutional consensus arises, argues Rawls, as the only workable alternative to endless destruction and strife.[77] The importance of this stage in Rawls' theory is both its historicity and its dynamism, its potential. For Rawls,

> at the first stage of constitutional consensus the liberal principles of justice, initially accepted reluctantly as *modus vivendi* … tends to shift citizens' comprehensive doctrines so that they at least accept the principles of a liberal constitution. To this extent the [state's principles] are reasonable if they were not before: simple pluralism moves toward reasonable pluralism and constitutional consensus is reached.[78]

Given the similarities in the background conditions of liberal and international society set out above it is not hard to amend this vital aspect of Rawls' consensual mechanism to fit his discussion of justice in 'LOP'. The 'dramatic change' in international law and the limited but shared history of international politics point to a developing consensus where politically organised peoples[79] who have traditionally accepted the rule of international law develop that traditional consensus, that *modus vivendi* and develop a shared background justification for international law capable of sustaining a thin theory of rights. The idea of the reasonable, the concept that Jones rightly points out does the job of discriminating between well-ordered and outlaw societies,[80] is developed reiteratively as the background justification for the move from *modus vivendi* to constitutional consensus. It indicates the willingness of agents to accept the burdens of public justification and to propose and abide by fair terms of cooperation.[81] In this model hierarchical societies are both rational (they care about the good of the society they represent) and reasonable (they do not try to extend their conception of the good to other peoples by war and aggression and are capable of political interaction). Further to this the rationality of states means that not only do they order their political structure on a common good sense of justice (albeit based on various comprehensive conceptions of justice) but they care about the benefits of peace and trade etc., and this also helps to ensure the protection of minimal human rights.[82] The concept doing most of the work here is the idea of the reasonable. It is shored up by the rationality of the agents in international politics but unless these agents can legitimately be characterised as reasonable there can be no move from *modus vivendi* to constitutional consensus and most definitely no move to overlapping consensus. The idea that international society can be said to enjoy a constitutional consensus on principles of international justice is not too hard to sustain. Let us just examine the three requirements that Rawls places upon international society, his construction of international community, and see whether it seems reasonable to use these ideas to support a constructivist theory of international justice. The three requirements of a stable constitutional consensus are weaker than those of overlapping consensus but nevertheless serve to engender a workable system of rights that is capable of policing and advancing international society. These modified requirements of society are:

1. The fact of reasonable pluralism must lead to consensus upon the need to fix the political situation and put such issues beyond particularist interest.
2. That applying principles of justice pays heed to the guidelines of public reason. These guidelines and rules must be specified in reference to forms of reasoning available to all.
3. (dependent on 1 and 2) Those involved believe the principles are just and thus the consensus works effectively.[83]

These requirements cohere with Rawls' insistence that the only appropriate account of international justice provides both 'the form that practical reason requires for its application … (and) the context within which practical questions and problems arise'.[84] These ideas are laid out in the background conditions of international society and model a realistic (if minimal) image of the firm areas of consensus in international politics. Jones' principal concern with 'LOP' is that the consensual materials needed to construct a conception of the well-ordered or the allied conception of the reasonable 'may not be available in our world'.[85] Yet for Rawls if there is an interest in putting issues of international justice beyond particularist interest, of achieving a degree of real stability then the appropriate materials are available albeit in a weaker form than they are found in *PL*. For Rawls the idea of the reasonable and associated concepts are constructed out of a consensus on the need to fix the political situation, something that Rawls, and more forcefully Frost, can convincingly argue exists. To be reasonable we must only be prepared to ask of other societies 'only what they can grant without submitting to a position of inferiority, much less to domination'[86] and this is something that emerges as peoples move towards constitutional consensus. Frost's account of the settled norms of the modern state domain of discourse is the most powerful expression of this point that I have examined in this argument but it models a similar starting point to the work of all three developmental communitarian theorists. Neither Frost nor Walzer and Rawls expect thorough transnational agreement on the best expressions of these norms but the way they model the international consensus can support a norm-oriented construction of principles of international ethics of the kind that Rawls provides.

The conception of human rights that Rawls' position underwrites is significantly different from the endorsement of human rights by liberal states but is sufficient to ensure a greater stability than a mere *modus vivendi*. These rights constitute a politically neutral class of rights for the present age[87] that fulfil three roles.

1 They are a necessary condition of a regime's legitimacy and of the decency of its legal order.
2 By being in place, they are also sufficient to exclude justified and forceful intervention by other peoples, say by economic sanctions, or in grave cases, by military force.
3 They set a limit on pluralism among peoples.[88]

This use of the idea of human rights is vital to an understanding of Rawls' theory. It is only this minimalist version of rights that can be said to be the object of a stable (and hence partly moral – in Rawls' constructivist sense of the word) consensus. Using the language of the cosmopolitans, it could be said that international actors have a reasonable expectation that agents will hold categorical allegiance to these principles – that they recognise them as just. At the level of constitutional consensus this does not require a homogenous understanding of what a just state will look like or what human rights ultimately entail. Rather it models a historically derived agreement that warmongering is wrong, that a legitimate state will exhibit that legitimacy through its dealings with all those in its territory and, following from these points, will therefore uphold the ideas of human rights that can be said to have international universality.

The main issue that Rawls wishes to address is the stability of reasonable pluralism both in domestic society and in international affairs. Stability of the right kind rests essentially on a 'wide' reflective equilibrium that endorses a thick conception of human rights compatible with a liberal conception of justice. The ideal of international justice (for the present age) is therefore vaguely liberal in its substance because the international arena has similar background conditions as the liberal democracy in *PL*. States agree on just (or fair) principles of interaction as persons with differing comprehensive doctrines would. There is no inconsistency here, Rawls argues, as

> a people sincerely affirming a non liberal conception of justice may still think their society should be treated equally in a just law of peoples, even though its members accept basic inequalities among themselves.[89]

There is however an additional point. A non-liberal society may well think it should be treated equally in a society of states *but* it would not be party to an overlapping consensus on the political conception of justice which is itself a thick moral conception including specific conceptions of society, the person and political virtue.[90] The idea of stability may well be central to the role of political theory in a liberal democracy but it does not make the transition to the realm of international relations theory intact. In admitting non-liberal societies to membership in good standing of a society of states Rawls must (and he argues that he does) relax the criterion of reasonableness,[91] but more importantly he *relaxes the criterion of stability*. Rawls, in order to try and make the case that non-liberal societies would respect human rights for the right reasons without imposing a liberal conception of the good shows that human rights must be agreed between and enforced by reasonable communities. These rights are said to result from the basic fact that a society cannot be legitimate unless it can impose moral rights and duties upon its subjects and are said to express the minimum standard of well-ordered political institutions necessary to achieve membership in good standing in the society of states.[92] Rawls' use of human rights does not have as much force as the first two requirements he places on hierarchical societies but this is more indicative of the issue he is looking at than of a major flaw in his construction. Human rights have indeed entered the discourse of international relations almost universally and they do, to some extent, weaken claims to domestic legitimacy based on simple pluralism but they cannot license interventionist policies against states that do not value individual autonomy the way a Kantian liberal might or that genuinely believe that an idea of the common good outweighs individual benefit. The claims advanced under this heading are still too easily subject to the charge of western value imperialism. In order to acknowledge this Rawls must not only relax the criterion of reasonableness but also of stability so that the analogue of a developing constitutional consensus becomes the current goal of international relations and so that this goal remains sensitive to the fact of pluralism (i.e. to the value of differing social and political cultures) while retaining some claim to universality. Essentially the idea of the equality of states in international society is reasonable (on the minimal reading of the term) because it is the basis of the fair terms of cooperation. All states which are prepared to engage in international politics rather than exploit international anarchy must, regardless of their historical cultural and economic development, have equal bargaining power if Rawls' theory is to be as impartial and fair as he believes. In accordance with this idea the principle of stability (which on a strong reading would base the equality of states on the value of reasonable pluralism) now reaches, Rawls' tells us, for a model in which all reasonable societies, 'affirm a peaceful society of peoples and benefit therefrom as liberal societies do. All have a common interest in changing the way in which politics among peoples – war and the threats of war – has hitherto been carried on.'[93]

This use of the idea of a shared history of international law fits the criterion of stability at the level of constitutional consensus perfectly and the idea of using constitutional consensus as a category in 'LOP' really seems to bring out the sense of Rawls' argument in a revealing manner. The argument is certainly not foundational. The argument runs, as I see it, like this: having a 'common good sense of justice' is a criterion of well-orderedness which is itself a criterion for entry into the society of states. This articulation of legitimacy is valued because it lends stability of the right kind to global justice (both through domestic and international organisation) which allows it to continue to develop from the normative stalemate of *modus vivendi* to (ideally) overlapping consensus. This ideal of legitimacy must therefore be capable of defending itself from the charge that it is an

> ideal of a global regime that is just by Rawlsian lights [and] may cohere well with *our* cultural heritage and *our* considered judgements but is nevertheless inappropriate on account of an existing intercultural diversity of traditions and moral judgements.[94]

Given that a 'long run aim' of the law of peoples is to bring all societies to honour that law and that the benefits gained by members in good standing of that law will be denied other states, it is not unreasonable to ask that the minimal conditions of social entry be appropriately universal and the universality of developmental communitarianism seems particularly suitable.

Review and conclusions: developmental communitarianism and human rights

The standard charge levelled against a theory of international justice such as the one developed by Rawls is that it has no real teeth; it cannot do the work we would wish a theory of human rights to do. This charge is drawn from the long history of human rights theory that insists that it is theoretically and politically possible to develop a conception of international justice from outside the practice of international politics. Yet it seems clear that it is impossible to develop an accessible account of international justice from anywhere but international politics. Theoretically human rights theory of this traditional sort builds in ideas that are not acceptable to many actors in world politics or are not provable before them. Politically this offers no publicly justifiable reason why any agent should accept these principles, particularly when the outcome of accepting such principles would be the requirement that they give up political position and moral beliefs and practices. The power of traditional human rights discourse is significantly weakened when its justification appears to belong to one particular political culture. The power of Rawls' theory (and of developmental communitarianism more generally) lies in the way it constructs its conception of international justice. Rawls, in articulating the only real hope for international justice argues that 'as the success of political cooperation continues, citizens gain increasing trust and confidence in one another'.[95] Indeed in his more optimistic moments Rawls permits himself the luxury of believing that constitutional consensus heralds the development of a full overlapping consensus on the moral status of a political conception of justice as it facilitates the historical development of truly shared principles. It is the further development of the process that has already led us from the uneasy *modus vivendi* of the Westphalian system of international politics to constitutional consensus. In order to understand just how different a developmental communitarian conception of human rights is in practice from a more traditional conception it is useful to briefly refer back to Moellendorf's reading of 'LOP'. Rawls' approach to international justice does not mean that he 'pierces' the idea of sovereignty in the name of human rights as Moellendorf claims. Rawls argues that given that the parties wish to cultivate the underdeveloped international political arena, it is both possible and necessary to develop traditional ideas of sovereignty and human rights in the name of political stability (of the right sort) in ways that do not conflict with the political will of the parties to undertake this international venture. Herein lies the importance of Rawls' position. Human rights, on a developmental communitarian reading of international politics, are seen to specify 'the outer boundary of admissible domestic law of societies in good standing in a just society of peoples'.[96] In explaining this position Rawls shows how the United Nations declaration on human rights of 1948 must be re-examined so that it can really be thought of as an expression of international justice rather than an expression of liberal intent. We are justly entitled to 'human rights proper' articulated by article 3 (rights to life and liberty and security of person), article 5 (denouncing torture etc.) and the special conventions on genocide and apartheid. What cannot be promulgated as universally relevant or accessible are article 1 ('all human beings are born free and equal in dignity and rights') and those articles which prescribe institutional expressions of welfare liberalism such as article 22 (the right to social security) and article 23 (equal pay for equal work).[97] For Rawls the only aims of international politics that we can reasonably expect the plurality of agents to agree upon culminate in the defence of the stability of the society of well-ordered peoples and this entails the long run aim of bringing all to honour the law of peoples and, in grave cases, the defence of the rights of those living under outlaw regimes.[98] The idea that all parties to the law of peoples wish to defend the stability of that order can do no more than this because the goal of stability identifies the object of and reiterates the relative strength of the consensus between peoples that an accessible theory is entitled to draw upon. To build any more into this conception of international justice would be to leave the acceptable boundaries of ethical constructivism and to precipitate a return to the conflict between comprehensive world views that characterises the unstable *modus vivendi* between absolute sovereign powers. International consensus on the value of political stability may be strong enough to ensure action in the case of genocide but to expect the international community to agree to take up arms against a state (or to refuse it entry in to the society of states) because it had inadequate social security provision (although it achieves the constructed standard of well-orderedness that Rawls draws from international consensus) is as unjust as it is ridiculous.

The idea that international society has attained a 'constitutional consensus' upon a conception of international justice outlines the limits of developmental communitarianism that Frost transcended and goes no small way beyond Walzer's contention that international society only temporarily attains a consensus on ethics. Frost's insistence that we are legitimately able to construct a substantive liberal understanding of the international consensus was seen to be problematic in chapter 5. In essence the liberal aspect of Frost's reasoning was seen to retain inaccessible aspects of metaphysical Hegelianism and inadmissible aspects of Dworkin's liberal constitutionalism. Rawls overcomes difficulties of this sort by remaining within the proper limits of ethical. He recognises the claims to sovereign legitimacy of a plurality of political societies and provides a genuinely accessible account of international society. This position does not, however, commit him to the very thin conclusions of Walzer who also remains within the acceptable boundaries of constructivist political theory. The principal reason why Walzer did not flesh out the consequences of the developing international consensus is partly because he believed that in times of extreme emergency states would robustly defend their right to self-determination and also because he is not convinced that the reiterated 'rights to life and liberty' are developed enough to truly be the object of a politically instantiated universal moral consensus. The first of these concerns does not affect Rawls' developmental communitarianism. In times of extreme emergency not only are each state's rights to self-determination upheld but each well-ordered society could legitimately expect the help of the society of well-ordered peoples. More importantly however Rawls develops an idea that can be adapted to respond to Walzer's second concern. The idea of an international constitutional consensus, adapted from Rawls' theory, offers an image of a substantive international consensus on political concerns and a developing, but still fairly thin and indeterminate, consensus on ethico-political principles. Walzer believes that at times of international and domestic tyranny the rights to life and liberty attain a thin but insistent expression but that this reiterated notion cannot find a suitable articulation in everyday political life. The world is too morally divergent to form a determinate consensus on this issue. The best we can do, Walzer suggests, is to employ a very diluted notion of these rights in our construction of the legalist paradigm and the war convention. Rawls, in more fully exploring the idea of a constructivist political and moral consensus, offers a more adequate conceptualisation of how divergent moral viewpoints might be incorporated within a workable political consensus. In constructivist political theory recognising that people have rights to life and liberty entails the recognition that there are many different expressions of what it means to have liberty or how a life might best be led. For Walzer this fact means that we cannot incorporate these thin moral ideas into the thickness of our everyday lives. For Rawls, however, although the moral/political consensus is primarily relevant to the stability of the society of states we can include these thin understandings in our everyday political arrangements as our domestic political and international political lives do overlap. This important overlap is, however, limited by the way we must construct justice from political interaction. The understanding that exists between peoples arises, as in Walzer and Frost, through *international interconnectedness*. The concept of human rights that we are justified in imposing on the relations between a government and its citizens are limited by (but not eradicated) by the source of an accessible and legitimately universalisable conception of justice. It is theoretically impossible and politically disastrous to attempt to develop such principles elsewhere and then to attempt to impose them regardless of the realities of international politics. Therefore, apart from requirements relating to a state's domestic legitimacy (requirements that stem from international consensus) we do not (and under the rules of ethical constructivism cannot) ask peoples to conform to any one understanding of the rights to life and liberty.

The force of the preceding interpretation of Rawls' 'LOP' goes comprehensively against the standard liberal interpretation. The idea that one may attempt to achieve a kind of universality from broadly particularist beginnings has dogged the intellectual footsteps of authors such as Walzer and it is vital that the same does not happen to Rawls' contribution to the debates concerning international justice. The project of theorists such as Walzer, Frost and, I have argued, Rawls are too important in this age of 'secular' liberalism to be dismissed superficially. In applying the full consensual mechanism of *PL* to 'LOP' and in drawing out the necessarily related interpretations of key but contentious ideas I do not think I have done Rawls an injustice. Rather the full sense of Rawls' project becomes clearer if we take seriously his claims to have attempted to come to terms with the difficult problems concerning the universality of international justice. What has been portrayed here as Rawls' broadly communitarian starting point allows him to take seriously the fact that liberals and non-liberals hold to the international law regarding human rights for different reasons and that even the *status quo* in international relations is the subject of endless dispute without requiring that he abandon any hope for international justice. There are perhaps two further benefits to reading Rawls in the manner prescribed in this chapter. Firstly it situates 'LOP' within the wider scope of Rawls' work and takes a serious look at Rawls' claims to have entered the debates concerned with international justice. Rawls should no longer be seen as a liberal political theorist who is unable to deal with international relations theory but as a philosopher who has made an important attempt to reconcile a considered theory of justice with the particular problems associated with international ethics. This chapter has argued that the attempt has made an important contribution to human rights discourse. Secondly, if we read 'LOP' as a hard case in Rawlsian political theory the full force of the methodological and philosophical shift from *TJ* to *PL* becomes clearer and the debate concerning the problem of universality in ethics in the age of 'secular' liberalism advances another step.

Notes and references

1 J. Rawls, '50 Years After Hiroshima', *Dissent*, summer 1995, pp. 323–327.
2 See particularly J. Rawls, *Theory of Justice*, Oxford University Press, 1972, §40 and compare with J. Rawls, *Political Liberalism*, Colombia University Press, 1993, Lecture III, §2.
3 S. Schwarzenbach, 'Rawls, Hegel, and Communitarianism', *Political Theory*, Vol. 19, No. 4, 1991, pp. 539–571.
4 R. Paden, 'Reconstructing Rawls's Law of Peoples', *Ethics and International Affairs*, Vol. 11, 1997, p. 231. B. Barry, 'John Rawls and the Search for Stability', *Ethics*, Vol. 105, 1995, pp. 904–905.
5 See particularly T. Pogge, 'Cosmopolitanism and Sovereignty', *Ethics*, Vol. 103, October 1992, p. 50 where Pogge argues that Rawls combines two types of cosmopolitanism. T. Pogge, 'An Egalitarian Law of Peoples', *Philosophy and Public Affairs*, Vol. 23, No. 3, summer 1994, p. 195 for a critique of Rawls' most recent attempt at international relations theory. C. Beitz, 'Cosmopolitan Liberalism and the States System', in C. Brown (ed.), *Political Restructuring in Europe: Ethical Perspectives*, Routledge, 1994, p. 123.
6 O. O'Neill, 'Transnational Justice', in D. Held (ed.), *Political Theory Today*, Polity Press, 1991, chapter 11.
7 Essentially Rawls' rejection of Kant's theory of constitutive autonomy (*PL*, Lecture III) and his focus upon *political* liberalism effect his transition to secular (and non-Kantian) liberalism.
8 Rawls, 'LOP', p. 44.
9 Rawls, *PL*, p. xvi.
10 Rawls, *PL*, p. 10.
11 P. Jones, 'International Human Rights: Philosophical or Political?', in S. Caney, D. George, and P. Jones (eds), *National Rights, International Obligations*, Westview Press, 1996, p. 189.
12 D. Moellendorf, 'Constructing the Law of Peoples', *Pacific Philosophical Quarterly*, Vol. 77, 1996, pp. 132–154.
13 While I do not have time to discuss it here, a critical assessment of the focal shift from *TJ* to *PL* can be found in B. Barry, 'John Rawls and the Search for Stability', *Ethics*, Vol. 105, No. 4, 1995, pp. 874–915.
14 Cf. K.C. Tan, 'Liberal Toleration in Rawls' Law of Peoples', *Ethics*, Vol. 108, January 1998, pp. 276–295.
15 Rawls, *PL*, Lecture III, §2, pp. 98–100.
16 Rawls, *PL*, p. 90.
17 Rawls, *PL*, p. 98. Here I should note that Rawls develops this understanding of his approach in *The Law of Peoples* (2000) and shows the distinct nature of his understanding of practical reason as opposed to that of Kant and cosmopolitanism more generally. Given the emphasis my reading of Rawls' project places on the norm-governed aspect of his method, this refinement is consistent with my characterisation of Rawls as both constructivist and communitarian. See Rawls, *Law Of Peoples*, 2000, §12.2.

18 Rawls, *PL*, pp. 18–19.
19 NB: Rawls rejects the notion that constructivism should provide a cosmopolitan conception of universality from the start. Cf. Rawls, 'LOP', p. 50, cf. chapter 4.
20 Cf. C. Beitz, *Political Theory and International Relations*, Princeton University Press, 1979.
21 Rawls, 'LOP', p. 46 and p. 50. See also Rawls, *PL*, Lecture VII.
22 Cf. Rawls, 'LOP', p. 49.
23 Rawls, 'LOP', p. 49. NB the idea that the parties represent free and equal peoples is significantly different from the idea that all persons are to be considered free and equal.
24 Rawls, 'LOP', p. 57. While the idea of 'peoples' as agent is explicitly contrasted with that of state (Rawls, 'LOP', note 1) it is still non-committal as a conception of agency. This too is indicative of Rawls' almost phenomenological approach to his subject. Rawls' point is that there is no ideal conception of agency; we construct principles of justice for the present structure while remaining agnostic about the seat of agency, the *status quo*. An ideal agent whether state or person would pre-empt questions of justice where the idea of 'Peoples' does not.
25 Rawls, 'LOP', p. 49.
26 Jones, 'International Human Rights', p. 187. Cf. Rawls' argument that reciprocity is relevant between citizens in a well-ordered society, *PL*, Lecture I, p. 17.
27 Cf. Brown, *International Relations Theory*, p. 173.
28 As a Rawlsian concept reciprocity applies between reasonable, free and equal citizens in a well-ordered society. In 'LOP' Rawls has to weaken the standard of the reasonable (due to the weaker background conditions of international society). The link between reasonable agents and reciprocal relations is mirrored in 'LOP' where agents are reasonable to a lesser degree and their relations reciprocal to a lesser degree. See the final sections of this chapter for the implications of this move.
29 This is essentially an expansion of remarks in Rawls' *Justice as Fairness: A Briefer Restatement*, p. 152, note 28.
30 Rawls, 'LOP', p. 43.
31 Rawls, *PL*, p. 144. See also p. xxiv.
32 Cf. Pogge's criticism of this line of reasoning in 'An Egalitarian Law of Peoples', *Philosophy and Public Affairs*, Vol. 23, No. 3, 1994, pp. 216–217. Here Pogge argues that Rawls' conception of toleration actually compromises liberal values (see also below).
33 Cf. T.W. Pogge, *Realizing Rawls*, Ithica and London, Cornell University Press, 1989, p. 268 and note 35.
34 Cf. Rawls, 'LOP', pp. 60–63.
35 Affirming the law of peoples for the right reasons confers stability of the right kind upon international society (see below).
36 Jones, 'International Human Rights', p. 194. See also my discussion of Pogge (below).
37 R. Paden, 'Reconstructing Rawls' Law of Peoples', *Ethics and International Affairs*, Vol. 11, 1997, p. 218.
38 Rawls, 'LOP', p. 54.
39 D. Moellendorf, 'Constructing the Law of Peoples', *Pacific Philosophical Quarterly*, Vol. 77, 1996, p. 137. Paden, 'Reconstructing the Law of Peoples', p. 222. Pogge, 'An Egalitarian Law of Peoples', p. 217. F. Teson, 'The Rawlsian theory of International Law', *Ethics and International Affairs*, Vol. 9, 1995, p. 79.
40 Moellendorf, 'Constructing the Law of Peoples', p. 137.
41 Moellendorf, 'Constructing the Law of Peoples', p. 139.
42 Moellendorf, 'Constructing the Law of Peoples', p. 144.
43 Moellendorf, 'Constructing the Law of Peoples', p. 143.
44 Even taking into account the role that 'reflective equilibrium' plays in Rawls' theory a refusal to accept principles of justice on the grounds that one's comprehensive viewpoint (which is not incompatible with the principles of justice) is not universalised and accorded a dominant position within the theory is viewed as unreasonable.

45 Paden, 'Reconstructing the Law of Peoples', p. 218, brackets mine.
46 Moellendorf, 'Constructing the Law of Peoples', p. 144.
47 Rawls, 'LOP', p. 55.
48 Rawls, 'LOP', p. 58.
49 Rawls, 'LOP', pp. 57–58.
50 Rawls, 'LOP', p. 59. For a fuller account of stability and consensus see Rawls, *PL*, Lecture IV, §2.
51 Rawls, '50 Years After Hiroshima', p. 324.
52 Rawls, 'LOP', p. 68.
53 See Rawls, 'LOP', pp. 60–63.
54 Rawls, 'LOP', p. 62.
55 Walzer, 'The Moral Standing of States: A Response to Four Critics', *Philosophy and Public Affairs*, Vol. 9, No. 18, 1980, p. 128.
56 Rawls, 'LOP', p. 69.
57 Pogge, 'An Egalitarian Law of Peoples', p. 215.
58 Pogge, 'An Egalitarian Law of peoples', p. 216.
59 Pogge, 'An Egalitarian Law of Peoples', p. 217.
60 Ibid.
61 Jones, 'International Human Rights', pp. 192–193.
62 Jones, 'International Human Rights', p. 195.
63 Jones, 'International Human Rights', p. 189.
64 Jones, 'International Human Rights', p. 197.
65 Jones, 'International Human Rights', pp. 199–200.
66 Jones, 'International Human Rights', p. 194.
67 Jones, 'International Human Rights', p. 189.
68 Jones, 'International Human Rights', p. 192.
69 Jones, 'International Human Rights', p. 193.
70 Rawls, 'LOP', pp. 60–63 and note 22, p. 224.
71 Rawls, *PL*, pp. xlii–xliii (introduction to the paperback edition). Here I have excluded Rawls' own references to previous sections of his introduction.
72 Rawls, *PL*, p. 147.
73 Rawls, *PL*, p. 148.
74 Rawls, 'LOP', p. 58
75 Rawls, *PL*, p. 147.
76 Rawls, *PL*, pp. 158–159. I am aware that there is no textual evidence to support the claim that this middle level of consensus would play a role in Rawls' international relations theory but as a vital element of his consensual mechanism (and if appropriately modified) I think it is fascinating to at least attempt the transition.
77 Ibid.
78 Rawls, *PL*, pp. 263–264.
79 On the adequacy of this conception of agency see note 25 (above).
80 Jones, 'International Human Rights', p. 195.
81 Rawls, *PL*, pp. 48–54.
82 Rawls, 'LOP', p. 64 and p. 67.
83 Rawls, *PL*, pp. 161–162.
84 Rawls, *PL*, p. 110.
85 Jones, 'International Human Rights', p. 195.
86 Rawls, 'LOP', p. 79.
87 Rawls, 'LOP', pp. 69–70.
88 Rawls, 'LOP', p. 71.
89 Rawls, 'LOP', p. 65.
90 Cf. Rawls, *PL*, p. 147.
91 Rawls, 'LOP', p. 78.
92 Ibid.

93 Rawls, 'LOP', p. 67.
94 Pogge, *Realizing Rawls*, p. 267.
95 Rawls, *PL*, p. 168.
96 Rawls, 'LOP', p. 71.
97 Rawls, *Law Of Peoples*, pp. 227–228.
98 Rawls, 'LOP', pp. 72–74.

Conclusions

Human rights play a vital role in international politics. However as these rights are currently laid down in convention, declaration and statute, as they are constructed by liberal political theorists, justified by philosophers and campaigned for by pressure groups, they are something of a double edged sword. This sword may be used, wittingly or unwittingly, to sustain the *status quo ante*, a system of international competition dominated by a western liberal hegemony. In doing so it may simply mask, rather than overcome, the continuation of a power oriented system of world politics. If, as the current situation in international relations suggests, we need a political tool capable of dealing adequately with the developing interconnectedness of agents, a liberal human rights culture would appear to offer a perfect solution. However, unless that theory of human rights is constructed along developmental communitarian lines it runs the risk of being nothing more than an extremely effective and well-disguised tool in the realist battle for political supremacy. This is not to suggest that those who favour cosmopolitanism or campaign for human rights violations to be subject to political and economic censure are duplicitous or Machiavellian. Neither is it to suggest that the development of human rights policies since the establishment of the League of Nations has been a front for the *Realpolitik* of the most powerful states. Rather, it is to suggest that the massive benefits that these developments have brought to the drive for international justice are in danger of dissipating unless we concentrate on the idea of justice that underpins the development of the international community. The extraordinary speed with which human rights discourse and policy has developed over the last half century has brought the twin ideas of international community and international justice to the fore. But this process can go no further unless we take adequate account of all those who make up the international community. We face a choice between a world structured on liberal principles of human rights where the most powerful economic states dictate the rules to the rest of the world and a genuine international community that would not live up to the principles of liberalism. The only way to choose is to think long and hard about what it must mean to act justly in the contemporary international world and what terms we (and our potential partners in world politics) could justly propose and abide by in good conscience.

A 'liberal' theory of international politics, and one that incorporates (often as a founding premise) the idea of human rights was seen in chapter 1 to be an important part of the development of international politics. As a theoretical and political tool it was cultivated to take account of the developing 'trans-stateness' and interconnectedness of the international sphere. However when the empirical evidence concerning interdependence, globalisation and interconnectedness was related to the theoretical difficulties in reaching certain widely held conclusions about contemporary international politics, it became clear that a lot more theoretical work had to be done if the generation of a liberal human rights culture was to be accepted as an unconditional good. The conclusions of theories advocating greater progress in the instantiation of a global human rights culture were shown to rely upon reasoning that was not derived from purely empirical evidence. Rather these arguments were shown to rely upon moral and philosophical predicates that had to be examined before any such conclusion, no matter how intuitively pleasing, could be justified. In recognising the role of theoretical arguments the focus of my study changed. It is not necessarily the content or policing of international law that gives us the most insight into the just nature (or otherwise) of those laws. Rather we need a standard by which to judge the arguments that support or oppose such laws. Such a standard, I have argued, is to be found in the constructivist turn in contemporary political theory

The requirements of constructivist political theory, as laid out by O'Neill, are simple. The criterion of accessibility captures the need to generate a theory that does not rely upon dubious or highly contestable predicates and that can be seen as appropriate by all relevant others. Therefore linking a defensible account of interconnectedness (a model of the empirical, political and moral issues surrounding globalisation and interdependence) with the requirement of theoretical accessibility offered the necessary tools with which we could examine the relative merits of contending liberal theories of international relations. Having compiled the necessary means to examine the central problem I turned to an examination of the most popular and widely held liberal international theory. Cosmopolitanism was shown to have a rich and much called upon history but the arguments it deployed in the defence of contemporary claims to create a greater global human rights culture, to have discovered the necessity of a greater *Ius Cosmopoliticum* or to urge the dissolution of state boundaries was shown to be wanting in many respects. Prime among these difficulties was a reliance upon unproven predicates and the assertion of the 'just' nature of liberalism's founding principles. In short, cosmopolitanism could not remain within the confines of constructivist theory. While a general survey of cosmopolitanism hinted at this conclusion a detailed examination of an avowedly constructivist cosmopolitanism, that of O'Neill, confirmed it. O'Neill's detailed and closely reasoned argument failed to show that a cosmopolitan-liberal theory was theoretically and politically necessary. In failing to show that taking account of 'all relevant others' required a recognition of individual, universal obligations to the rest of humanity O'Neill's argument relied upon her secondary claim that no non-cosmopolitan theory of international ethics could account for the circumstances of international justice. In responding to this argument I constructed the tradition of developmental communitarianism. The principles generated by Walzer, Rawls and in part by Frost, derived from legitimate premises. In doing so the developmental communitarians had to modify the case for human rights (without ever rejecting their importance to international relations) and a full exploration of their position constituted the final chapters of this book.

Without reiterating the claims made by Frost, Walzer and Rawls I believe it possible to state the role that developmental communitarianism can play in international relations theory once more. If human rights or, more generally, liberalism is to play a lead role in completing the development of international to a more global politics its principles need to be (potentially at least) the object of a real consensus of all relevant agents. Without this liberalism is simply one more distinctive and local way of life competing for international supremacy. To be sure liberalism has the upper hand in the current battle but if we are to take seriously the idea of international justice then it must be recognised that the victor in a dispute of this kind can only claim political and not ethical supremacy. Developmental communitarianism takes seriously the idea that, if we are to derive a system of international justice from the consent of all relevant parties then, some exclusively liberal values will have to be withdrawn from international politics (not from national politics) in the name of accessibility. The same process, they point out, is undertaken by all parties.

The importance of viewing the contributions of Frost, Walzer and Rawls as being part of a unified and developing tradition is twofold. Firstly, in building an image of this tradition, we begin to develop a better understanding of how we can think about ethical issues in world politics. The developmental communitarian method meets the requirements of constructivism. That is, it shows how it is possible to make ethical demands of agents in world politics without relying on one ethical or political tradition and without making inaccessible or incomprehensible claims about the nature of morality. It is only the developmental communitarian tradition, I have argued, that meets this necessary condition. In building this tradition it becomes clearer that the goals of Frost, Walzer and Rawls are the outcome of a desire both to say something clear and positive about the future development of international justice and to do so in an ethical register that is accessible to all. It is possible to build a clearer understanding of this type of international political theory by drawing the best from all three philosophers and laying out the core elements of what is the most successful attempt to offer principles for the developing international community. For example, if my argument that these three theorists can be seen to be a part of a new tradition in international relations theory is successful then one can draw on the strengths of these thinkers and lay out the structure of developmental communitarian reasoning in the following way. Drawing on Frost's account of the settled norms of the current domain of discourse and the need to construct a background justification capable of settling hard cases it becomes clear that the role of political theory in contemporary international relations has changed. Drawing on Walzer's account of the reiterative development of settled norms gives us a clearer insight into the character of the norms of international politics and an understanding of the possibilities and limitations of using universal norms such as human rights to structure the development of the international community. Drawing on Rawls' account of the search for consensus reinforces the recognition that the way we think about international ethics must change and shows how we could go about providing ethical principles for the modern world. If we recall the third condition of constitutional consensus we get, I think, a very simple description of the general philosophy of these theorists. To paraphrase Rawls' point; if those involved believe the principles of international ethic to be just *then* the political consensus will work effectively. Building the tradition of developmental communitarianism shows us the method and the reach of the contemporary political theory of international relations.

The second benefit is critical in character. The arguments offered in this book show the difficulties we face if we continue to search for the universal first principles of ethics and then seek to apply them to international politics. The cosmopolitan method purports to give powerful principles of international ethics, but at what price? The developmental communitarian tradition can offer universal principles without requiring that the peoples of the world conform to a liberal understanding of moral agency. In taking account of the requirements of constructivism all three developmental communitarians develop principles of justice that derive from a shared international political culture. The principles they derive are capable of doing the necessary discriminatory or critical work but not to the same extent that cosmopolitan principles of international justice can do so. Thus the charge of conservatism. But is developmental communitarianism really conservative? The new and continually developing circumstances of international politics require constructivism. Adopting a constructivist philosophical approach can hardly be called conservative. Applying this approach to the developing political character of international politics is, in the first instance at least, conservative in as much as it has to take account of the historical development of shared principles. It was the failure of cosmopolitans to adequately take account of this factor, the necessary and initial construction of international community, that led to my rejection of their position. But seeking to show that a just international community requires a sea change from liberal led politics to shared principles can hardly be called conservative. In showing the differing conclusions that can be reached from genuinely accessible reasoning that takes proper account of interconnectedness I believe I have proven two important points. The first is that liberal reasoning in international affairs must take the form of developmental communitarianism. The second is that if we take seriously the claim that Rawls adequately models the developmental communitarian tradition (and given the refutation of the claim that Rawls imposes liberal ideas from outside his chain of reasoning I believe I have proven that this strategy is both necessary and useful) it is possible to conclude that this necessary approach to liberal international relations theory is not overly conservative. It shows the real route to making human rights a key aspect of a genuinely accessible and genuinely shared international politics. Until liberal theory becomes accessible to all relevant others the international arena remains the place in which competing worldviews struggle for their expression. The idea behind the drive to create a more liberal international politics is that it will sustain and protect the growing interdependence of political actors. The only liberal theory that can achieve this goal is developmental communitarianism. In showing how this tradition is able to deal theoretically with the two prime concerns of world politics, a concern for sovereignty and for human rights, I believe that I have made the case for a re-examination of liberal international relations theory, its form and its role in the construction of an interconnected world order.

Of course, an argument of this sort does not lay out the ways in which human rights legislation should be reworked. What it does do is highlight the basic criterion by which such reworking might be judged. Key among these criteria is the constructivist understanding of universality. For a principle of international justice to be considered correct it must be appropriately universal. Here universality has a different meaning to the way it has been traditionally understood in the history of political thought and, in particular, in much cosmopolitan theory. A constructivist theory is universalisable if it is accessible to and followable by all relevant agents. Here universality relies on the construction of the scope of ethics, upon the characterisation of the relevant others. The fact that we have, over history, come to view the relevant others as individual agents with rights to life and liberty is the key. It is simply not possible to argue convincingly that morality necessarily requires that we adopt this view. Rather, the best hope for constructing a just international community lies in the way we model the claims that actors do make, are prepared to make and wish to make. We cannot rule out, as a matter of principle, non-cosmopolitan aspirations for the international community. Following Walzer and Frost we can convincingly argue that agents do commonly make claims about individual rights such as the rights to life and liberty. But we cannot go as far as O'Neill or Frost and argue that this practice requires that we view such individual rights as having priority over the other rights that individuals as citizens and their governments make (such as the right to self-determination). Walzer's characterisation of these rights as reiterative, yet very thin, has much to commend it. We cannot prioritise individual rights over communal rights when it is clear that both sets of rights do a lot of work in world politics. The advantage that Rawls' theory has over Walzer's is that it treats the construction of principles of international justice as an ongoing and overtly political exercise. In working towards a form of political consensus we are obliged to build a mode of discourse that all can understand. The construction of an international community has to be an overtly political exercise and it has to be recognised that what the nascent international community is proposing to build is not merely an extension of the United Nations system of international politics, governed and guided by liberal states and principles, but the opportunity to create something that is genuinely shared.

Bibliography

Ackerman, B. 'Political Liberalisms', *The Journal of Philosophy*, Vol. 41, No. 7, July 1994, 364–386.

—— 'Rooted Cosmopolitanism', *Ethics*, Vol. 104, April 1994, 516–535.

Alejarndro, R. 'Rawls' Communitarianism', *Canadian Journal of Philosophy*, Vol. 23, No. 1, 1993, 75–100.

Alker, H. and Biersteker. 'The Dialectics of World Order: Notes for a Future Archaeologist in International Savoir Faire', *International Studies Quarterly*, Vol. 28, No. 2, 1984, 121–142.

Ashley, R. 'Untying the Sovereign State: A Double Reading of the Anarchy Problematique', *Millennium: Journal of International Studies*, Vol. 17, No. 2, summer 1988, 227–262.

—— 'Living on Border Lines: Man, Poststructuralism and War', in J. Der Derian and M. Shapiro (eds), *International/Intertextual Relations: Postmodern Readings in World Politics*, Lexington Books, Maxwell Macmillan International, 1989.

—— 'The Achievements of Post-Structuralism', in S. Smith, K. Booth and M. Zalewski (eds), *International Theory: Positivism and Beyond*, Cambridge, Cambridge University Press, 1996.

Ashley, R. and Walker, R. 'Speaking the Language of Exile: Dissidence in International Studies', *International Studies Quarterly*, Vol. 34, No. 3, 1990, 259–268.

Avineri, S. *Hegel's Theory of the Modern State*, Cambridge, Cambridge University Press, 1972.

Avineri, S. and de-Shalit, A. (eds), *Communitarianism and Individualism*, Oxford, Oxford University Press, 1992.

Barry, B. 'Do Countries Have Moral Obligations? The Case of World Poverty', in S. McMurrin (ed.), *The Tanner Lectures on Human Values*, Vol. 2, Salt Lake City, University of Utah Press, Cambridge, London, Sydney, Cambridge University Press, 1981.

—— 'Humanity and Justice in Global Perspective', in J. Pennock and J. Chapman (eds), *Ethics, Economics and the Law*, Nomos xxiv, New York and London, New York University Press, 1982.

—— 'Can States be Moral? International Morality and the Compliance Problem', in A. Ellis (ed.), *Ethics and International Relations*, Manchester, Manchester University Press, 1986.

—— 'John Rawls and the Search for Stability' *Ethics*, Vol. 105, 1995, 874–915.

—— 'Justice and International Order', unpublished paper, Conference on Egalitarian Justice, Senate House, London University, 22 June 1996.

Barry-Jones, R.J. 'Concepts and Models of Change in International Relations', in B. Buzan and R.J. Barry-Jones (eds), *Change in the Study of International Relations*, London, Frances Pinter, 1981.

Beitz, C. 'Justice and International Affairs', *Philosophy and Public Affairs*, Vol. 4, summer 1975, 360–389.

—— *Political Theory and International Relations*, Princeton, Princeton University Press, 1979.

—— 'Bounded Morality: Justice and the State in World Politics', *International Organisation*, Vol. 33, No. 3, summer 1979, 405–424.

—— 'Nonintervention and Communal Integrity', *Philosophy and Public Affairs*, Vol. 9, No. 4, 1980.

—— 'Cosmopolitan Ideals and National Sentiment' *The Journal of Philosophy*, Vol. 80, No. 10, October 1983, 591–600.

—— 'Cosmopolitan Liberalism and the States System', in C. Brown (ed.), *Political Restructuring in Europe: Ethical Perspectives*, Routledge, 1994.

Bellamy, R. 'Justice in the Community: Walzer on Pluralism, Equality and Democracy', in D. Boucher and P. Kelly (eds), *Perspectives on Social Justice*, London, Routledge, 1998.

Bellamy, R. and Hollis, M. 'Liberal justice: Political and Metaphysical', *The Philosophical Quarterly*, Vol. 45, No. 178, January 1995, 1–19.

Bernstein, R. *The New Constellation: The Ethical-Political Horizons of Modernity/Postmodernity*, Cambridge, Polity Press, 1991.

Blocker, G. and Smith, E. (eds), *John Rawls' Theory of Social Justice*, Athens, Ohio University Press, 1980.

Boucher, D. 'Inter-Community and International Relations in the Political Philosophy of Hobbes', *Polity*, Vol. 23, No. 2, winter 1980, 207–232.

—— 'The Character of the History of the Philosophy of IR and the Case of Edmund Burke', *Review of International Studies*, Vol. 17, 1991, 127–148.

—— 'Political Theory, International Theory and the Political Theory of International Relations', in A. Vincent (ed.), *Political Theory: Tradition and Diversity*, Hong Kong, Cambridge University Press, 1997.

—— *Political Theories of International Relations: From Thucydides to the Present*, Oxford, Oxford University Press, 1998.

Brown, C. *International Relations Theory: New Normative Approaches*, New York, London, Harvester Wheatsheaf, 1992.

—— '"Really Existing Liberalism" and International Order', *Millennium: Journal of International Studies*, Vol. 21, No. 3, winter 1992, 313–328.

—— 'The Ethics of Political Restructuring in Europe: The Perspective of Constitutive Theory', in C. Brown (ed.), *Political Restructuring in Europe: Ethical Perspectives*, London, Routledge, 1994.

—— 'Critical Theory and Postmodernism in International Relations', in A. Groom and M. Light (eds), *Contemporary International Relations: A Guide to Theory*, London, Pinter Publishers, 1994.

—— 'International Theory and International Society: The Viability of the Middle Way?', *Review of International Studies*, Vol. 21, 1995, 183–196.

—— *Understanding International Relations*, Basingstoke and London, Macmillan, 1997.

—— 'International Social Justice', in D. Boucher and P. Kelly (eds), *Perspectives on Social Justice*, London, Routledge, 1998.

Brown, P. and Shue, H. (eds), *Boundaries: National Autonomy and its Limits*, Totowa NJ, Rowman and Littlefield, 1981.

Brown, S. *The Causes and Prevention of War*, New York, St Martin's Press, 1994.

—— *International Relations in a Changing Global System: Toward a Theory of the World Polity*, Boulder Colorado and Oxford, Westview Press, 1992, 1996.

Bruggencate, H. ten, 'Hegel's Views on War', *Philosophical Quarterly*, Vol. 1, 1950.

Burchill, S. and Linklater, A. with Detevak, R. Paterson, M. and True, J. *Theories of International Relations*, London, Macmillan Press, 1996.

Caygill, H. *A Kant Dictionary*, Oxford, UK and Cambridge, MA, Blackwell, 1995.

Chambers, S. *Reasonable Democracy: Jurgen Habermas and the Politics of Discourse*, Ithaca, NY, Cornell University Press, 1996.

Charvet, J. *A Critique of Freedom and Equality*, Cambridge, Cambridge University Press, 1981.

—— 'Contractarianism and International Political Theory', in D. Boucher and P. Kelly (eds), *The Social Contract from Hobbes to Rawls*, London, Routledge, 1994.

Cochran, M. 'Cosmopolitans and Communitarians in a Post-Cold War World', in J. MacMillan and A. Linklater (eds), *Boundaries in Question: New Directions in International Relations*, London and New York, Pinter, 1995.

—— 'Postmodernism, Ethics and International Political Theory', *Review of International Studies*, Vol. 21, No. 3, 1995, 237–250.

—— 'The Liberal Ironist, Ethics and International Relations', *Millennium: Journal of International Studies*, Vol. 25, No. 1, 1996, 29–41.

—— *Normative Theory in International Relations: A Pragmatic Approach*, Cambridge, Cambridge University Press, 1999.

Connolly, W.E. 'Identity and Difference in Global Politics', in J. Der Derian and M. Shapiro (eds), *International/Intertextual Relations: Postmodern Readings in World Politics*, Lexington Books, Maxwell Macmillan International, 1989.

Cox, R. 'Social Forces, States and World Orders: Beyond International Relations Theory', *Millennium: Journal of International Studies*, Vol. 10, No. 2, 1981.

Crowder, G. 'Pluralism and Liberalism', *Political Studies*, Vol. 42, 1994, 293–303.

Danielson, P. 'Theories, Intuitions and the Problems of World Wide Distributive Justice', *Philosophy and Social Science*, Vol. 3, 1973, 331–340.

Der Derian, J. 'A Reinterpretation of Realism: Genealogy, Semiology, Dromology', in J. Der Derian (ed.), *International Theory: Critical Investigations*, Basingstoke, Macmillan, 1995.

Der Derian, J. and Shapiro, M. (eds), *International/Intertextual Relations: Postmodern Readings in World Politics*, Basingstoke, Lexington Books, Maxwell Macmillan International, 1989.

Detevak, R. 'Incomplete States: Theories and Practices of Statecraft', in J. MacMillan and A. Linklater (eds), *Boundaries in Question: New Directions in International Relations*, London, Pinter, 1995.

—— 'Postmodernism', in S. Burchill, A. Linklater *et al.*, *Theories of International Relations*, London, Macmillan, 1996.

Dewey, J. *Egotism in German Philosophy*, London, Dent, 1940.

Donnelly, J. 'Twentieth Century Realism', in T. Nardin and D.R. Mapel (eds), *Traditions of International Ethics*, Cambridge, Cambridge University Press, 1992.

Doppelt, G. 'Walzer's Theory of Morality in International Relations', *Philosophy and Public Affairs*, Vol. 8, No. 1, 1978, 3–26.

—— 'Statism Without Foundations', *Philosophy and Public Affairs*, Vol. 9, No. 4, 1980, 398–403.

Doyle, M. 'Kant, Liberal Legacies, and Foreign Affairs', *Philosophy and Public Affairs*, Vol. 21, No. 3, 1983, 203–235.

Dubik, J. 'Human Rights, Command Responsibility and Walzer's Just War Theory', *Philosophy and Public Affairs*, Vol. 11, No. 4, 354–371.

Dunne, T. 'Mythology or Methodology? Traditions in International Theory', *Review of International Studies*, Vol. 19, 1993, 305–318.

Dworkin, R. *Taking Rights Seriously*, London, Duckworth, 1981.

—— *Law's Empire*, London, Fontana Press, 1991.

Fain, H. *Normative Politics and the Community of Nations*, Philadelphia, Temple University Press, 1987.

Freeman, S. 'Reason and Agreement in Social Contract Views', *Philosophy and Public Affairs*, Vol. 19, 1990, 122–157.

—— 'Contractualism, Moral Motivation and Practical Reason', *The Journal Of Philosophy*, Vol. 88, No. 6, June 1991, 281–303.

Frost, M. *Towards a Normative Theory of International Relations*, Cambridge, Cambridge University Press, 1986.

—— *Ethics and International Relations: A Constitutive Theory*, Cambridge, Cambridge University Press, 1996.

—— 'Reply to Peter Sutch's "Human Rights as Settled Norms"', *Review of International Studies*, Vol. 26, 2000.

Gallie, W.B. 'Wanted a Philosophy of International Relations', *Political Studies*, Vol. 27, No. 3, 1978, 484–492.

Galston, W. 'Community, Democracy, Philosophy: The Political Thought of Michael Walzer', *Political Theory*, Vol. 17, No. 1, February 1989, 119–131.

Greene, D. *Greek Political Theory*, University of Chicago Press, 1967.

Griffiths, M. 'Order and International Society: The Real Realism', *Review of International Studies*, Vol. 18, 1992.

—— *Realism, Idealism and International Relations: A Reinterpretation*, London, New York, Routledge, 1992.

Gross, L. 'The Peace of Westphalia 1648–1948', in R. Falk and W.F. Hanreider (eds), *International Law and Organization*, Philadelphia, Lipincott, 1968.

Guignon, C. and Hiley, D., 'Biting the Bullet: Rorty on Private and Public Morality', in A. Malachowski (ed.), *Reading Rorty: Critical Responses to Philosophy and the Mirror of Nature and Beyond*, Oxford, Blackwell, 1990.

Hart, H. 'Are There any Natural Rights?', *Philosophical Review*, Vol. 64, 1955, 175–191.

Hegel, G.W.F. *Early Theological Writings*, trans. T.M. Knox, Chicago, 1948.

—— *The Philosophy of History*, trans. J. Sibree, Dover, 1956.

—— *Hegel's Political Writings*, trans. T.M Knox, introductory essay by Z. Pelczynski, Oxford, Oxford University Press, 1964.

—— *Jena Realphilosophie*, cited S. Avineri, *Hegel's Theory of the Modern State*, Cambridge, Cambridge University Press, 1972.

—— *Elements of the Philosophy of Right*, ed. A. Wood, trans. H.B. Nisbet, Cambridge texts in the history of political thought, Cambridge University Press, 1991.

Held, D. *Democracy and the Global Order: From the Modern State to Cosmopolitan Governance*, Cambridge, Polity Press, 1995.

Hobbes, T. *Leviathan*, ed. C.B. Macpherson, Harmondsworth, Penguin Books, 1985.

Hoffman, M. 'Critical Theory and the Inter-Paradigm Debate', *Millennium: Journal of International Studies*, Vol. 16, No. 2, summer 1987, 231–249.

Hoffman, S. *Duties Beyond Borders: On the Limits and Possibilities of Ethical International Relations*, Syracuse University Press, 1981.

Hoffman, S. and Fidler, D. (eds), *Rousseau on International Relations*, Oxford, Clarendon Press, 1991.

Hurrell, A. 'Kant and the Kantian Paradigm in International Relations', *Review of International Studies*, Vol. 16, 1990, 183–205.

Jackson, R. 'Pluralism in International Political Theory', *Review of International Studies*, Vol. 18, 1992, 271–281.

Jones, P. 'International Human Rights: Philosophical or Political?', in S. Caney, D. George and P. Jones (eds) *National Rights, International Obligations*, Boulder, CO, Westview Press, 1996.

Kant, I. *Perpetual Peace and Other Essays on Politics, History, and Morals*, trans. T. Humphrey, Indianapolis, Hacket Publishing Co., 1983.

—— *Ethical Philosophy*, trans. J. Ellington, Indianapolis, Cambridge, Hacket Publishing Co., 1983.

—— *The Moral Law: Kant's Groundwork of the Metaphysic of Morals*, trans. H.J. Paton, London, Routledge, 1991.

—— *The Metaphysics of Morals: Metaphysical First Principles of the Doctrine of Right*, trans. M. Gregor, Cambridge, Cambridge University Press, 1991.

Kaufmann, W. (ed.), *Hegel's Political Philosophy*, New York, Atherton Press, 1970.

Kymlikca, W. *Multicultural Citizenship: A Liberal Theory of Minority Rights*, Oxford, Clarendon Press, 1995.

Legutko, R. 'Cosmopolitans and Communitarians: A Commentary', in C. Brown (ed.), *Political Restructuring in Europe: Ethical Perspectives*, London, Routledge, 1992.

Linklater, A. *Beyond Realism and Marxism: Critical Theory and International Relations*, Basingstoke, Macmillan, 1990.

—— *Men and Citizens in the Theory of International Relations*, Basingstoke, Macmillan, 1990.

—— 'The Problem of Community in International Relations.', *Alternatives*, Vol. 14, No. 2, 1990.

—— 'The Question of the Next Stage in International Relations Theory: A Critical Theoretical Point of View', *Millennium: Journal of International Studies*, Vol. 21, No. 1, 1992, 77–98.

—— 'Citizenship and Sovereignty in the Post-Westphalian State', *European Journal of International Relations*, Vol. 2, No. 1, Sage, 1996, 77–103.

—— 'The Achievements of Critical Theory', in S. Smith, K. Booth and M. Zalewski (eds), *International Theory: Positivism and Beyond*, Cambridge, Cambridge University Press, 1996.

Linklater, A. and Macmillan J. (eds), *Boundaries in Question: New Directions in International Relations Theory*, London, New York, Pinter, 1995.

Luban, D. 'Just War and Human Rights', in *Philosophy and Public Affairs*, Vol. 9, 1980, 160–181.

—— 'The Romance of the Nation-State', *Philosophy and Public Affairs*, Vol. 9, No. 4, 1980, 392–398

Mackie, J.L. *Ethics: Inventing Right and Wrong*, Harmondsworth, Penguin Books 1977.

Magrew, A. (ed.), *The Transformation of Democracy? Globalization and Territorial Democracy*, Cambridge, Polity Press, 1997.

Meinecke, F. *Machiavellism: The Doctrine of Raison D'Etat and its place in Modern History*, London, Routledge, 1962.

Miller, D. *On Nationality*, Oxford, Clarendon Press, 1995.

Milo, R. 'Scepticism and Moral Justification', *The Monist*, Vol. 76, 1993.

—— 'Contractarian Constructivism', *Journal of Philosophy*, Vol. 92, No. 4, April 1995, 181–204.

Mitias, M. 'Hegel on International Law', *Clio*, Vol. 9, No. 2, 1980.

Moellendorf, D. 'Constructing the Law of Peoples', *Pacific Philosophical Quarterly*, Vol. 77, 1996, 132–154.

Morgenthau, H.J. *Politics Among Nations: The Struggle for Peace*, New York, Alfred A. Knopf, 1948.

Mulhall, S. and Swift, A. *Liberals and Communitarians*, Oxford, Blackwell, 1992.

Nardin, T. *Law, Morality and the Relations Between States*, Princeton, Princeton University Press, 1983.

O'Neill, O. *Faces of Hunger: An Essay on Poverty, Justice and Development*, London, Allen and Unwin, 1986.

—— 'Who Can Endeavour Peace', *Canadian Journal of Philosophy*, Supplement, Vol. 12, 1986, 41–73.

—— 'Abstraction, Idealization and Ideology in Ethics', in J. Evans (ed.), *Moral Philosophy and Contemporary Problems*, Supplement to Philosophy: Vol. 22, Cambridge University Press, 1987, 55–69.

—— 'Ethical Reasoning and Ideological Pluralism', *Ethics*, Vol. 98, 1988, 705–722.

—— *Constructions of Reason: Explorations of Kant's Practical Philosophy*, Cambridge, Cambridge University Press, 1989.

—— 'Transnational Justice', in D. Held (ed.), *Political Theory Today*, Cambridge, Polity Press, 1991.

—— 'Justice and Boundaries', in C. Brown (ed.), *Political Restructuring in Europe: Ethical Perspectives*, London, Routledge, 1994.

—— *Towards Justice and Virtue: A Constructive Account of Practical Reasoning*, Cambridge, Cambridge University Press, 1996.

—— 'Rawls and the use of Public Reason', Plenary lecture at Brave New World 2, Second Graduate Conference in Political Theory at Manchester, 18 June 1997.

Paden, R. 'Reconstructing Rawls' Law of Peoples', *Ethics and International Affairs*, Vol. 11, 1997, 217–232.

Palan, R. and Blair, B., 'On the Idealist Origins of the Realist Theory of International Relations', *Review of International Studies*, Vol. 19, 1993, 385–399.

Paskins, B. and Dockrill, M. *The Ethics of War*, Duckworth, 1979.

Patomaki, H. 'From Normative Utopias to Political Dialectics: Beyond a Deconstruction of the Brown-Hoffman Debate', *Millennium Journal of International Studies*, Vol. 22, No. 1, 1992, 53–75.

Peterson, V. Spike 'Shifting Ground(s): Epistemological and Territorial Remapping in the Context of Globalization(s)', in E. Kofman and G. Youngs (eds), *Globalization: Theory and Practice*, London, Pinter, 1996.

Pettman, R. (ed.), *Moral Claims in World Affairs*, London, Croom Helm, 1979.

Pogge, T.W. 'Liberalism and Global Justice: Hoffman and Nardin on Morality in International Affairs', *Philosophy and Public Affairs*, Vol. 15, No. 1, 1986, 67–82.

—— *Realizing Rawls*, Ithica and London, Cornell University Press, 1989.

—— 'Cosmopolitanism and Sovereignty', *Ethics*, Vol. 103, October, 1992, 48–75.

—— 'An Egalitarian Law of Peoples', *Philosophy and Public Affairs*, Vol. 23, No. 3, summer 1994, 195–224

Popper, K.R. *The Open Society and Its Enemies, Vol. II, The High Tide of Prophesy: Hegel and Marx*, London, New York, Routledge and Kegan Paul, 1945.

—— *Conjectures and Refutations*, London, New York, Routledge and Kegan Paul, 1969.

Rawls, J. *A Theory of Justice*, Oxford, Clarendon Press, 1972.

—— 'Justice as Fairness: Political not Metaphysical', *Philosophy and Public Affairs*, Vol. 14, 1985, 223–251.

—— *Political Liberalism*, New York, Columbia University Press, 1993.

—— 'The Law of Peoples', *On Human Rights, The Oxford Amnesty Lectures*, S. Shute and S. Hurley (eds), New York, Basic Books, 1993.

—— 'Justice as Fairness: A Briefer Restatement', unpublished manuscript, Cambridge, MA, Harvard University, 1989.

—— '50 Years after Hiroshima', *Dissent*, summer 1995, 323–327.

—— *The Law of Peoples: With 'The Idea of Public Reason Revisited'*, Harvard University Press, 1999.

Rengger, N. 'A City Which Sustains all Things: Communitarianism and International Society', *Millennium: Journal of International Studies*, Vol. 21, No. 3, 1992.

—— Book Review, *Millennium: Journal of International Studies*, Vol. 24, No. 3, 1995.

Ripstein, A. 'Foundationalism in Political Theory', *Philosophy and Public Affairs*, Vol. 16, No. 2, spring 1987, 115–138.

Rorty, R. *Philosophy and the Mirror of Nature*, Oxford, Blackwell, 1980.

—— 'Method, Social Science and Social Hope; Ungrounded Hope, Dewey vs Foucault', in *The Consequences of Pragmatism*, New York, London, Harvester Press, 1982.

—— 'Thugs and Theorists: A Reply to Bernstein', *Political Theory*, Vol. 15, No. 4, 1987.

—— *Contingency, Irony and Solidarity*, Cambridge, Cambridge University Press, 1989.

—— 'Human Rights, Rationality and Sentimentality', in S. Shute and S. Hurley (eds), *On Human Rights: The Oxford Amnesty Lectures*, New York, Basic Books, 1993.

Rosenberg, J. *The Empire of Civil Society: A Critique of the Realist Theory of International Relations*, London, New York, Verso, 1994.

Rousseau, J.J. 'Abstract and Judgment of Saint-Pierre's Project for Perpetual Peace', in S. Hoffman and D. Fidler (eds), *Rousseau on International Relations*, Oxford, Clarendon Press, 1991.

Ruggie, J. 'Territoriality and Beyond: Problematising Modernity in International Relations', *International Organisation*, Vol. 47, No. 1, 1993.

Schwarzenbach, S. 'Rawls, Hegel, and Communitarianism', *Political Theory*, Vol. 19, No. 4, November 1991, 539–571.

Scruton, R. *A Dictionary of Political Thought*, London, Pan Books in association with Macmillan Press, 1982.

Smith, M. 'Liberalism and International Reform', in T. Nardin and D.R. Mapel (eds), *Traditions of International Ethics*, Cambridge, Cambridge University Press, 1992.

Smith, S. 'Positivism and Beyond', in S. Smith, K. Booth and M. Zalewski (eds), *International Theory: Positivism and Beyond*, Cambridge, Cambridge University Press, 1996.

—— 'The Self Images of a Discipline: A Genealogy of International Relations Theory', in S. Smith and K. Booth (eds), *International Relations Theory Today*, Cambridge, Polity Press, 1995.

Smith, S. and Hollis, M. *Explaining and Understanding International Relations*, Oxford, Clarendon Press, 1990.

Suganami, H. *The Domestic Analogy and World Order Proposals*, Cambridge, New York, Cambridge University Press, 1992.

Sutch, P. 'Human Rights as Settled Norms: Mervyn Frost and The Limits of Hegelian Human Rights Theory', *Review of International Studies*, Vol. 26, No. 2, 2000, 215–231.

—— 'Global Civil Society and International Ethics; Frost's Restatement of Constitutive Theory', *Review of International Studies*, Vol. 26, No. 3, 2000, 485–489.

—— 'Constructing International Community' in M. Evans (ed.), *The Edinburgh Guide to Contemporary Liberalism*, Edinburgh University Press, 2000.

Taylor, P. 'The Modern Multiplicity of States', in E. Kofman and G. Youngs (eds), *Globalization: Theory and Practice*, London, Pinter, 1996.

Taylor, T. 'The Concept of Justice and the Laws of War', *Colombia Journal of Transnational Law*, Vol. 13, 1974, 189–207.

Teson, F. *Humanitarian Intervention: An Inquiry into Law and Morality*, New York, Transnational Publishers Inc., 1988.

—— 'The Rawlsian Theory of International Law', *Ethics and International Affairs*, Vol. 9, 1995, 71–101.

Thompson, J. *Justice and World Order: A Philosophical Inquiry*, London, Routledge, 1992.

Thucydides *History of the Peloponnesian War*, trans. R. Warner, Harmondsworth, Penguin Books, 1954.

Treitschke, H. von. *Politics*, 2 vols, trans. B. Dugdale and T. de Bille, London, Constable and company, 1916.

Vincent, A. 'The Hegelian State and International Politics', *Review of International Studies*, Vol. 9, 1983.

Vincent, R.J. *Human Rights and International Relations*, Cambridge, Cambridge University Press, 1986.

Wain, K. 'Strong Poets and Utopia: Rorty's Liberalism, Dewey, and Democracy', *Political Studies*, Vol. 41, No. 3, 1993.

Walker, R. *Inside/Outside: International Relations as Political Theory*, Cambridge, Cambridge University Press, 1993.

Waltz, K. *Man, the State and War*, New York, Columbia University Press, 1959.

Walzer, M. *Obligations: Essays on Disobedience, War and Citizenship*, Cambridge, MA, Harvard University Press, 1970.

—— *Just and Unjust Wars: A Moral Argument with Historical Illustrations*, New York, Basic Books, 1977 (2nd edition 1992).

—— *Interpretation and Social Criticism*, Cambridge, MA, Harvard University Press, 1987.

—— 'The Moral Standing of States: A Response to Four Critics', in *Philosophy and Public Affairs*, Vol. 9, No. 18, 1980, 209–229.

—— 'Political Decision Making and Political Education', in M. Richter (ed.), *Political Theory and Political Education*, Princeton, Princeton University Press, 1980.

—— *Spheres of Justice: A Defence of Pluralism and Equality*, Oxford, Blackwell, 1983.

—— *The Company of Critics: Social Criticism and Political Commitment in the Twentieth Century*, London, Peter Halibran, 1989.

—— 'Nation and Universe', *The Tanner Lectures on Human Values XI 1989*, G. Peterson (ed.), Salt Lake City, University of Utah Press, 1990.

—— 'The Communitarian Critique of Liberalism', *Political Theory*, Vol. 18, No. 1, February 1990, 6–23.

—— *Thick and Thin: Moral Arguments at Home and Abroad*, Notre Dame, Indianapolis, London, University of Notre Dame Press, 1994.

—— 'Response to Veit Bader', *Political Theory*, Vol. 23, No. 2, 1995, 250–253.

—— (ed.), *Towards a Global Civil Society*, Providence, Oxford, Berghahn Books, 1995.

Wight, G. and Porter, B. (eds), M. Wight, *International Theory: The Three Traditions*, Leicester, Leicester University Press, 1991.

Wight, M. 'Why there is no International Theory', in H. Butterfield and M. Wight, *Diplomatic Investigations: Essays in the Theory and Practice of Diplomacy*, London, Allen and Unwin, 1966.

—— *Power Politics*, Leicester, Leicester University Press, 1978.

Williams, H. *International Relations in Political Theory*, Milton Keynes, Philadelphia, Open University Press, 1992.

Williams, M. 'Rousseau, Realism and *Realpolitik*', *Millennium: Journal of International Studies*, Vol. 18, No. 2, 1989, 185–203.

—— 'Rethinking Sovereignty', in E. Kofman and G. Youngs (eds), *Globalization: Theory and Practice*, London, Pinter, 1996.

Wood, A. 'Hegel's Ethics', in F.C. Beiser (ed.), *The Cambridge Companion to Hegel*, Cambridge, Cambridge University Press, 1993.

Wright Mills, C. *The Sociological Imagination*, Oxford, Oxford University Press, 1959.

Index